The Non-Independent Territories of the Caribbean and Pacific: Continuity and Change

Edited by Peter Clegg and David Killingray

ISBN 978-0-9569546-0-2

Institute of Commonwealth Studies
School of Advanced Study
University of London

Institute of
Commonwealth Studies
SCHOOL OF ADVANCED STUDY · UNIVERSITY OF LONDON

Contents

Acknowledgements

Most of the chapters in this book were originally written for, or inspired by, a day-long conference held at the Institute of Commonwealth Studies (ICwS), University of London in May 2011. The event was made possible with funding from the Political Studies Association, the University of the West of England, Bristol and the ICwS. The editors would like to thank these institutions for their support, without which the conference and this book would not have been possible. We would also like to thank the Foreign and Commonwealth Office and the UK Overseas Territories Association for their assistance in helping to frame the scope of the conference and therefore the book.

There are also a number of individuals the editors would like to thank for their vital support from the initial idea of holding the conference through to the writing of the book. These include Professor Philip Murphy, Director of the ICwS; Professor Gert Oostindie; Janice Panton, Chair of the UK Overseas Territories Association; Sukey Cameron; Andrew Allen; Frank Savage; Vijay Krishnarayan; and Ian Orr. We would also like to thank the authors for their perceptive chapters and for meeting our very tight editorial deadlines.

Finally, we would like to thank Taylor and Francis for granting us permission to reprint two articles included in the book. The original details of publication are: 'The UK Overseas Territories: a decade of progress and prosperity' by Peter Clegg and Peter Gold, *Commonwealth and Comparative Politics* 49 (1) (2011), pp. 115–35; and 'Looking for Plan B: What next for island hosts of offshore finance?' by Mark P. Hampton and John Christensen, *The Round Table* 100 (413) (2011), pp. 169–81.

Abbreviations

ACP	African Caribbean and Pacific
ALM	Antilliaanse Luchtvaart Martschippij
BBC	British Broadcasting Corporation
BDEEP	British Documents on the End of Empire
BES	Bonaire, Sint Eustatius and Saba
BIOT	British Indian Ocean Territories
BIS	Bank for International Settlements
BVI	British Virgin Islands
CARICOM	Caribbean Community
CDOM	Collectivité Département d'Outre-Mer
CFATF	Caribbean Financial Action Task Force
CI	Cayman Islands
CO	Colonial Office
COM	Collectivités d'Outre-Mer
CTOM	Collectivité Territoriale d'Outre-Mer
DFID	Department for International Development
DO	Dominions Office
DOM	Département d'Outre-Mer
DROM	Département et Région d'Outre-Mer
DT	Dependent Territories
EDF	European Development Fund
EEC	European Economic Community
EGOM	États Généraux de l'Outre-Mer
EPA	Economic Partnership Agreement
EU	European Union
FAC	Foreign Affairs Committee
FATF	Financial Action Task Force
FCO	Foreign and Commonwealth Office

FI	Falkland Islands
FINCEN	Financial Crimes Enforcement Network
FOT	French Overseas Territories
GDP	Gross Domestic Product
GFC	Global Financial Crisis
HMG	Her Majesty's Government
HTCI	Harmful Tax Competition Initiative
IBC	International Business Company
ICCPR	International Covenant on Civil and Political Rights
ICESR	International Covenant on Economic and Social Rights
IJ	International Jurisdiction
IMF	International Monetary Fund
IT	Integrated Territories
LAT	Living Apart
LODEOM	Loi pour le Développement Économique des Outre-Mer
LOOM	Loi d'Orientation pour l'Outre-Mer
MoD	Ministry of Defence
MS	Member State
NAO	National Audit Office
NIC	Non-Independent Countries
NICC	Non-Independent Caribbean Countries
NSGT	Non Self-Governing Territories
OCT	Overseas Countries and Territories
OCTA	Overseas Countries and Territories Association
ODA	Overseas Development Administration
OECD	Organisation for Economic Cooperation and Development
OECS	Organisation of Eastern Caribbean States
OFC	Offshore Financial Centre
OR	Outermost Regions
OT	Overseas Territories
OTCC	Overseas Territories Consultative Committee
PFII	Permanent Forum on Indigenous Issues
REI	Racial Equality Index
ROM	Région d'Outre-Mer
SGC	Self-Governing Countries

SIDS	Small Island Developing States
SIE	Small Island Economies
STD	Savings Tax Directive
STR	Suspicious Transaction Reports
TA	Technical Assistance
TAFF	Terres Australes et Antarctiques Françaises
TCI	Turks and Caicos Islands
TIEA	Tax Information Exchange Agreement
TOM	Territoires d'Outre-Mer
UK	United Kingdom
UKOT	United Kingdom Overseas Territories
UKOTA	United Kingdom Overseas Territories Association
UNDP	United Nations Development Programme
UNESCAP	United Nations Economic and Social Commission for Asia and the Pacific
UNESCO	United Nations Education, Scientific and Cultural Organisation
UNHCHR	United Nations High Commissioner for Human Rights
UNO	United Nations Organisation

Contributors

Ian Bailey joined the Foreign and Commonwealth Office (FCO) in 1987 after periods working in local government and the private sector. He has had postings in Muscat (Oman), Seoul and Hong Kong. His first FCO job was on the Falkland Islands desk. Since September 2010, he has been Head of the Strategy and Co-ordination Section of the Overseas Territories Directorate in the FCO, which leads on cross-cutting issues relevant to the Overseas Territories as a whole. In the interim Ian has also worked in London on export licensing issues; on the Hong Kong desk; and on conflict prevention work dealing with the Middle East and North Africa.

John Christensen is co-founder of the Tax Justice Network and directs its London-based International Secretariat. Trained as an auditor and economist, he has worked in a variety of the world's poorer countries and for 11 years was economic adviser to the government of the British Channel Island of Jersey. John is a board member of the New Rules for Global Finance Coalition (Washington, DC) and represents civil society on the Task Force on Tax and Development launched by the OECD in January 2010.

Peter Clegg is a Senior Lecturer in Politics at the University of the West of England, Bristol, and formerly a Research Fellow at the Sir Arthur Lewis Institute of Social and Economic Studies, The University of the West Indies, Jamaica. He has published widely on the politics and international relations of the Caribbean. Peter has also provided advice on the Caribbean to the British and Jamaican governments, Transparency International and the OECD.

Carlyle Corbin is an international advisor on governance, and former Minister for External Affairs for the US Virgin Islands. He has provided advice to the United Nations on self-determination and is the author of two UN studies on non-independent countries. Carlyle has been constitutional advisor to the Anguilla Government; independent expert to UN missions to Bermuda and the Turks and Caicos Islands; and he is senior editor of *Overseas Territories Review*.

Peter Gold is Emeritus Professor of Hispanic Studies at the University of the West of England, Bristol. He has published extensively on Gibraltar, including the monograph *Gibraltar: British or Spanish?* (Routledge, 2005), and more recently through articles in *Mediterranean Politics* (2009), *Diplomacy and Statecraft* (2009) and *Geopolitics* (2010).

Ian Hendry was an FCO legal adviser from 1971 to 2005, including postings to the British Military Government, Berlin 1982–5 and the UK Permanent Representation to the European Union, Brussels 1991–5. During his career he spent many years, at different stages, dealing with British overseas territories matters. Since 2005 Ian has been a constitutional adviser to the FCO on Overseas Territories and led the UK delegation that negotiated new constitutions for the territories.

Mark Hampton is a Senior Lecturer at the University of Kent, and Director of the Centre for Tourism in Islands and Coastal Areas (CENTICA). He has given over 80 international conference papers and published around 30 journal articles and book chapters (including in *Environment & Planning A*; *World Development*; *Third World Quarterly*; *Annals of Tourism Research*; and *Geografiska Annaler B*). Mark has field experience in South-East Asia, the Caribbean, South Atlantic and Europe. His research has been funded by the FCO; Department for International Development; Ministry of Tourism Malaysia; British Academy; and the British Council. He is a Fellow of the Royal Geographical Society and Visiting Professor at Universiti Teknologi Malaysia.

Lammert de Jong served nine years between 1985 and 1998 as resident-representative of the Netherlands government in the Netherlands Antilles. Prior to this, he was attached to the National Institute of Public Administration in Lusaka, Zambia (1972–6). In the People's Republic of Bénin, he was director of the Netherlands Development Aid Organization (1980–4). Lammert concluded his civil service career as counsellor to the Netherlands government on Kingdom Relations. Since then he has written as a freelance scholar on extended statehood in the USA, French, Dutch and British Caribbean. His most recent book, *Being Dutch, more or less*, explores Dutch identity (Rozenberg, 2010).

David Killingray is Emeritus Professor of History at Goldsmiths College London, a Senior Research Fellow at the Institute of Commonwealth Studies (ICwS) and Honorary Professor of History at the University of Stellenbosch. He is the author or editor of a number of books and articles on Africa, the Caribbean, Imperial History, and also English local history.

Nathalie Mrgudovic is a Lecturer in French Studies at Aston University (Birmingham). Her research is focused on the French Overseas Territories and on the South Pacific. She is particularly interested in the notions of self-determination, sovereignty and also regional integration. Nathalie is the author of *La France dans le Pacifique Sud. Les enjeux de la puissance* (L'Harmattan, 2008), for which Michel Rocard, former Prime Minister of France, wrote the preface.

Paul Sutton was formerly Professor of Caribbean Studies at London Metropolitan University, and Reader of Politics at the University of Hull. He has published many books and articles on the Caribbean and is a former chair of the Society for Caribbean Studies. Professor Sutton has lectured in the Caribbean, United States and European Union. He has been a consultant on the Caribbean to various international organisations, including bodies such as the West Indian Commission.

Ron van der Veer studied political science at the University of Amsterdam. He worked for the Department of Kingdom Relations in Curaçao and Sint Maarten between 1993 and 1998, at the same time as Lammert de Jong. From 1998–2005 he worked for the Ministries of the Interior and Justice in The Hague on aspects of international police and law enforcement co-operation. Since 2005 Ron has been attached to the Kingdom Council of State, where he was involved in an advisory capacity in the restructuring of the Kingdom. He is also Executive Secretary of the Kingdom Committee for NGO co-operation (*Comité Koninkrijksrelaties*).

William Vlcek is Lecturer in International Relations at the School of International Relations, University of St Andrews, and was previously Lecturer in International Politics at the ICwS, University of London. The author of *Offshore Finance and Small States: Sovereignty, Size and Money* (Palgrave, 2008), his research on offshore financial centres and initiatives to combat the financing of terrorism has been published in a variety of journals.

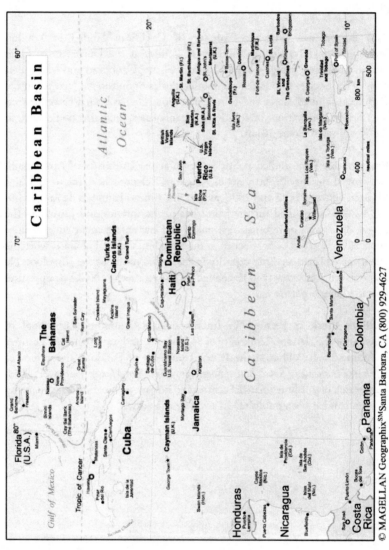

Map of the Caribbean, courtesy of http://maps.caribseek.com.

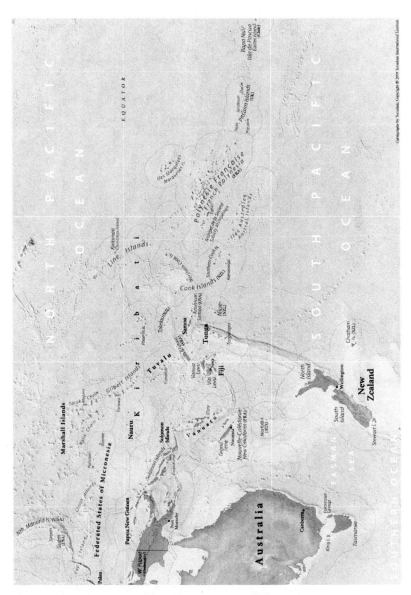

Map of the Pacific, courtesy of Victoria University Press.

Introduction

One hundred years ago the map of the world was littered with small pieces of territory, enclaves and islands that belonged to neighbouring or distant countries. For example, the Aegean island of Thasos, with its Greek-speaking population, belonged to the Khedive of Egypt, a strange reversal of imperialism in an age of European colonialism. Many internal borders also bore the marks of patchy acquisition, with bits and pieces of German states, and English counties, isolated or cut off and surrounded by areas subject to a different jurisdiction. Since then maps have been tidied up – partly as a result of conflict, but often in the process of administrative convenience, although there are also many examples of people firmly resisting any change to historic claims and loyalties. And yet, scattered around the world are the remnants of recently deceased empires, territories that for various reasons have failed, or resisted attempts, to take the path to full sovereignty in a world where many small states exist. A good number of these – islands in the Caribbean and the Pacific – are the subject of this book of essays resulting from a conference at the Institute of Commonwealth Studies in the School of Advanced Study, University of London.

This conference was marked by the presence of British officials from the United Kingdom Overseas Territories Directorate of the Foreign and Commonwealth Office, who have contributed to the book. Other contributors are Dutch colleagues who in recent years have been closely involved at an official level in discussions on the future of the Netherlands dependencies in the Caribbean. A further constituency represented at the conference were members of the UKOT Association, the body in London that serves as a forum for the United Kingdom Overseas Territories. Also present were citizens of British Overseas Territories living in Britain. An additional insider view of offshore financial affairs came from a contributor with first-hand experience of advising a British Crown Dependency government. And finally there were the academics, not always armchair observers of events far away but activists who welcome opportunities to see the subject of their study at first hand. It would seem that the number of scholars interested in small island affairs and governance is increasing in number. It is a rich field of multi-disciplinary study which embraces political scientists, economists, geographers, historians, sociologists, ecologists and also environmentalists.

This collection of essays looks at 'continuity and change' in the Caribbean and the Pacific. It is hardly surprising that non-independent territories, which have had their status defined by metropolitan decree, and that are subject to a measure of control from distant metropoles, are eager to push to the limits of autonomy while maintaining those essential links that help to secure their social and economic well-being. Thus there is a continuous challenge to the status quo with attempts to redefine the relationship with the former colonial power. Those debates embrace future constitutional relationships, greater fiscal powers and freedoms, the ongoing and important relationships with the European Union (EU), the necessary engagement with neighbouring foreign states, and how best to secure and protect the environmental wealth of island territories.

There are inevitably restraints on this process; those economically weak territories dependent upon aid from the metropole have limited room for manoeuvre. And few would wish to lose the right of citizenship of a non-independent territory which also guarantees free movement to and from, plus right of abode within, the countries of the EU. There are powerful incentives to maintain the status quo which serve to put the brake on local political ambitions to seek independence, as in Bermuda or the French territory of New Caledonia. Many local electorates have voted strongly in support of integration, even if it means that this is to be achieved by a gradual process with the loss of certain traditional legal rights, as in Mayotte.

Claims for greater autonomy are not solely directed at the metropole. Within non-independent territories there are inter-territorial disputes, especially where islands have been attached to neighbours for economy of management. Such integrations may work. However, they also provide potential grievances, over access to and allocation of resources and equable share of budgets, which lead to demands for further devolution of power and autonomy, not from London or Paris, but from a local political union of metropolitan design. This has happened in the last decade, particularly in the French and Dutch Caribbean islands, and similar reactions by aggrieved populations are possible in the future.

Integration of non-independent territories with the metropole inevitably means that the overseas territories become a political issue within the metropole. This has been so in both France and the Netherlands. Over the last decade French and Dutch policies of decentralisation and constitutional changes have offered options for a greater measure of local autonomy, including full sovereignty. To describe the former Netherlands territories in the Caribbean as 'Dutch' is to court severe criticism from the indigenous inhabitants who are conscious of their own identity. Autonomy and the preservation and promotion of identity are key issues. The aim has been to gain from the Dutch state as much autonomy as possible without losing the advantages of association. It is often a difficult line to draw for all non-independent territories when the price of association means adhering to ideas and practices on economic matters and human rights determined in Europe. In both France and the Netherlands, the electorates have an eye on the costs of the relationship with overseas territories, especially with centre-right governments and economies weakened by the financial crisis of 2008. In the UK the overseas territories have little impact on domestic politics, only becoming significant when threats are made by a foreign power, such as Spanish claims on Gibraltar and the Argentine invasion and subsequent war over the Falklands Islands in 1982. Although Parliament changed the status of the dependent territories to UK Overseas Territories ten years ago, this passed virtually unnoticed by the British electorate. Few Britons are even aware that the off-shore Crown Dependencies of the Isle of Man and the Channel Islands are autonomous and outside the EU.

Non-independent territories adhere to the metropoles for a variety of reasons, most importantly economic advantage, although security and sentiment also play a part. Association and consequent 'dependency' are a safeguard against being reduced to the economic and social condition of neighbouring states which opted for full independence. The global financial crisis since 2008 has had a double impact; on the economies of the overseas territories, but it has also encouraged metropolitan governments to look for relationships that save money.

Many overseas territories are vulnerable in a variety of ways. One problem is weak administrative structures and poor government. Faced with ministerial corruption in the Turks and Caicos Islands, Britain suspended the constitution in 2009 and imposed temporary direct rule in an attempt 'to restore good governance and sound financial management'. Although most local politicians denounced Britain's action, many citizens approved the intervention. In the Caribbean, in particular, corrupt government has lead to politicians and officials embezzling public funds and also being involved with the illegal traffic in drugs and arms. Certain islands suffer from isolation, for example, Pitcairn with a population of around 60 people, and St Helena in the south Atlantic, although the island with its 7,700 people is scheduled to have an airport funded by the Department for International Development. However, such development also threatens the vulnerable ecology of the island's environment. Several non-independent territories are 'dependent' because they have suffered from dramatic natural disasters, the obvious instance being the volcanic eruption in Montserrat in 1995. Although the Cayman Islands suffered seriously from the destructive effects of Hurricane Ivan in 2004, its stronger economy, largely based on offshore finance, enabled it to recover more easily.

So in short, this edited collection provides a comprehensive insight into the complexities, contradictions, challenges and opportunities that today help to define the non-independent territories of the Caribbean and Pacific, and their long-standing but sometimes awkward ties with their respective metropolitan powers.

Chapter 1

British decolonisation and the smaller territories: the origins of the UK Overseas Territories[1]

David Killingray

Introduction

By the end of the 20th century the once great modern European empires had gone – well, almost! Today, scattered around the world, there are small territories, remnants of empire that for one reason and another have eschewed independence and retained links of various kinds with the former imperial power. These territories, the result of unfinished decolonisation, have a status that varies greatly from integration through different degrees of autonomy to almost full sovereignty. The Imperial fragments are related to Britain (United Kingdom Overseas Territories – UKOT), France (*départements d'outre-mer*, and *territoires d'outre-mer* until 2002), the Netherlands (Aruba and the countries of the former De Nederlandse Antillen), Portugal (Azores, Madeira), Spain (Balearic Islands, Canary Islands, Ceuta and Melilla), Denmark (Greenland, Faeroes), the United States (Commonwealth of Puerto Rico, US Virgin Islands, Guam, Freely-Associated States in the Pacific), Australia (External Territories) and New Zealand (Territories Overseas and Self-Governing Territories) (for the British territories see Aldrich and Connell, 1998; Drower, 1992; Winchester, 2003; for the French territories see Aldrich and Connell, 1992; and for the Dutch territories see Oostindie and Klinkers, 2003).

This chapter looks at the debate on the future constitutional status of those British colonies generally referred to as 'smaller territories' during the latter years of decolonisation, and the remnant described, in 1999, as the UK Overseas Territories. It is a story of discarding imperial possessions, sometimes with accelerated haste, in a world where Empire was no longer acceptable. There are a

---

1   This is an amended version of a chapter originally published in David Killingray and David Taylor (eds.) (2005) *The United Kingdom Overseas Territories: Past, Present & Future* (London: Institute of Commonwealth Studies).

few moments of high drama (the Falklands War), some of petty farce (Anguilla), as well as of disgraceful dealings (Diego Garcia), in an account dominated by the search for a status for territories that either declined independence or were unsuited to sovereignty. It might be useful to offer a tentative periodisation for Britain's relationship with her declining dependent territories over this nearly 50-year period of Cold War, Britain's changing position in the world, and her accession to what is now the European Union (EU). The first period, 1947–62, was marked by attempts to discharge responsibility for many of the smaller territories by systems of federation, for example, in the abortive West Indies Federation. By the late 1950s 'smaller' colonies once thought unsuited to independence now became accepted as likely members both of the United Nations (UN) and the Commonwealth. In the second period, 1962–73, small territories such as Jamaica, Sierra Leone and Malawi became independent and less-viable colonies were named 'Associated states'; in the third, 1973–83, the UK as a new member of the European Economic Community (EEC) retreated from the idea of 'associated states' encouraging them to become independent. The fourth period, 1983–97, was shaped by the Falklands War and to a lesser extent by the US invasion of Grenada, which highlighted Britain's neglect of her former and remaining dependent territories. As Simon Winchester wrote in his engaging account, *Outposts*, '[t]he islands that remain are not, by and large, places for which London has any time to spare' (Winchester, 2003: 343). Independence remained an option for dependent territories but efforts were made to increase aid and investment and, under the aegis of the Maastricht Treaty 1993, to deal with specific external questions related to the dependent territories. The final period, post-1997, with the passing of Hong Kong to China, enabled new policies to be shaped for the dependent territories and its approximately 190,000 people.

The following analysis is based mainly on official sources. Various volumes in the *British Documents on the End of Empire* (BDEEP) series have been most helpful for the period up to the early 1970s. The 30-year rule on access to official papers obviously places limits on analysis of the finer points of London's policies to the dependent territories and so, for the more recent period, I have relied on official reports and various unofficial sources.

Decolonisation and 'smaller territories'

From 1946 the aim of successive British governments was constitutional change in the colonial Empire (Cmd 7433, para. 3, 1948). The great diversity of territories in geographical size, population, levels of economic development (or underdevelopment) and constitutional status inevitably meant that this process of change would not be single and smooth. Decolonisation was interpreted and applied in a variety of ways. Policy was not consistent and inevitably subject to both national and international considerations: Britain's status as a great power, the Cold War, the interests of the US, the role of the UN, and the decolonisation policies and strategies of other European imperial powers.

In 1949 a Colonial Office Committee of Enquiry envisaged that full self-government was unlikely to be achieved 'under any foreseeable conditions' except by Nigeria, the Gold Coast, and the Federation of Malaya with Singapore. Independent status, it was argued, could only be achieved by the colonies in south east Asia, the Caribbean, east Africa and central Africa by some form of closer union, a policy promoted with varying degrees of vigour in the 1950s. Territories labelled 'intermediate' or 'less mature' – and this included most African colonies – were subject to slow constitutional advance with no timetable for a transfer of power (CAB 129/33/2, CP (49)62, 1949). A Cabinet paper of 1955 correctly stated that '"Self-government" does not mean the same thing for all territories, irrespective of their characteristics'. However, it was less than accurate when it went on to say that 'it is ... generally assumed ... that at present all colonial territories are on one and the same ladder leading up to a common goal of "Dominion" status' (CAB 129/77, CP (55)133). This was only possible within grand schemes of association and federation, some of which were unlikely to be achieved. Many 'smaller territories' – and the nomenclature changed over time – clearly were not going to follow that optimistic trajectory, and nor was it intended that strategically located 'fortress' colonies such as Cyprus should become independent. Leaving aside considerations of imperial defence and strategic value, an essential qualification for independence then, and in to the 1960s, was that colonies should be economically self-sustaining and not in receipt of budgetary grants-in-aid. That ruled out the many colonies that had small populations and weak economic and social structures.

The question of 'smaller' territories had exercised the first Attlee government in 1948–9 (CAB 134/55, CA 8(48)2 & 3, 1948). The recommendation of the Rees committee (it included two distinguished Imperial historians, Vincent Harlow and Margery Perham) that reported in early 1951 was for a new constitutional status to which smaller territories might aspire, 'something between a dependency and a fully self-governing territory under the title of "Island or City States"' (CO 967/146, no. 1, 1951). This would require new structures in Whitehall, a minister for Commonwealth Affairs, and permanent territorial representatives in London, ideas not far removed from those that unfolded at various times over the next 50 years. Integration with Britain, proposed for Gibraltar in 1947 (CO 847/36/1), and also suggested for other territories most notably Malta in 1953–6, the Seychelles, and the Falklands at a later date, was ruled out in the early 1970s although thereafter it continued to be discussed from time to time. The idea that distant colonies might emulate the constitutional relationship of the Crown Dependencies, the Isle of Man and the Channel Islands, to Britain was generally deemed impracticable although it was often listed as a remote possibility until the early 1990s (CO 1032/412, no. 18, 1965). In the mid 1950s the Conservative government, worried at the implications for the future of the Commonwealth, attempted to put a brake on the pace of the colonial devolutionary process. A Colonial Policy Committee was established to 'assist the Cabinet in controlling constitutional development in colonial territories' (CO 1032/60, no. 1, 1955). The first issue addressed by the new committee was the smaller territories (CAB 19/77, CP (55)133, 1955). It proposed the term 'statehood' for those 'Colonies which [were] too small or remote to be able to look forward to independent national status, either alone or as components of a regional federation'. British Honduras, the Gambia and Mauritius were looked at in detail. 'Statehood' was given another look in 1958 but then steadily buried. The view in the Colonial Office in the late 1950s was that the small territories should be dealt with on an ad hoc basis. Five years later Andrew Cohen argued that finding 'a single managed solution' for ending colonial status was impossible.

By the end of the 1950s the pace of decolonisation had moved into a higher gear. Iain Macleod's period at the Colonial Office, from October 1959 to October 1961, saw rapid constitutional change, particularly in Africa, and the reluctant acceptance that the Central African Federation could not survive. Inevitably, ministerial thought continued as to the constitutional future of the smaller territories, a designation increasingly confined to genuinely small colonies now that independence had been scheduled for Sierra Leone and Cyprus. The collapse of the West Indies Federation in 1961, quickly followed by the promise of independence for Jamaica, a status also soon demanded by Trinidad and Tobago, meant that the future status of the smaller Caribbean islands had to be decided upon.

Decolonisation: Commonwealth and UN membership?

The decolonisation of small territories was subject to a number of important considerations other than the size, political development and economic viability of each colony. Britain's national interests, particularly in terms of defence and Cold War strategy, invariably were pre-eminent. In one case, that of the Chagos Islands and Diego Garcia, the interests and wishes of the indigenous *Ilois* peoples were blatantly disregarded because their presence conflicted with Cold War strategic considerations; following the creation of the British Indian Ocean Territories in 1965 the people were removed in order to make way for a US military base (Curteis, 2003).[2] Despite this, Britain was concerned at the international image of its colonial stewardship before other Commonwealth countries, the US and the often highly critical UN. A further concern was the

---

2   British official documents, including the White Paper of 1999, continue to promote the falsehood that these islands had no permanent population – only 'contract employees'.

interests of the US in the Caribbean, an area of much greater sensitivity to Washington following the Cuban revolution in 1959.

Decolonisation of small territories also involved the knotty question of Commonwealth membership. London's purpose was to selectively expand the Commonwealth and also to keep it together. Marrying the older white 'Dominions' with the newly independent Asian and African states was beset with problems. Current rules dictated that sovereign independence entitled a state to full membership of the Commonwealth and the right of attendance at the Commonwealth prime minister's conference. That this right be extended to small states was questioned by Cabinet papers in October 1954 and May 1956 (CAB 129/71, C 54(307); CAB 134/1203, CA (0)56). The idea of a 'two-tier' membership of the Commonwealth, discussed but not proceeded with in the final days of the previous Labour government (DO 35/2218, 1951), was ruled out in 1955 largely because of the negative image first- and second-class membership would have on peoples in Africa and the Caribbean. The idea refused to die and was only finally put to rest in 1960 due largely to the hostility of Ghana (CAB 129/77, CP (55)133, 1955).[3] By July 1960, the principle was accepted of Commonwealth membership irrespective of size (CAB 133/200, C (60)1222). This was just as well for, in April 1962, it was envisaged that membership would reach 17 the following year, possibly 24 in 1965, and increase to between 32 and 35 members by the end of the decade (CO 1032/226, no. 169).

Post-war British governments were increasingly sensitive to UN criticism of colonial rule and official irritation also existed due to a widespread feeling that the problems of decolonisation that British policies sought to meet were not properly understood. Concerns remained about removing colonies from the category of 'non self-governing' territories covered by Chapter XI of the UN Charter. Dropping the term 'colony' in favour of 'dependent territory' in 1956 was one response. There was little sense that small territories, such as Cyprus, could be fully independent or a member of the Commonwealth. The Working Party on Smaller Territories in 1959 offered the title of 'Commonwealth State' as a comfortable half-way house' between self-government and independence, but this term was not adopted (CAB 134/2505, no. 2, 1959). By the early 1960s overseas colonies were an increasing embarrassment even to Conservative governments (CO 936/733, 1962). The official line was that the 'colonial relationship [was] becoming outdated' and adversely affecting Britain's 'position in the UN and our relations with other countries' (FO 371/172610,

---

3 'Statehood' as an alternative to Dominion status was rejected as 'illusory' by a number of new Commonwealth countries at the Commonwealth Prime Minister's meeting in January 1956. Six years later, Norman Brook, secretary to the Cabinet, argued that a search should continue for a 'general formula for constitutional change that would meet this need'.

no. 13, 1963). Thus it was necessary 'to devise new "post-colonial" forms of association which will honour our obligations to their people and preserve our interests'. This became even more urgent with the collapse of the West Indies Federation following the Jamaican referendum in 1961 (Ashton and Killingray, 1999: 'Introduction'). Unsuccessful attempts were made to encourage first an Eastern Caribbean federation of eight, then of seven, and finally six member states. This latter attempt had effectively collapsed by May 1965 (Alomar, 2003 and 2009). Britain's desire was to be rid of the burden of the West Indian colonies and also the Pacific island territories; neither possessions nor regions had a strategic or economic value while Caribbean territories had long been regarded as a drain on metropolitan resources. Clare Short's ill-uttered public jibe in the 1990s about Montserrat's fiscal demands and 'golden elephants' merely echoed a sentiment once regularly voiced in the Colonial Office (*The Independent*, 1997).

Ending 'the stigma of colonialism'

A Labour government was elected in October 1964. The new Colonial Secretary, Anthony Greenwood, was told by Harold Wilson, the prime minister, to work 'himself out of a job as soon as possible' (CO 1031/4409, no. 495, 1965). Labour was ideologically committed to decolonisation and happy to follow the terms of the UN Special Committee on Decolonisation, the Committee of 24, established in November 1961.[4] Greenwood toured the Caribbean in February and March 1965 hoping that a strong federation could still be created in the eastern Caribbean. His visit did not reassure him and the various territories were reluctant to follow Jamaica, Trinidad & Tobago and Barbados to independence. In many territories there was little or no sense of 'nationalism'; insular particularism maybe, as in Anguilla and Ocean Island that created headaches for London; certain territories also had a very strong notion of being British. In May, Greenwood circulated a minute explaining that 'at this stage in our colonial history our main task must be to liquidate colonialism', either by granting independence or evolving other forms of government which would secure democratic rights for the people (CAB 148/21, OPD (65)89, 1965).

A smaller territories conference held in Oxford, in July 1965, chaired by Greenwood, discussed various schemes. The Colonial Office hoped that this would help to pave the way for a general omnibus piece of legislation entitled the 'Overseas Territories Bill'. A possible model for the dependent territories was the 'free association' relationship established between New

---

4   On the UN Special Committee see Aldrich and Connell, 1998: 156–61. On Labour Party thinking see the pamphlet, *Labour's Colonial Policy – III Smaller Territories* (London, June 1957). The Labour Government 1974–9 co-operated with the UN Committee but the Thatcher Government resigned from it in 1985 and refused to co-operate further.

Zealand and the Cook Islands and Western Samoa in 1962. This was in accord with the wording of UN Resolution 1541 (XV) of December 1960 where 'free association' was the 'free and voluntary choice by the people of the territory concerned, expressed through informed and democratic processes' to be 'associated with an independent state'. The model met the desire of the new Labour government to end the 'stigma of colonialism' and the needs of the territories of the failed federation schemes in the Caribbean, as well as the future of other small colonies dotted about the world. The main aim was to devise an omnibus piece of legislation that would deal with the remaining colonial territories. What emerged from the conference was the idea of 'associated state'.[5] This offered small territories a new relationship with Britain or perhaps with a Commonwealth or foreign state. Free association was not viewed favourably by the Foreign Office (which saw complications with the US over Puerto Rico), certain departments found fault with an omnibus piece of legislation to deal with the remaining colonies, and other legislation was piling up that took Parliamentary time. Pressed for time the Colonial Office dropped the proposed 'Overseas Territories Bill' (Morgan, 1980: 236–47). The six small territories of the failed Eastern Caribbean Federation became 'Associated States', the West Indies Act of 1967 describing them to be in a 'free and voluntary' association with Britain which handled their foreign relations and security (CO 1032/226, no. 169, 1967; Thorndike, 1979). It was a status that some UN members viewed as a camouflage for continuing colonialism. Britain was eager to be shot of the commitment in the Caribbean hoping that the US would assume greater fiscal responsibility for the island economies. Washington wanted Britain to remain in the region as a safeguard against the trouble that might result from 'any multiplication of mini-states in the area'. As for British policy, the intention of the UK government from the late 1960s 'was not … to delay independence for those who want it, nor … to impose it on those who do not want it' (FCO 86/60, 1972).

An alternative to independence

The new constitutional arrangement in the Caribbean with six associated states was soured by local difficulty. The merger of the small island of Anguilla, population 6,000, with the new associated state of St Christopher (Kitts) and Nevis was opposed by the Anguillans mainly over economic questions. In February 1969 the island unilaterally seceded. As it developed, the story involved an undignified retreat from the island by a visiting parliamentary under-secretary and a heavy-handed and costly (£1.23 million a year by 1970) invasion by a British force of soldiers and police to 'restore order'. This was

---

5   Morgan, 1980: 66, says that the term 'Associated State' appears to have been first suggested informally at a meeting within the Colonial Office in October 1952.

greeted by international criticism comparing the Caribbean venture with Britain's military inactivity towards rebellious Southern Rhodesia. Britain acknowledged that the islanders could not be forced against their wishes to rejoin St Kitts and Nevis, a policy which damaged relations between London and the islands. Anguilla returned to dependent status in 1971, being formally separated from St Kitts and Nevis in 1980. The crisis revealed that under free association 'Britain carried responsibility but had no executive authority, while the associated state had the authority without the responsibility' (Ashton and Louis, 2004: xciv). The experiment of free association was not tried elsewhere (Crossman, 1977: 510), being refused to the Seychelles in the late 1960s, while the Foreign Secretary told Bermuda in 1973 that Britain was not willing to create any more associated arrangements. Although Anguilla's size and economic reliance on Britain ruled out independence this did not necessarily deter other small territories. Nauru had become independent in 1968 with an economy totally reliant upon a rapidly depleting resource of phosphates.

The loss of the Overseas Territories Bill meant the policy continued of dealing with each territory on its individual merits. Reviews of dependent territories were undertaken in 1967 (CAB 148/31, OPD (67)11, 1967; CO 1058/17, 1966) and again in 1969 (FCO 44/127, 1969). In mid 1970, a further official study of future constitutional possibilities for the dependent territories was carried out. The inconclusive result was the rather unsurprising view that there would be 'a hard core of territories remaining dependent in some form or another' (Sir David Scott, quoted by Drower, 1992: 27). This was followed in 1973 by a *Programme Analysis and Review*, an inter-departmental cost-benefit analysis prepared by the Foreign and Commonwealth Office (FCO), Ministry of Defence (MoD), and Overseas Development Association (ODA) with the emphasis on political decolonisation (Sir David Scott, quoted by Drower, 1992: 27). Under the new Labour administration, from March 1974, decolonisation was pushed even more rapidly especially by Ted Rowlands, appointed Minister at the FCO in mid 1975 (Rowlands, 1979: 361–2). According to the recollections of Evan Luard, Rowlands believed decolonisation was 'what he was there to do and the quicker we got rid of these places [the DTs] the better' (quoted by Drower, 1992: 29). Rowlands certainly regarded himself as 'Minister of Decolonisation' (Cmnd 6409: 14), and when he left office in 1979 he said he regretted not having decolonised more (Rowlands, 1984). Decolonisation had continued apace under the Heath and Wilson/Callaghan governments, administrations of different hues but singly intent on retreating rapidly, albeit decently, from the responsibilities of Empire. This process continued into the early 1980s. Fiji and Tonga became independent in 1970, the Seychelles in 1976. Between 1973 and 1983 the Associated States of Bahamas, Grenada, Dominica, St Lucia, St Vincent, Belize, Antigua, and St Kitts-Nevis all chose independence. In the Pacific region the Solomon Islands, Tuvalu, Kiribati and Vanuatu all became independent between 1978 and 1980.

However, at that time in certain Caribbean territories – the Cayman Islands, British Virgin Islands, and the Turks and Caicos Islands – there were no strong local demands for independence.[6]

The European Union

In 1973 the UK joined the EEC. This had implications for the dependent territories (Sutton, 1991). Current and newly independent colonies were concerned that this would threaten the terms of the Commonwealth Sugar Agreement and the subsidy that came to sugar producers. Protocol 22 of the treaty of accession offered overseas territories future association with the EEC and also membership of the Lomé conventions that gave protection to both sugar and banana production, as well as access to the European Development Fund (Sutton, 2001: 45–6). Twenty-two years later the Maastricht Treaty provided for a common foreign and security policy encompassing dependent territories and dealt with questions of asylum, movement of people including immigration, drugs, fraud and other criminal activities. For example, in 1996 the EU provided £23.5 million in a five-year programme to combat drug trafficking in the Caribbean region, including the dependent territories.

What to do with the remnants?

With small territories becoming independent up to 1983, the question to be addressed was what to do with those colonies that remained as dependent territories. The most populous was Hong Kong but in 1984 it was agreed that it should return to China in 1997. A seminar held at the Institute of Development Studies, University of Sussex, in September 1979, chaired by Nicholas Ridley, looked at the decolonisation prospects of smaller territories and the various constitutional options. According to Sir Richard Stratton (then under-secretary at the FCO and responsible for dependent territories), the seminar set out 'to talk with various outside experts, whether journalists or academics, or possibly even former administrators, to see whether they thought the manner in which we were proceeding was more or less on the right lines' (Drower, 1992: 31). The official view remained that the UK would not force independence on the remaining Dependent Territories. The conclusion was again not altogether surprising: there was no single answer, most of the remaining territories would remain dependent, and even if any became independent they were likely to continue to be a charge on the British exchequer for aid and defence (Institute for Development Studies, 1979; Selwyn, 1978). At no point did the idea occur of Britain simply abdicating all responsibility for the smaller territories. Among Colonial Office officials, and their successors within the FCO, there

6   Richard Posnett had recently been appointed adviser on dependent territories at the FCO.

was a long-standing, strong and abiding sense of moral responsibility for the political, economic and social welfare of the dependent territories. Britain's international image for good stewardship in administering even the remnants of a fading empire remained an important imperative before the gaze of the US, the Commonwealth countries and the UN.

Dilemmas of the Dependent Territories

The retention of and responsibility for small colonies in the Atlantic, Caribbean and Pacific during the 1980s and 1990s did not come without dilemmas for Britain. First, many of the islands had weak economies that were dependent upon a single product vulnerable to sudden price changes on the international market. Remoter islands lacked good external communications. Two islands had active volcanoes, while sudden tropical storms could undo years of investment in a few hours. Several territories relied upon budgetary grants-in-aid and although some underwent rapid economic development after the 1970s, most notably the Cayman Islands and the British Virgin Islands, there was little prospect of St Helena, let alone philatelic-reliant Pitcairn, following suit.[7] Although Shackleton's report in 1976 had pointed up the economic neglect of the Falkland Islands only the shock of the Argentine invasion in 1982 forced economic reforms and investment, at considerable cost, on that distant, ill-developed, economically depressed and thinly inhabited possession. In the 1970s and 1980s London continued to hope that the economic burdens of overseas territories might be shared with, or even passed to, other powers. The option of independence remained for certain territories, in the 1970s thought most likely to be Bermuda and Montserrat, but sovereignty had to be based on a high degree of economic independence. The level of aid to be given (in the Caribbean, British aid looked mean when compared to the largesse of the French and the Dutch) troubled officials in London who argued that it should not raise local standards of living to levels beyond that which the territory would be able to sustain if it progressed to independence (FCO 86/75, 1973).

A second dilemma was that several dependent territories were threatened by more powerful and predatory neighbours. Since Peron's time Argentina had stridently laid claim to the Falklands; Guatemala claimed British Honduras but independence and the 1981 agreement did not completely negate the need for troops with the attendant costs; and Spain demanded Gibraltar. For Britain these were regular irritants that disturbed regional politics and incurred additional defence costs. Britain's publicly stated policy was that there would be no change to the dependent territories without the consent of the local population. However, this did not prevent covert negotiations with a view to

---

7   The Cayman Islands GDP (US$): 1970 $2,760, 1995 $30,500; Turks and Caicos Islands 1984 $3,320, 1992 $6,000.

ceding sovereignty taking place with Buenos Aires and Madrid. From 1964 to 1981, both Labour and Conservative governments lacked the political will to uphold the economic and security interests of the Falklands. Dependent territories with strategic value were more secure but political change, for example democratisation in Spain after 1975 and the end of the Cold War, significantly reduced the value of garrison colonies and a naval base such as Gibraltar.

The Argentine invasion of the Falklands in 1982 highlighted the degree of neglect by London of its existing and former small territories. It also led to a reappraisal of policy that Baroness Young, the minister of state responsible for the Caribbean, described as 're-engagement rather than disengagement', and an increase in trade and investment. Independence was not a wise option, she argued: 'The last 20 years have witnessed the emergence of a large number of small independent states which are incapable of providing for their own economic or political security' (HC541, 1983–4).

A third dilemma was on the question of race and nationality. This was highlighted by the British Nationality Act 1981, the purpose of which was to bring nationality and immigration legislation into line, and also with Europe. But the Act, by conferring on people in the Empire's remnants the title of 'Citizenship of Dependent Territories', wrote Ian Spencer, in effect 'disposed of remaining claims to enter the United Kingdom from groups who were not recently descended from British emigrants' (Spencer, 1997: 148). This racial nature of the Act, and the loss of a 'sense of Britishness' held by many people in dependent territories, was compounded when Gibraltarians were granted British citizenship rights in 1981, a status extended to Falkland Islanders by the British Nationality (Falkland Islands) Act of 1983. Whites were citizens while non-whites were not! The old Empire of race had not gone away. This was clear from the arbitrary removal of the black *Ilois* from Diego Garcia compared to the talk of generous compensation if the white population of the Falklands was to be evacuated. Many people in the dependent territories were predictably aggrieved and angry that they could not have free entry to and right of residence in Britain. Various local campaigns, for example in St Helena, demanded rights of UK citizenship.[8] For Britain, the big headache was Hong Kong with its eight million British 'subjects' whose status was defined further by the Hong Kong Act 1985, although post-Tiananmen the British Nationality (Hong Kong) Act granted right of abode to highly selected and highly qualified Hong Kong residents. The return of Hong Kong to China cleared the board by removing the weight of numbers leaving dependent

8   The St Helena campaign began in 1992 and the eventual demand was for the 'restoration' of UK citizenship for the British Island that would enjoy rights similar to the Channel Islands and the Isle of Man, like those Crown Dependencies outside of the EU.

territories with approximately 190,000 people, few of whom were likely to want to come and live permanently in Britain.

Self-governing dependent territories posed further dilemmas: qualities of governance and levels of corruption; judicial policies; and offshore financial dealings. Corrupt local administrations in the Caribbean had long worried London, for example Grenada under Gairy (CO 1031/3974, no. 22C, 1962), and self-government increased opportunities for corrupt political and economic practices. Caribbean territories also were well-placed geographically to take advantage of offshore banking and a range of other commercial activities that helped to underpin and strengthen their economies, but also to be involved in drug smuggling, gun running and money laundering. In 1985 and 1986 the chief minister and other senior figures of the Turks and Caicos Islands government were arrested in Miami on narcotics charges and imprisoned. Subsequently, the Blom-Cooper enquiry of 1986 led to ministers resigning, the suspension of constitutional government and Britain assuming direct control until 1988 (Cmnd 21. 1986; Thorndike, 1987: 259–65).

In the wake of this scandal, and pressured by Parliament, the FCO conducted an internal review of policy towards Bermuda and the remaining Caribbean territories in late 1987. The review engaged in a cost-benefit analysis of the dependent territories and examined the pros and cons of independence and also alternative constitutional possibilities. It concluded that dependent territories would remain for the foreseeable future, that existing policy was basically sound but the quality of local administrative personnel needed improving. It also contained the statement that the UK government should in no way attempt to influence opinion in the territories on the question of independence. Tim Eggar, minister at the FCO, told the Commons: 'We would not urge them [the dependent territories] to consider moving to independence, but we remain ready to respond positively when this is the clearly and constitutionally expressed wish of the people' (HC Debates, 102, 1986: 863–6; HC Debates, 124, 1987, col. 574; Sutton, 2001: 47–8). In a further review of Caribbean dependent territories in late 1991–early 1992, the prominent questions were on drug trafficking, money laundering, good governance and economic development. The regulation of offshore financial services was improved and governors' powers were increased. British security in the region relied on a frigate based in Bermuda and 1,600 troops in Belize.

By 1990 the dependent territories were reduced to Hong Kong, whose future had been determined six years earlier for transfer to China in 1997, and a number of small islands and enclaves that seemed unlikely or unwilling to change their existing relationship with Britain. These included colonies with strategic and communications value: Ascension Island in the Atlantic administered by the BBC, and the Chagos and Diego Garcia islands that had been turned into US military bases. Two territories were threatened by the annexationist claims of neighbours: Gibraltar, by Spain, and the Falklands by

Argentina, in both cases strongly resisted by populations that spoke English, claimed to be British and were overwhelmingly opposed to any change of national status. There were also remote islands with small populations and weak economies heavily dependent upon budgetary grants-in-aid (St Helena and Pitcairn); and also Montserrat hit hard by Hurricane Hugo in 1989, and then, as economic recovery began, dealt a more disastrous blow by the volcanic eruption of 1995 which led to widespread devastation, economic and demographic dislocation, thus removing any idea that the island might be independent.

There were only two dependent territories with levels of economic growth and good governance that made them possible candidates for independence: the Cayman Islands and Bermuda. In neither was there any strong indication that the electorate wanted to alter the existing relationship with the UK. Bermuda held a referendum in 1995 that, on a low turnout of 59 per cent, showed 73 per cent against independence. John Swan, leader of the United Bermuda Party, was reported as saying in 1982: 'With the Americans to feed us and the British to defend us, who needs independence' (quoted Connell, 1994: 99). The Constitutional Commission of the Cayman Islands stated: 'There is no wish whatsoever to alter the present state of the islands as a dependent territory on which, it must be said, much of the islands' prosperity may depend'. In 1990 Ralph O'Neal, deputy chief minister of the British Virgin Islands, told the visiting UN Special Committee that 'the British Virgin Islands will not be bullied, provoked, coerced or sweet mouthed into independence' (Connell, 1994: 93–4, 96). There were few, if any, benefits to be had on the uncertain and costly waters of independence; economic independence not sovereignty put food on the table. Independence might flatter the vanity of certain Caribbean politicians but it was widely known that people in the French, Dutch, US, and British dependent territories enjoyed a higher standard of living than those in the independent states, even territories of comparable geographical size and population (Oostindie and Klinkers, 2003: 154–5).

A new direction in policy

A new approach to the dependent territories gradually developed in the 18 months after Labour won the 1997 election. Labour in power did not demonstrate great sensitivity initially to the dependent territories or to the Caribbean, even though a substantial majority of the 600,000 voters of Caribbean origin had voted for the party. The imminent handover to China of Hong Kong, the continuing volcano activity in Montserrat with the deaths of 19 people on 25 June 1997, an increased awareness of the economic problems of the poorer territories, and the growing significance of the offshore financial centres, led the new Foreign Secretary, Robin Cook, to announce a thorough review of Britain's relationship with the dependent territories. In May 1997 the National Audit Office had published an updated *Report on Contingent Liabilities in the Dependent Territories*. Following the deaths in Montserrat in June, there had been House of Commons enquiries into Montserrat initiated by the International Development Committee, which reported in November 1997, and by the Foreign Affairs Committee into the Dependent Territories generally, which reported in January 1998. The White Paper, *Partnership for Progress and Prosperity*, resulting from Cook's review, was issued in March 1999. Introducing this in the Commons, Cook said that it provided 'the basis for a renewed contract and a modern partnership between the United Kingdom and the dependent territories' (HC Debates, 327, col. 1125). The outcomes were that the 190,000 people in the dependent territories were offered British citizenship with right of abode; the territories were to be renamed the UK Overseas Territories (effected by the British Overseas Territories Act, 2002); there were to be responsible ministers of state within the FCO and DFID; and plans were laid down to help the territories advance both economically and politically. In return, the dependent territories were expected to meet the terms and standards laid down by the UK and international treaty obligations relating to financial institutions, observing human rights and good governance. An Overseas Territories Consultative Council, formed by chief ministers or their equivalents from each territory, met annually in London. Each territory also had representatives in the metropolitan capital where they established the UKOT Association.

It would appear that most, if not all, of the UK Overseas Territories will remain related to Britain. Serious challenges certainly remain: on sovereignty – Britain is unlikely to cut a deal with Argentina over the Falklands but would clearly like to do so with Spain over Gibraltar; of constitutional modernisation which initially was a languid process (Fergus, 2005; Hendry, chapter 4 below); on reconciling Territory desire for full self-government with the UK's need to retain the powers and levers needed to fulfil overall responsibilities; and progress to promote good governance, policing and judicial reform (the Pitcairn child sex abuse trials of 2004). In 2000 six territories were dependent on British development assistance the major recipients being Montserrat and St Helena.[9] In December 2003 the Foreign Secretary announced publication of a comprehensive strategy for the next five to 10 years; the eighth strategic international priority was related to the security and good governance of the UKOTs. However, these are small islands, some far away, many weak and insignificant, and despite the recent rhetoric their welfare and interests (the Falklands may be the exception) probably have little weight in the corridors of Whitehall.

---

9   In 2008, 70 per cent of people living in the dependent territories enjoyed average living standards higher than the UK.

References

Primary sources: The United Kingdom, The National Archive, Kew

CAB 19/77, CP (55)133, 'Smaller colonial territories, 27 Sept. 1955.

CAB 129/33/2, CP (49)62, 10 March 1949, 'Constitutional development in smaller colonial territories', Cabinet Memo. by Arthur Creech Jones.

CAB 129/77, CP (55)133, 'Smaller colonial territories', Cabinet memo. by Alan Lennox-Boyd, Appendices, 27 Sept. 1955.

CAB 129/71, C 54(307), 11 Oct. 1954.

CAB 129/77, CP (55)133, App. B, 'Smaller colonial territories', 27 Sept. 1955.

CAB 132/225, no. 99, to CO, 17 Jan. 1961.

CAB 133/200, C (60)1222, 'The constitutional development of the Commonwealth', 23 July 1960.

CAB 134/55, CA 8(48)2 & 3, 'Constitutional reform in Gibraltar', Cabinet Commonwealth Affairs Committee mins, 29 Oct. 1948.

CAB 134/1203, CA (0)56, 25 May 1956.

CAB 134/2505, no. 2, 'Future status of smaller colonial territories within the Commonwealth', 24 March 1959.

CAB 148/21, OPD (65)89, 'Future of remaining colonial territories', 31 May 1965.

CAB 148/31, OPD (67)11, memo by Judith Hart, 'The outlook for the dependent territories', 2 March 1967.

CO 847/36/1. Mins by Thomas, Jan.–May 1947.

CO 936/733, nos. 43–53, 20 June–16 July 1962.

CO 967/146, no. 1, 'Interim recommendations to the S of S for the Colonies by the Committee of Enquiry into Constitutional Development in the Smaller Colonial Territories', March 1951.

CO 1031/3974, no. 22C, on maladministration in Grenada, June 1962.

CO 1031/4409, no. 495, 'Future of dependent territories', 22 June 1965.

CO 1032/60, no. 1, letter, Sir Norman Brook to Sir Charles Jeffries, 23 Sept. 1955.

CO 1032/226, no. 169, 'Evolution of the Commonwealth', 24 April 1962.

CO 1032/412, no. 18, 'Future of the remaining colonial dependencies', 18 Aug. 1965.

CO 1058/17, no. 14, paper by Hilton Poyton on 'Future policy in the smaller colonial territories', 15 July 1966.

DO 35/2218, CRO note of discussion, 1 June 1951.

FCO 44/127, numbers 14 and 15, 1969.

FCO 86/60, 'Programme and analysis review', Anthony Kershaw, 12 June 1972.

FCO 86/61, 86/75, and the full report at 86/76, dd. Nov. 1973.

FCO 86/75, Anthony Royle to Lord Balneil, 8 Nov. 1973.

FO 371/172610, no. 13, 'The future of British colonial territories', CO memo, [27] Sept. 1963.

HC541 (1983–4) *First Special Report from the Foreign Affairs Committee: The Economic and Political Security of Small States.*

Official: United Kingdom

CM 4264, *Partnership for Progress and Prosperity: Britain and the Overseas Territories* (1999).

Cmd 7433, *The Colonial Empire 1947–1948* (1948).

Cmnd 21, *Turks and Caicos Islands Commission of Enquiry*, London, Dec. 1986.

Cmnd 6409, *The Seychelles Constitutional Conference* (1976).

HC Debates, Vol. 102, 25 July 1986, pp. 863–6.

HC Debates, Vol. 124, 16 Dec. 1987, col. 574.

HC Debates, Vol. 327, col. 1125, 17.

Secondary sources

R. Aldrich and J. Connell (1992) *France's Overseas Frontier: Départements et Territoires d'Outre-Mer* (Cambridge: Cambridge University Press).

— (1998) *The Last Colonies* (Cambridge: Cambridge University Press).

R.C. Alomar (2003) 'Britain's withdrawal from the Eastern Caribbean, 1965–7: a reappraisal', *Journal of Imperial & Commonwealth History* 31 (3), pp. 74–106.

— (2009) *Revisiting the Transatlantic Triangle. The constitutional decolonisation of the Eastern Caribbean* (Kingston, Jamaica: Ian Randle).

S.R. Ashton and D. Killingray (eds.) (1999) *BDEEP: The West Indies* (London: HMSO).

S.R. Ashton and W.R. Louis (eds.) (2004) *BDEEP: East of Suez and the British Commonwealth, 1964–1971* (London: HMSO).

Bishop of St Helena's Commission on Citizenship (1996) *St Helena: The last county of England* (St Helena).

J. Connell (1994) 'Britain's Caribbean colonies: the end of the era of decolonisation', *Journal of Commonwealth & Comparative Politics* 32 (1), pp. 87–106.

R.H.S. Crossman (1977) *Diaries of a Cabinet Minister,* vol. 3 (London).

M. Curteis (2003) *A Web of Deceit* (London: Verso).

G. Drower (1992) *Britain's Dependent Territories: A Fistful of Islands* (Aldershot: Dartmouth).

F. Fergus (2005) 'Constitutional reform in some British Overseas Territories in the Caribbean: modernisation or colonial entrenchment', in D. Killingray and D. Taylor (eds.) *The United Kingdom Overseas Territories: Past, Present and Future* (London: Institute of Commonwealth Studies).

The Independent (1997) 'Volcano island gives Short shrift', 25 Aug. Available at www.independent.co.uk/news/volcano-island-gives-short-shrift-1247214.html (accessed 28 Oct. 2011).

Institute for Development Studies (1979) *Seminar on the Future of Britain's Remaining Dependent Territories,* Seminar no. 157, Sept. (University of Sussex).

Labour Party (1957) *Labour's Colonial Policy – III Smaller Territories,* June (London).

W.D. McIntyre (1996) 'The admission of small states to the Commonwealth', *Journal of Imperial and Commonwealth History* 24 (2), pp. 244–77.

D.K. Morgan (1980) *The Official History of Colonial Development: Towards Self-Government in British Colonies 1941–1971,* vol. 5 (London: Macmillan).

G. Oostindie and I. Klinkers (2003) *Decolonising the Caribbean: Dutch policies in a comparative perspective* (Amsterdam: Amsterdam University Press).

R. Posnett (1978) 'Britain's Dependent Territories', Institute of Commonwealth Studies, seminar paper, 3 Nov.

T. Rowlands (1979) 'The end of Empire', *Royal Society of Arts Journal,* May.

— (1984) *The Small States of the Commonwealth* (London: Royal Commonwealth Society).

P. Selwyn (1978) 'Small, poor and remote: Islands at geographical disadvantage', IDS Discussion Paper 123 (University of Sussex).

I.R.G. Spencer (1997) *British Immigration Policy since 1939: The Making of Multi-racial Britain* (London: Routledge).

P. Sutton (1991) 'The European Community and the Caribbean: main dimensions and key issues', in P.K. Sutton (ed.) *Europe and the Caribbean* (Basingstoke: Macmillan).

— (2001) 'Two steps forward, one step back: Britain and the Commonwealth Caribbean', *Itinerario* XXV (2), pp. 42–58.

A.E. Thorndike (1979) 'The concept of Associated Statehood in the eastern Caribbean', PhD thesis, University of London.

— (1987) 'When small is not beautiful: the case of the Turks and Caicos Islands', *Corruption and Reform* 2 (3), pp. 259–65.

N. Turner (1997) *St Helena: A British Island. The Second Report Produced for the Citizenship Commission* (Raynes Park, London).

S. Winchester (2003) *Outposts: Journeys to the Surviving Relics of the British Empire* (London: HarperCollins).

Chapter 2

The UK Overseas Territories: a decade of progress and prosperity?[1]

Peter Clegg and Peter Gold

Introduction

This study analyses the complex relationship between the UK and its permanently populated Overseas Territories (OTs) with a particular focus on the last decade up to the British general election of May 2010. In 1999, the 'New' Labour government published a White Paper, Partnership for Progress and Prosperity, which was an attempt to refocus and renew the links between the UK and its OTs. For many years prior to that the relationship was rather ad hoc – a situation that can be traced back to the compromises, fudges and deals characteristic of 'pragmatic' British colonial administration. The chapter details the efforts on the part of the Labour government to overcome the legacy of only intermittent UK interest, through the imposition of greater coherence across the territories via a new partnership based on mutual obligations and responsibilities. It focuses on the two most important aspects of the White Paper: governance (including good governance, constitutional reform and human rights) and economic growth and sustainability. An assessment is made of the progress achieved in these areas since 1999 and the problems that remain. The concluding section provides a number of recommendations in terms of how the relationship can be improved over the next ten years.

A mandate for reform

A crisis in Montserrat and a UK National Audit Office (NAO) report highlighted Britain's inadequate organisational and regulatory framework as it related to the then-named Dependent Territories in the mid 1990s. The crisis in Montserrat began in July 1995 (towards the end of the British Conservative

1   This article first appeared in *Commonwealth and Comparative Politics* 49 (1), pp. 115–35, Feb. 2011. Inevitably some bibliographical details may have changed.

Party's term in office) when the Soufrière Hills Volcano erupted, precipitating a period of great uncertainty and insecurity for the island. The eruption of the volcano devastated the country and by December 1997 almost 90 per cent of the resident population of over 10,000 had been relocated at least once, while over two-thirds had left the island. Much of the infrastructure had been destroyed or put out of use, while the private sector had collapsed and the economy had become largely dependent on British aid (Department for International Development, 1999). Three reports were published on the disaster, all of which highlighted several deficiencies in the UK-Montserrat relationship, including a confused division of responsibility for Montserrat between the Department for International Development (DFID) and the Foreign and Commonwealth Office (FCO), the overly complex UK government management systems for Montserrat and the absence of contingency planning in terms of how the FCO and DFID would manage an emergency in a Dependent Territory (International Development Committee, 1997, 1998; Department for International Development, 1999).

At about the time the Montserrat crisis was at its height and the first reports on the situation were being published, the NAO investigated the action taken by the FCO to minimise the risk of potential contingent liabilities falling on the UK as a result of the actions of the territories. As the report stated: 'Given the Foreign Office's responsibilities, there exists a continuing exposure to potential liabilities ... Under English and Dependent Territory law, the governments of the Territories are answerable for their own actions. However, if the Territories' resources are insufficient, the UK government may come under pressure to provide assistance. Legal liability may fall on the UK if Territories fail to comply with international law, especially treaty obligations' (National Audit Office, 1997: 1).

The report found that, despite the FCO having undertaken a number of past initiatives to identify and minimise the risk of contingent liabilities in the territories, the UK remained exposed. In particular, the NAO noted that the UK was vulnerable to 'financial sector failures, corruption, drug trafficking, money laundering, migrant pressure and natural disasters' (National Audit Office, 1997: 7). The NAO worryingly described the UK government as having 'extensive responsibilities but limited power' (National Audit Office, 1997: 17). In a follow-up report by the House of Commons Committee of Public Accounts, its concern over the situation was starkly highlighted. The Committee wrote: 'We are worried by the mismatch between the extent of these responsibilities [for the Dependent Territories] and the inadequacy of the FCO's powers, strong in theory but limited in practice, to manage them'. The Committee further stated: 'As a result of this mismatch, the UK taxpayer continues to be exposed to very significant liabilities in the Territories and, from time to time, these materialise. More generally, we are concerned at the Foreign Office's admission that everything is not wholly under control and that all risks are not weighed and properly covered' (Committee of Public Accounts, 1998: v). Both the NAO and the Committee recommended a number of reforms to reduce Britain's potential contingent liabilities and encouraged the UK government to strengthen its control over the territories.

Partnership for progress and prosperity: a new beginning

The arrival of the 'New' Labour government, the ongoing crisis in Montserrat and the NAO and Committee of Public Accounts reports, led to the initiation of a review of the UK's relationship with its OTs in August 1997. The purpose of the review was 'to ensure that the relationship reflected the needs of the Territories and Britain alike and to give the Territories confidence in our commitment to their future' (Foreign and Commonwealth Office, 1999: 8). It was based on the principle that 'Britain's links to the Dependent Territories should be based on a partnership, with obligations and responsibilities for both sides' (Foreign and Commonwealth Office, 1999: 8). In particular, it was noted, 'the relationship ... needs to be effective and efficient, free and fair. It needs to be based on decency and democracy' (Foreign and Commonwealth Office, 1999: 7). During the review, the UK government consulted with a range of interested parties but it was clearly a British-led initiative.

In March 1999, the completed review was published as a White Paper entitled Partnership for Progress and Prosperity (Foreign and Commonwealth Office, 1999). The White Paper set out a number of recommendations on issues such as the constitutional link, citizenship, financial standards, good governance and human rights. The latter issues highlighted Britain's desire that the territories should meet certain standards set by the UK government and the wider international community. On the constitutional issue, the White Paper reported that there was a clear wish on the part of the territories to retain their connection with Britain and not move towards independence. However, it was agreed that a process of constitutional review would be carried out in an attempt to update existing provisions and that if any territory wanted independence in the future Britain would not stand in its way. Further, the White Paper documented the changes that had been introduced to streamline the administrative links between the UK and the territories, including for the first time a dedicated minister for the territories and the establishment of a new department within the FCO (the OTs Department). Also, a new political forum, the OTs Consultative Council, was established to bring together British ministers and territory representatives to discuss matters of concern.

Most of the reforms were undertaken out of public view, but two gained widespread publicity and perhaps best represented the UK government's new approach to the territories. One decision related to a change in nomenclature from 'Dependent Territory' to 'Overseas Territory'. Several officials from the territories had asked for the name change believing that it better reflected the nature of a post-colonial 'partnership' at the end of the 20th century. Many of the territories at this point were not receiving any budgetary assistance from the UK (today only Montserrat, Pitcairn and St Helena, which all have significant natural and structural barriers to growth, receive such assistance), and they felt, therefore, that they were not dependent on the UK government. The second change to the relationship came with the announcement that British citizenship – and so the right of abode – would be offered to citizens of all of the territories (hitherto only the Falkland Islanders and Gibraltarians had enjoyed such status).

The review of the OTs undertaken by the British Labour government was certainly the most wide-ranging for many years. The desire of a new administration to assert its influence over a problematic policy area, as the OTs were deemed to be, was an important factor underpinning the FCO-led examination. In addition, the fact that the Labour Party had been out of power for 18 years heightened the expectations of new thinking and new approaches. In many ways, the outcome of the Partnership for Progress and Prosperity White Paper indicated that the Labour government was serious about its attempts to overcome long-standing problems in the UK-OT relationship. However, as will be seen, the realities of overseeing such a disparate and in most cases distant group of territories have meant that only some aspects of the Partnership for Progress and Prosperity agenda have been fulfilled. Indeed, it is evident from particular developments that fundamental structural problems in the relationship remain unattended.

Governance

In the White Paper, there was a clear commitment to the promotion of good governance, democracy and the rule of law. Further, the White Paper highlighted a series of action points to achieve these ends, including through measures to promote more open, transparent and accountable government; to improve the composition of legislatures and their operation; to improve the effectiveness, efficiency, accountability and impartiality of the public service; to promote representative and participative government and to secure freedom of speech and information (Foreign and Commonwealth Office, 1999: 13). The record of achievement in these areas is patchy and was undermined significantly by the serious allegations of corruption highlighted recently in the Turks and Caicos Islands (TCI). The case is certainly not representative of the OTs as a whole, but the deep-seated problems in the TCI must be acknowledged because they highlight grave failures in the post-1999 approach to UK-OT relations. The weaknesses in governance were seen most starkly in regard to the TCI, but it can be argued that they exist more generally in the relationship. To illustrate the point, the situation in the TCI must be considered.

The TCI

A detailed picture of the state of affairs in the TCI was revealed by a Commission of Inquiry led by Sir Robin Auld, a former British High Court Judge. The Commission was appointed on 10 July 2008, an interim report was completed in late February 2009 and the full report was released five months later on 18 July. Sir Robin's criticisms were numerous, but fundamentally he argued that 'there is a high probability of systemic corruption in government and the legislature and among public officers in the TCI ...' (TCI Commission of Inquiry, 2009: 11).

Particular areas of concern included the '... bribery by overseas developers and other investors of Ministers and/or public officers, so as to secure Crown (public) land on favourable terms, coupled with government approval for its commercial development'; the '... serious deterioration ... in the Territory's systems of governance and public financial management and control'; the '... concealment of conflicts of interest at all levels of public life, and consequent venality'; the manipulation and abuse of Belongerships (a status which confers rights normally associated with citizenship, including the right to vote and to be a recipient of the disposal of Crown land); and the misuse of wide discretionary powers given to Ministers in the 2006 Constitution (TCI Commission of Inquiry, 2009: 11–12). Stemming from these and many other criticisms, Sir Robin recommended the institution of criminal investigations in relation to former Premier Michael Misick (who resigned in March 2009 after the Commission's interim report was published) and three of his former cabinet ministers.

The criticisms and recommendations against high-profile members of the government were, of course, highly damaging, but what was perhaps even more significant was the Commission's emphasis on the systemic nature of the corruption. Throughout the Commission's report, fundamental weaknesses in the system of governance in the TCI were highlighted. The outcome was that the TCI's '... democratic traditions and structures [were] tested almost to beyond breaking point' (TCI Commission of Inquiry, 2009: 215). Because of these broader concerns Sir Robin called for '...urgent and wide-ranging systemic change' (TCI Commission of Inquiry, 2009: 218) and in particular the partial suspension of the 2006 Constitution, interim direct rule from Westminster and reforms to the constitution and other aspects of the system of governance in the TCI to help prevent future abuses of power (TCI Commission of Inquiry, 2009).

After such wide-ranging criticisms, the UK government had little choice but to act. As former FCO minister, Gillian Merron, stated after the Commission's interim report was published: 'These are some of the worst allegations that I have ever seen about sitting politicians ...' and '... when things go badly wrong ... we need to act' (*Hansard*, 2009a). An Order in Council, the TCI

Constitution (Interim Amendment) Order 2009, was implemented on 14 August 2009. Once executed, the Order suspended ministerial government and the House of Assembly for a period of up to two years (although this has since been extended). In their place, the Governor was given the power to take charge of government matters, subject to instruction from the FCO, supported by a range of other British officials and guided by an Advisory Council and Consultative Forum, both of which are composed entirely of Belongers (Foreign and Commonwealth Office, 2009). Soon afterwards an anti-corruption team was dispatched to the TCI to investigate and prosecute criminal cases arising out of the Commission's report (*Financial Times*, 2009).

One other aspect of the Commission of Inquiry's report which has not yet been touched upon is the parallels it draws with the Inquiry undertaken by Louis Blom-Cooper in 1986 into allegations of arson, corruption and related matters in the TCI (Report of the Commissioner Mr Louis Blom-Cooper QC, 1986). Blom-Cooper's findings are disturbingly similar to those of the 2009 Inquiry, when he talks about 'persistent unconstitutional behaviour' and 'maladministration by both Ministers and civil servants at every level of government', leading to 'constant blights upon a ... society which is already displaying signs of political instability' and to an economy that 'at present is precariously poised' (Report of the Commissioner Mr Louis Blom-Cooper QC, 1986: 98–9). Commenting on these observations, the report of the 2009 Inquiry states that '[Blom-Cooper's] general conclusions ... suggest that little has changed over the last 20 or so years leading to this Inquiry, except as to the possible range and scale of venality in public life' (TCI Commission of Inquiry, 2009: 23). This remark is deeply troubling and is perhaps the most significant aspect of the entire report as it strikes right at the heart of UK government policy in relation to many of its OTs, not just the TCI, over the last decade and indeed beyond.

There had in fact been strong indications for many years that there were deep-rooted problems in the TCI. Numerous studies were undertaken that highlighted issues of concern (TCI Commission of Inquiry, 2009: 94 –5). As the Commission of Inquiry report argued: '... [criticisms] have been identified time and again in official and independent reports in different contexts ... but to little result' (TCI Commission of Inquiry, 2009: 102). The FCO was certainly aware of some of the problems in the TCI and it did upgrade the post of the governor, but largely it took a softly, softly approach to enacting change. Further, the FCO was not proactive in investigating the allegations of more systemic corruption that were coming to the fore. Indeed, until very late in the day, the FCO argued there was insufficient evidence to justify either prosecutions or a Commission of Inquiry regarding developments in the TCI (Foreign Affairs Committee, 2008: 67). The UK government's position may have remained the same if it had not been for a Foreign Affairs Committee (FAC) investigation on the OTs.

The largest number of submissions received by the FAC came from the TCI, and many of the authors had taken the unusual step of asking for confidentiality. During the course of the investigation, the committee said that many of these submissions suggested 'a substantial measure of financial impropriety [is] taking place', including, it was claimed, at the government level (Caribbean Insight, 2008: 1). The subsequent report also criticised the 'climate of fear' in the territory, with some citizens too afraid to discuss their concerns about the standards of governance in the TCI. Under such circumstances, the FAC recommended that the UK government establish a commission of inquiry, with full protection for witnesses (Foreign Affairs Committee, 2008: 7).

While recognising that it is sometimes difficult to assess whether an issue is serious enough to merit intervention, the FAC report stated quite clearly that in regard to the TCI '[the UK government's] approach has been too hands off'. As a consequence, the Committee argued, 'the Government must take its oversight responsibility for the OTs more seriously – consulting across all OTs more on the one hand while demonstrating a greater willingness to step in and use reserve powers when necessary on the other' (2008: 131). The call for a Commission of Inquiry indicated how seriously the committee viewed the situation in the TCI, and a few days later the UK government announced that one would be established. Despite this final act, the TCI's collapse in governance suggests that, rather than being too interventionist as some of its critics would suggest, the UK government has been far too lax in its dealings with at least some of the OTs and thus many of the original objectives of the 1999 White Paper have not been met – in the TCI's case, clearly so.

The balance of power in UK-OT relations

The breakdown of good governance in the TCI shows that the UK government failed to meet its own objectives as defined by the White Paper. However, was the TCI an isolated case or is there a more general problem with UK oversight of – and good governance in – the OTs? It can certainly be argued that Misick and his government pushed the system of governance to breaking point and behaved in an unacceptable manner. In contrast, there have been allegations of corruption in several other OTs, such as in relation to the Bermuda Housing Corporation, but these appear to have been more isolated (Foreign Affairs Committee, 2008). So it does appear that standards of governance are relatively good in the other territories. However, there are several underlying problems in the UK's relationship with its OTs that might indicate that its failings are more deep-seated than just in relation to the TCI.

Each constitution allocates government responsibilities to the Crown (i.e. the UK government and the governor) and the OT, according to the nature of the responsibility. Those powers generally reserved for the Crown include defence and external affairs, as well as responsibility for internal security and the police, international and offshore financial relations and the public service. The Crown also has responsibility for the maintenance of good governance. Meanwhile, individual territory governments have control over all aspects of policy that are not overseen by the Crown, including the economy, education, health, social security and immigration. However, ultimate control rests in the hands of the UK as the territories are constitutionally subordinate (Davies, 1995). Nevertheless, because the arrangements were not intended to be permanent – they were rather meant to be 'stepping-stones on the route to independence' (Taylor, 2005: 21) – there are problems.

In terms of the direct relationship the UK government, via the governors, is reluctant to use its full powers, even in areas where the governor has responsibility – rather consensus and persuasion are preferred. The UK is aware of the importance of maintaining good relations with democratically elected governments and this is particularly true when OTs are no longer in receipt of UK government funding – as is the case with most of them at present. A further constraint in advancing the good governance agenda is the limited power the governor has in certain circumstances. There remains a problem with issues that are in the mid-spectrum. Of course, the governor can use his constitutional powers – including Commissions of Inquiry – and the UK government can introduce Orders in Council, but there is a reluctance to do this because of the controversy they cause. As has been argued, 'Governors have few intermediate levers between ... influence on the one hand and the constitutional power on the other, despite the responsibilities they must discharge' (National Audit Office, 2007: 26). Problems can be exacerbated because key UK responsibilities depend on funding from local governments, which is not always sufficient. Also, governors often lack the experience and skills to carry out this very particular and difficult role, meaning they have to learn on the job and make decisions which may not always be appropriate. Further, the views and priorities of the governor and those of the FCO can diverge. In consequence, concerns that are serious but not extremely so are sometimes left unattended and allowed to fester or are dealt with inappropriately. Another issue is that the constitutions provide continuous opportunities for turf wars between the governor and local ministers. As Taylor argues: 'In my time in Montserrat Ministerial attempts to encroach on the Governor's areas of responsibility and to challenge his powers were the normal stuff of day-to-day administration as they are to a greater or lesser extent in all the Territories' (2000: 339). Tensions are made worse by the fact that the British government and the local government have different agendas and face conflicting pressures. Local governments are subject to short-term electoral pressures, while the UK government is concerned with maintaining good governance and minimising its contingent liabilities.

Problems also exist in Whitehall, particularly in terms of continuity of personnel and the limited resources available for the promotion of good governance. In terms of staffing, both at ministerial and civil service levels, there is little continuity. There was a high turnover of individuals filling the post of Parliamentary Under-Secretary of State under Labour – six between 1999 and 2010. Further, the ministerial position, as well as dealing with the OTs, involved several other responsibilities as part of the portfolio, including the European Union (EU), Eastern Europe and Russia, South America and Australasia and Pacific. Within this list, the OTs were certainly not central priorities. In addition, the qualifications of the people filling the ministerial role have sometimes been inadequate. Some of the deficiencies at ministerial level have also been replicated within the civil service. For example, the OTs team has had six heads in 12 years, while FCO desk officers for the territories tend to remain in post for 18 months to two years, reflecting general practice in the FCO and across Whitehall (National Audit Office, 2007). As the NAO argued '... the resulting lack of continuity and loss of Territory-specific knowledge has been a concern for some stakeholders' (National Audit Office, 2007: 28). A final important concern is the limited funds the FCO has available to encourage good governance and to build capability in the OTs. For example, the department was only able to provide £215,000 in 2006–7 for improvements that extended across all the OTs (National Audit Office, 2007: 68).

At the level of the OTs, most are faced with governance challenges that relate to their small size. For example, 'close communities with personal or extended family relationships between officials and citizens, and small legislatures with a lack of separation of duties and membership between the executive and the elected assembly' (National Audit Office, 2007: 31). Further, some lack a developed civil society and a vibrant media, both of which can reduce the level of checks and balances on the executive. In addition, the very limited electoral franchise in many OTs, particularly in the Caribbean, helps to distort the political and democratic process. The source of this problem is the special immigration status that exists, called 'Belonger', which only applies to certain members of the permanent resident population. Those that have 'Belonger' status have the right to vote; other residents do not. As a consequence, the franchise is much restricted. For example, in the TCI prior to the partial suspension of the constitution only about 7,000 people were allowed to vote out of a total population of 36,000 and these 7,000 were spread across 15 constituencies, the smallest of which had 190 voters. There is evidence to suggest that Misick's Progressive National Party took advantage of the limited franchise to win power (TCI Commission of Inquiry, 2009: 79).

Constitutional review and human rights

Before concluding this section on governance, it is necessary to consider two other issues that emanated from the White Paper: constitutional reform and the requirement of the territories to reform and modernise their human rights provisions. On the first issue, the UK government maintained that reform should be evolutionary and during 2001 set in motion a constitutional review process for the OTs. For the first time, the process was supposedly 'locally owned and driven rather than directed from London' (Foreign Affairs Committee, 2004: 7). Despite this, the UK had clear lines beyond which reform was not possible unless independence was the end objective. In a memorandum submitted on 27 October 2003 by the FCO Minister Bill Rammell to the FAC, strict limits were placed on territories' constitutional room for manoeuvre. The final sentence of the memorandum stated: 'OT governments should not expect that in the Constitutional Reviews ... the UK will agree to changes in the UK Government's reserved powers, or which would have implications for the independence of the judiciary and the impartiality of the civil service' (Foreign Affairs Committee, 2004: 9). Whereas Gibraltar and the Falkland Islands can both now claim 'post-colonial' constitutions – in the sense that both the administering power and the territory agree that the responsibilities set out in the constitution have resulted in a relationship that is no longer a colonial one – in the constitutions agreed recently for British Virgin Islands, Cayman Islands, St Helena (plus Ascension and Tristan da Cunha), Pitcairn and TCI only limited new responsibilities were devolved to the territories. However, even these changes further exacerbated rather than addressed the structural and operational problems in the UK-OT relationship considered above. Indeed, the new TCI constitution introduced in 2006 actually helped to facilitate the breakdown in good governance that occurred. As the Commission of Inquiry stated: 'The 2006 Constitution, to a far greater extent than its 1988 predecessor, leaves individual Cabinet Ministers with a wealth of discretions, by way of grants, exemptions, concessions, discounts etc. to override or side-step matters of principle or orderly and fair administration' (2009: 216).

With regard to the issue of human rights, the UK government made clear that 'high standards of observance' were required (Foreign and Commonwealth Office, 1999: 20). The White Paper indicated three particular issues on which the UK government wanted reform: judicial corporal punishment, capital punishment and legislation outlawing homosexual acts between consenting adults in private. Progress was made on the first two issues but the issue of decriminalising homosexuality was more problematic. Despite lengthy consultations there remained strong resistance to decriminalisation. Many in the territories believed the issue was a local one and local views and predispositions should take precedence over British demands. However, in early 2001, despite widespread controversy the UK government passed an Order in Council to force the change in legislation. It is interesting to note, however, that although the law was changed the view of many has not and in some territories (for example, Bermuda and Gibraltar) local differences remain, with the age of consent for male homosexuals remaining higher than for other citizens.

Since then, the FCO, sometimes in collaboration with DFID, has maintained an interest in human rights in the OTs, which includes an objective to extend all the key human rights conventions to the OTs. In addition, the UK government has the responsibility for ensuring that the OTs fulfil their obligations from the conventions which have been extended to them. To assist in this process, DFID is funding a £1 million four-year programme to build human rights capacity in the OTs (Foreign Affairs Committee, 2008: 82). Some real progress was made when in their new constitutions Gibraltar, the Falkland Islands, British Virgin Islands, Cayman Islands, TCI and St Helena included sections protecting human rights. However, even here there is disappointment. Concerns have been raised about an aspect of the new Cayman Islands constitution – the narrow scope of section 16 dealing with non-discrimination (The Cayman Islands Constitution Order, 2009: 17–18). Human Rights Watch criticised the language highlighting the absence of a free-standing guarantee of equality before the law and the limitation of anti-discrimination protections only to rights expressly included in the constitution (Human Rights Watch, 2009). Furthermore, section 16 limits the scope of protection to discrimination by the government – thus horizontal discrimination by private entities is not forbidden. Hence, it is likely that the new constitution will be inadequate to properly safeguard the rights of certain groups within society. Indeed, it was alleged that the scope of section 16 was narrowed by the Cayman government at the last moment after representations were made by religious and other civil society groups. The intention was to deny protections to lesbian, gay, bisexual and transgender people (Human Rights Watch, 2009). The result is that the Cayman Islands new constitution is likely to be at variance with its commitments under various UN conventions and the European Convention on Human Rights and Fundamental Freedoms. Such a situation is unfortunate in its own terms, but it also reflects badly on the UK as it is ultimately responsible if the OTs are not fulfilling their obligations.

If all these issues are brought together, there is certainly more than a nagging suspicion that despite the changes enacted under the White Paper problems of oversight and engagement continue. One former FCO official has suggested that HMG [Her Majesty's Government] still treats the OTs 'as being mostly of peripheral interest' (Foreign Affairs Committee, 2008: 131). Weaknesses in Whitehall, exacerbated by a loss of institutional memory through the high turnover of ministers and civil servants and the restricted powers of governors, can and do have a serious detrimental impact on policy. This is, of course, important, as proper UK oversight is vital in territories where institutional capacity, developed civil society, strong legislatures and vibrant media are lacking. Nevertheless, the structure and dynamics of the UK-OT relationship seem just about adequate when there is good faith and responsibility on both sides. When the system of governance is really tested, however, as in the case of the TCI, the imbalances and weaknesses in the system are starkly highlighted and standards of governance can deteriorate quite significantly.

Economic growth and sustainability

Beyond the political sphere the White Paper focused on the need to improve the regulation of the offshore financial service industries in the OTs and to encourage sustainable economic development, in part by improving financial procedures and controls via, for example, improved auditing and financial accountability (Foreign and Commonwealth Office, 1999: 6, 25). As with the political issues considered above, progress on the economic agenda has been variable and there has been a degree of complacency on the part of HMG, particularly in relation to the sustainability of certain OT economies. Consideration of this aspect of the White Paper comes later, but first an assessment is made as to whether the commitment to improve the regulation of the offshore financial service industries has been achieved.

Offshore financial services

The offshore financial sector is extremely important to the economies of many OTs both in terms of Gross Domestic Product (GDP) and employment. For example, in the Cayman Islands over 50 per cent of GDP is derived from offshore financial services and a quarter of all employment. Bermuda, British Virgin Islands and Gibraltar also have significant interests in the sector, while Anguilla and TCI have a more modest interest (Foot, 2009: 24). Each territory provides a particular niche service: Bermuda is the third largest centre for reinsurance in the world and the second largest captive insurance domicile, Cayman Islands is the world's leading centre for hedge funds, while British Virgin Islands is the leading domicile for international business companies (Foot, 2009: 16). Notwithstanding, concerns have been raised about the probity of the offshore financial sector. A key source of criticism came in 1997 from the NAO report on contingent liabilities. The report concluded that the offshore sector was vulnerable to abuses by money launderers and drug traffickers and the territories faced possible financial sector failure as a consequence (National Audit Office, 1997). In response, the UK government commissioned consultants KPMG in 1999 to undertake a report reviewing the OTs' compliance with international standards and best practice in financial regulation. The report recommended a number of proposals that the OTs agreed to implement. The key measures were the establishment of independent regulatory authorities, the introduction of investigative powers to assist enquiries by overseas regulators and the creation of comprehensive anti-money laundering frameworks (KPMG, 2000).

It is important to recognise, however, that bilateral efforts involving the UK and the OTs to improve regulatory oversight of the offshore financial sector have not been carried out in a vacuum. International demands for greater control over offshore finance have also been very important with the involvement of organisations such as the Financial Action Task Force (FATF) which promotes policies to combat money laundering and terrorist financing; the Financial Stability Board (formerly the Financial Stability Forum) which promotes the implementation of effective regulatory and supervisory policies; the International Monetary Fund via its Financial Sector Assessment Programme; the EU via its savings tax directive; and the Organisation for Economic Cooperation and Development (OECD) formerly through its 'Harmful Tax Competition Initiative' (HTCI) and more recently via its Global Forum and 'internationally agreed tax standard' to encourage financial centres to share information with tax authorities. The level of oversight over the offshore financial sector is thus now substantive, but in several cases the process of adopting new regulation has been controversial. For example, in relation to the ultimately unsuccessful HTCI, Persaud argued: 'Rule-making by the OECD for non-OECD states is of questionable international legality' (Persaud, 2001: 202), while Sanders called the OECD action the 'usurpation of global governance' (Sanders, 2003: 6). Further, the Cayman Islands raised 'holy hell' about the lack of consultation over the EU savings tax directive (Foreign Affairs Committee, 2008: 46).

Regulatory standards today

It is clear that the UK government has taken a significant interest in the territories' financial service industries. As a consequence, the OTs are largely compliant with the key international regulatory regimes. For example, all territories meet the OECD's internationally agreed tax standard, and in addition, improvements have been made in the regulatory environment more generally. For example, the size of the regulatory authority in each territory has generally been on a rising trend. Bermuda and Gibraltar have more than doubled the number of staff employed since 2002, while the British Virgin Islands has increased staff resources by more than 60 per cent (Foot, 2009: 41). The NAO commended these changes as 'major improvements' (National Audit Office, 2007: 21).

However, as the IMF's Financial Sector Assessment Programme highlights, there are still improvements to be made, both in terms of delivering effective regulation in banking, insurance and securities and in fighting financial crime. For example, Gibraltar in 2007 and Bermuda in 2008 were assessed as needing to do more in order to meet particular FATF recommendations (International Monetary Fund, 2007, 2008). Further, concerns have been raised about the limited number of suspicious transaction reports (particularly in Anguilla, British Virgin Islands and TCI) and the low level of prosecutions for finance-related crime (for example, there was just a single money laundering prosecution in Bermuda in 2008) (National Audit Office, 2007; Foot, 2009: 53, 55).

Nevertheless, the larger territories are doing better than the smaller ones. As the NAO found, Bermuda, British Virgin Islands, Cayman Islands and Gibraltar were 'leaving in their wake the weaker regulatory capacity' of Anguilla, Montserrat and TCI (National Audit Office, 2007: 5). As Foot argued, the scope for improvement 'is most evident in the smaller Territories, where compliance costs bear most heavily because of a lack of economies of scale and the difficulty of attracting staff with the necessary expertise' (2009: 39). This is particularly true for Anguilla and TCI, both of whom employ fewer than ten staff to supervise financial services providers. It is argued that this is below the 'critical mass' to keep up with the ever-evolving international regulatory framework (National Audit Office, 2007: 6; Foot, 2009: 41). This is worrying as the Governor retains direct responsibility for the regulation of international finance in these small territories. Indeed, mirroring the criticisms made in relation to safeguarding good governance, it can be argued that the UK government via its governors has not been sufficiently engaged in overseeing good practice in the offshore financial industries of the smallest territories, despite the enactment of high-profile reforms such as the EU savings tax directive. As the Committee of Public Accounts noted, the 'Governors have not used their reserve powers to rectify [weak investigative capacity]' and the UK has been 'complacent' in not acting more decisively (Committee of Public Accounts, 2008: 5).

Although the OTs are making attempts to comply with global standards of financial regulation, there are still concerns that small jurisdictions lack the necessary resources for proper supervision. Bermuda, British Virgin Islands and Cayman Islands are small countries with large financial sectors in proportion to their size and this remains problematic in terms of proper oversight of the industry. Presently, Cayman Islands is listed on the US State Department's list of countries of primary concern in relation to money laundering (US State Department, 2010). Further, the then US presidential candidate Barack Obama made specific mention of Cayman Islands and its role in alleged tax evasion. Obama stated: 'There's a building in the Cayman Islands that houses supposedly 12,000 US-based corporations [referring to Ugland House, the Cayman Islands' office of the law firm Maples and Calder]. That's the biggest building in the world or the biggest tax scam in the world, and we know which one it is' (*The Guardian*, 2009). Despite such concerns, a recent report commissioned by the UK government to review the UK's offshore financial centres said little on these matters (Foot, 2009). As a consequence, there is no threat to the OTs' offshore financial sector in the foreseeable future. Nevertheless, it can be argued that regulation of the offshore financial service industries in the OTs has been patchy since the White Paper – particularly so for the smaller jurisdictions – and this is troubling.

Sustainable economic development

Over much of the last decade, there is no doubt that many OTs have experienced rapid economic growth. For example, real GDP growth in Bermuda averaged 4.4 per cent a year between 2003 and 2007, while in Gibraltar growth in 2008–9 was estimated at 6 per cent (Foot, 2009: 25). Growth in the Caribbean territories has also been strong. This in turn has consolidated the territories' excellent GDP per capita figures. Bermuda, for example, had a GDP per capita of US$91,477 in 2007 (Bermuda Department of Statistics, 2009: 7), while Cayman Islands had a GDP per capita of US$57,016 in the same year (Cayman Islands Economics and Statistics Office, 2009). However, in the last couple of years, the effects of the global economic downturn have had a very big impact on many OTs and this has undermined the UK's stated aim in the White Paper to 'help [the OTs] achieve sustainable development' through 'sensible economic and financial management' (Foreign and Commonwealth Office, 1999: 30).

Despite the OTs' relatively high levels of economic development, most rely on a few key industries – particularly financial services, tourism and construction – for both government revenue and employment. The proportion of government revenue generated by financial services and tourism is approximately 50 per cent for the majority of territories, while they account for between 23 per cent and 48 per cent of employment (Foot, 2009: 23). The vulnerability of government revenue is particularly acute since the Caribbean territories and Bermuda have a narrow revenue base. There are no taxes levied on income, profits and capital gains, nor are there sales or value-added taxes. Rather, revenue is derived from a combination of import duties, financial sector licence fees and other specific charges (Foot, 2009: 24). Thus many OT economies are 'particularly exposed to economic shocks' (Foot, 2009: 25). The one exception to this is Gibraltar because it has one of the most diversified economies amongst the territories, with income from shipping, tourism, financial services and internet gaming. In addition, the Falklands economy continues to diversify, with greater emphasis on tourism and commercial fishing and the future possibility of oil extraction.

The Caribbean territories and Bermuda have suffered during the recession from reduced activity in their financial services sector and declines in tourist arrivals and construction. For example, in the British Virgin Islands new international business company incorporations fell by 44 per cent between September and December 2008 compared with the same period in 2007, while Anguilla and the Cayman Islands suffered declines in tourist arrivals in 2009 of 22.6 per cent and 10.2 per cent, respectively (Foot, 2009: 26; Caribbean Tourism Organisation, 2010). Therefore, the negative impact on public finances has been significant, particularly for Anguilla, Cayman Islands and TCI (the latter's situation being exacerbated by the previous government's corruption and mismanagement). In response, the UK has shown a new determination to help correct the structural imbalances in the OT economies and this is of course welcome and necessary. However, it is unfortunate the UK waited so long to act despite the commitments enshrined within the White Paper. It can be argued that the impressive levels of economic growth during the mid 2000s helped to hide the serious structural problems present in the OT economies and, as a consequence, the UK felt that any reforms could be delayed. Unfortunately, the shortcomings of this approach can now be seen.

One further example that illustrates the impact of the recent global economic downturn on the economic development of the OTs is the case of St Helena, the second poorest of the territories in terms of GDP per capita (National Audit Office, 2007: Appendix 2). For many years, the principal link with the isolated island, which is 2,000km from its nearest neighbour, has been the ageing supply and passenger vessel RMS St Helena, which calls at the island from the UK twice a year and is due to be withdrawn from service. After several years of lobbying, DFID agreed in 2005 that St Helena should have its own airport within five years as an essential means of attracting inward investment, enabling the island to develop its economy – including tourism – and to offset its limited natural resources, high import dependency, relatively large public sector and outward migration. However, in December 2008, DFID decided to freeze the airport plan in view of the economic climate and took the opportunity to consider potential savings to the airport contract and a possible public private partnership (*Hansard*, 2009b). This decision was reversed by the Coalition Government on 22 July 2010 when the Secretary of State for International Development announced that 'provided certain conditions are met, the best long-term solution from an economic and financial perspective for both HMG and St Helena is to construct an airport' (*Hansard*, 2010). Provided that this decision is followed through, the population decline noted by the National Audit Office (2007: 55) may eventually be halted and the current level of aid – £35.7 million in bilateral aid in 2008–9 – will ultimately be reduced.

Beyond the broad economic vulnerabilities of the OTs, concerns have also been raised about the inadequate financial procedures and controls in place. In its 2007 report, the NAO highlighted the fact that many territories 'have difficulty producing timely, audited public accounts' and most significantly suggested 'the situation appears much the same as it was 10 years ago, when half of populated Territories were two years or more "behind"' (National Audit Office, 2007: 31). The NAO also stated that 'a capable external audit function is not seen as a priority by all Territory governments' (National Audit Office, 2007: 31). For example, staffing levels in the Auditor General's office in the British Virgin Islands was one-third below complement in 2007 (National Audit Office, 2007: 31). There were also concerns over the independence of audit officers. To overcome such problems both Anguilla and the Falkland Islands have their accounts audited by external agencies. Other difficulties were highlighted more recently in the Foot report. Foot noted 'the absence of timely and reliable data and of the expertise to analyse [economic] trends' (Foot, 2009: 29). He also criticised the 'weaknesses in data quality' (Foot, 2009: 29) in some territories. For example, Anguilla, Cayman Islands and TCI overestimated significantly their expected revenue take during 2008 – 9 (Foot, 2009: 29). The weaknesses in data quality and auditing procedures have largely been left unattended since the White Paper. If they had been corrected, the worst effects of the global economic downturn might have been mitigated.

Conclusions and recommendations

The 1999 White Paper set out a clear, necessary and generally comprehensive plan of action to improve the governing arrangements between the UK and its OTs. However, the results ten years on have been only partially successful. There are three main reasons for this. First, the nature of the relationship remains very complex and dynamic which provides continuous challenges for the UK government, the governors and the local territory governments to overcome. Second, governors' powers remain limited in several respects and this inhibits the UK government's ability to deal with problems in the OTs. Third, the UK government and the OT governments failed to act with due care and attention when it came to properly maintaining the relationship. The UK did not fully engage and intervene in the OTs even when its interests were at stake, while in many cases the territories (particularly those in the Caribbean) showed a disregard for maintaining the highest standards of good governance and financial probity – illustrated recently and most clearly in the TCI. So in light of these problems, what improvements should be made to the relationship over the next decade?

First, links between the UK and the OTs should be strengthened, deepened and in some areas made more nuanced. Thus, we endorse the view taken by the FAC who suggested that the partnership concept between the UK and the OTs must be based on something more than an annual meeting of the Overseas Territories Consultative Council (OTCC) and who argued that 'properly consulting and representing the OTs on issues that affect them is an important part of creating the type of "modern partnership" which may prevent the need for direct intervention' (2008: 130). This would also mean more varied approaches and policies to deal with the diversity among the territories. In addition, there should be more regular consultation by the UK government with the OT representatives based in London, as well as greater openness in publishing documents and reporting on meetings of the OTCC. In addition, the FAC's recommendation that governors of the OTs ought to use their reserve powers to bring in more external investigators or prosecutors to strengthen investigative capacity (2008: 98) should be implemented. Indeed, the UK's entire approach towards the OTs must be more consistently pro-active than before. However, there are worrying signs in regard to the TCI that the UK is still reluctant to use all its available powers and to undertake all the necessary reforms to clean up the political system. If the UK fails in its task, it will be a dereliction of its duty and will risk 'undermining its own credibility in its use of reserved powers in not just the TCI but in the other OTs' (Foreign Affairs Committee, 2010: 13).

Second, the position of the UK government and its governors must be strengthened. For example, there should be greater continuity in the appointment of ministers responsible for the OTs and a requirement that the incumbent holds fewer responsibilities so that they can devote more time to the territories. Further, the process of familiarising newly appointed governors with the OTs should be reinforced and OT administration and governance should be developed as a distinct specialism and career path within Whitehall.

Third, there needs to be better sharing of information and good practice across the OTs via cross-Territory training and conferences and support for short-term secondments and personnel exchange. Importantly, this training and support must be overtly focused on specific objectives. Above all, the development of a stronger culture of integrity in the OTs is a necessity; otherwise any initiatives will come to nought.

Clearly, further change is needed if the objectives of the 1999 White Paper are to be finally met. However, the recent spending cuts announced by the new Conservative-led coalition government will not make real reform any easier to achieve. The FCO's budget is scheduled to be cut, and this could have a negative impact on the administrative and financial support given to the OTs. It is true that DFID's budget will increase but its main interests lie not with the territories. Under such circumstances, the UK's level of engagement with the OTs may well decline. The key message emerging from this chapter is that this would be a mistake, and potentially a costly one. The failure to maintain and more importantly improve standards of governance in the territories would undoubtedly lead to increased financial and legal liabilities in the future.

References

Bermuda Department of Statistics. (2009) Facts and Figures 2009. Available at www.gov.bm/portal/server.pt/gateway/ PTARGS_0_2_980_227_1014_43/http%3B/ptpublisher.gov. bm%3B7087/publishedcontent/publish/cabinet_office/statistics/dept___ statistics___additonal_files/facts___figures_2009_0.pdf (accessed 31 March 2010).

Caribbean Insight (2008) 'UK MPs express concern over Turks and Caicos', *Caribbean Insight*, 31(12), 31 March.

Caribbean Tourism Organisation (2010) Latest Statistics 2009. Available at www.onecaribbean.org/statistics/tourismstats/ (accessed 31 March 2010).

Cayman Islands Economics and Statistics Office (2009) *Statistical Compendium: The Cayman Islands at a Glance*. Available at www.eso.ky/docum1/docum85.pdf (accessed 31 March 2010).

Committee of Public Accounts (1998) *Foreign and Commonwealth Office: Contingent Liabilities in the Dependent Territories*, Thirty-Seventh Report, House of Commons, 11 May (London: The Stationery Office).

— (2008) *Foreign and Commonwealth Office: Managing Risk in the Overseas Territories*, Seventeenth Report, House of Commons, 31 March (London: The Stationery Office).

E. Davies (1995) *The Legal Status of British Dependent Territories: The West Indies and North Atlantic Region* (Cambridge: Cambridge University Press).

Department for International Development (1999) *An Evaluation of HMG's Response to The Montserrat Volcanic Emergency*, Vol. 1, EV635, Dec. (London: The Stationery Office).

Financial Times (2009) 'Anti-corruption team sent to Turks & Caicos', 25 Aug.

M. Foot (2009) *Final Report of the Independent Review of British Offshore Financial Centres*, Oct. (London: Office of Public Sector Information).

Foreign Affairs Committee (2004) *Overseas Territories: Written Evidence*, HC 114, House of Commons, March (London: The Stationery Office).

— (2008) *Overseas Territories*, House of Commons, Seventh Report of Session 2007–8, HLC 147–1, July (London: The Stationery Office).

— (2010) *Turks and Caicos Islands, Seventh Report of Session 2009–10*, HC469, March (London: The Stationery Office).

Foreign and Commonwealth Office (1999) *Partnership for Progress and Prosperity: Britain and the Overseas Territories*, Cm 4264, March (London: The Stationery Office).

— (2009) *A Major Step in Clean up of Public Life in Turks and Caicos*, 14 Aug. Available at www.fco.gov.uk/en/news/latest-news/?view=News&id=20700728 (accessed 9 Sept. 2009).

The Guardian (2009) 'Brown targets Switzerland in global tax haven crackdown', 19 Feb. Available at www.guardian.co.uk/business/2009/feb/19/gordon-brown-tax-avoidance-switzerland?INTCMP=SRCH (accessed 20 Feb. 2009).

Hansard (2009a) Written ministerial statement – Turks and Caicos Islands: Governance, Columns 39–40WS, *Hansard*, 16 March. Available at www.publications.parliament.uk/pa/cm201011/cmhansrd/cm101209/wmstext/101209m0001.htm (accessed 9 Sept. 2009).

— (2009b) Written ministerial statement – St Helena, Columns 114–15WS, *Hansard*, 15 December. Available at www.publications.parliament. uk/pa/cm200910/cmhansrd/cm091215/wmstext/91215m0004. htm#09121583000009 (accessed 10 March 2010).

— (2010) Written ministerial statement – St Helena (Access), Columns 46–7WS, *Hansard*, 22 July. Available at www.publications.parliament. uk/pa/cm201011/cmhansrd/cm100722/wmstext/100722m0001.htm (accessed 23 July 2010).

Human Rights Watch (2009) 'Cayman Islands: ensure equality for all', *Human Rights Watch*, 11 March. Available at www.hrw.org/ news/2009/03/11/cayman-islands-ensure-equality-all (accessed 31 March 2010).

International Development Committee (1997) *Montserrat, First Report*, House of Commons, 18 Nov. (London: The Stationery Office).

— (1998) *Montserrat – Further Developments*, Sixth Report, House of Commons, 28 July (London: The Stationery Office).

International Monetary Fund (2007) *Gibraltar: Assessment of Financial Sector Supervision and Regulation* including reports on the observance of standards and codes on the following topics: banking supervision, insurance supervision, and anti-money laundering and combating the financing of terrorism, IMF Country Report No. 07/154, May (Washington, DC: IMF).

— (2008) *Bermuda: Assessment of Financial Sector Supervision and Regulation*, IMF Country Report No. 08/336, Oct. (Washington, DC: IMF).

KPMG (2000) *Review of the Financial Regulation in the COTs and Bermuda*, Cm 4855 (London: Foreign and Commonwealth Office).

National Audit Office (1997) *Foreign and Commonwealth Office: Contingent Liabilities in the Dependent Territories*, report by the Comptroller and Auditor General, HC 13 1997/98, 30 May (London: The Stationery Office).

— (2007) *Foreign and Commonwealth Office: Managing Risk in the Overseas Territories*, report by the Comptroller and Auditor General, HC 4 2007 – 08, 16 May (London: The Stationery Office).

B. Persaud (2001) 'OECD curbs on offshore financial centres: a major issue for small states', *The Round Table*, 359, pp. 199–212.

Report of the Commissioner Mr Louis Blom-Cooper QC (1986) *Allegations of Arson of a Public Building, Corruption and Related Matters*, December (London: HMSO).

R. Sanders (2003) *The War Against Terror and the Erosion of Rights* (London: Hansib Publications).

D. Taylor (2000) 'British colonial policy in the Caribbean: the insoluble dilemma – the case of Montserrat', *The Round Table*, 355, pp. 337–44.

— (2005) 'The British Overseas Territories in the Caribbean: recent history and current policy', in David Killingray and David Taylor (eds.), *The United Kingdom Overseas Territories: Past, Present and Future*, pp. 19–23 (London: Institute of Commonwealth Studies).

Turks and Caicos Islands Commission of Inquiry (2009) *Turks and Caicos IslandsCommission of Inquiry (2008 – 2009)*, Report of the Commissioner The Right Honourable Sir Robin Auld. Available at www.fco.gov.uk/en/news/latest-news/?view=News&id=20700728 (accessed 9 Sept. 2009).

US State Department (2010) *International Narcotics Control Strategy Report, VolumeII: Money Laundering and Financial Crimes.* Available at www.state.gov/p/inl/rls/nrcrpt/2010/vol2/index.htm (accessed 31 March 2010).

Chapter 3

The UK Coalition Government's policy towards the UK Overseas Territories

Ian Bailey

I am Head of the Strategy and Co-ordination Section of the Overseas Territories Directorate in the Foreign and Commonwealth Office (FCO), which leads on cross-cutting issues relevant to the Overseas Territories (OTs) as a whole, rather than bilateral issues with individual territories. I have been fortunate to arrive in the Overseas Territories Directorate at an interesting time. The Coalition government has made it clear that it wants a step change in the relationship with the OTs. The Conservative Party had spelt out its vision in its Policy Green Paper: 'One World Conservatism – A Conservative Agenda for International Development'. In the section entitled 'Building vibrant and successful British Overseas Territories', the party said:

> [We] see the Territories as important assets to be protected and
> nurtured ... [We will] look at new ways to intensify the effectiveness
> of the support we give to the Overseas Territories. Our ultimate
> goal will be, wherever possible, to help them take advantage of their
> unique advantages and move towards self-sufficiency ... Our overall
> vision is of flourishing and vibrant Territories freer from financial
> dependence on Whitehall, proudly retaining their British identity and
> generating wider opportunities for their people (Conservative Party,
> 2009: 22).

When the Coalition government took office in May 2010, it inherited 14 diverse OTs, some of which were suffering – like many parts of the world – with the fall-out of the global economic crisis. The situation in the Turks and Caicos Islands (TCI) was particularly unique. The previous UK government suspended parts of TCI's constitution in August 2009, following a Commission of Inquiry report into allegations of corruption by TCI ministers, which concluded that there was a high probability of systemic corruption in the former TCI government (TCI Commission of Inquiry, 2009; see also chapter 2). In the South Atlantic, there was continuing Argentine pressure over the

Falkland Islands sovereignty issue, as well as challenges involved in supporting and developing the remoter territories with their small populations. These were quite different to the challenges facing the government in the more accessible – and more populated – Caribbean.

Henry Bellingham – FCO Minister for the Overseas Territories – announced in June 2010 that there would be a review of our relationship with the OTs. He said, in reply to a Parliamentary Question: 'We aim to bring renewed focus to the UK's relationship with the Overseas Territories and the important strategic, historic and cultural links that we share' (*Hansard*, 2010a). In order to demonstrate its intent, the government soon announced conditional approval of the Air Access Project for St Helena, and in the Strategic Defence and Security Review, the government confirmed that defence of the OTs was a core defence mission for the UK (HM Government, 2010).

The Foreign Secretary elaborated further during oral evidence to the Foreign Affairs Committee on 8 September 2010. He said:

> I think there should be a clear strategy in this country for the overseas territories. I think we should be able to assist them in their economic development. You can see the evidence of a change in approach under the new Government. For instance, the Department for International Development has made its announcement about the airport at St Helena.
>
> I think we have a responsibility to ensure the security and good governance of the overseas territories, as well as to support their economic well-being. They can create substantial challenges for the United Kingdom in many different ways, and we must recognise that … We need to manage those risks quite carefully, but I think we've moved quickly in the past few months to tackle certain problems. There have been fiscal crises in some of the Caribbean territories, and a very severe problem in the Turks and Caicos Islands, as we know (Foreign Affairs Committee, 2011: Ev 10–11).

On a visit to Anguilla later in September, Mr Bellingham was quoted in the Anguillan press as saying:

> I take the view that the territories are a huge asset to Britain; they are part of the British family; they want to remain British and we should cherish that and respect that (*The Anguillan*, 2010).

The overall direction from Ministers was clear. There would not be a change from the basic constitutional model, but Ministers were keen to make sure it worked better. They were determined to increase engagement with the territories and to help raise the profile of the territories in the UK.

British Ministers have high regard for the OTs and their peoples. In Henry Bellingham's words, the territories are 'part of the British family'. So, at the annual Overseas Territories Consultative Council (OTCC) meeting in London in November 2010, territory leaders were invited for an Audience with Her Majesty the Queen – the first time this has happened in that context. And, more recently, it was good to see the territories formally represented at the Royal Wedding – which I know attracted as much interest back home as it did here. We will be looking at even more ways to involve the territories as we move into the celebrations of the Queen's Jubilee in 2012. Whilst these are in some respects small things, they illustrate clearly the warm sentiment with which the government approaches the OTs and their relationship to the UK. This high regard and greater engagement was also demonstrated by the record number of Ministers from other government Departments who attended the OTCC meeting. Ministers from the Departments for International Development (DFID), Transport, Environment, Energy and Climate Change, the Treasury, Home Office, and the Ministry of Defence attended. This sent a clear signal that the OTs were a priority right across the government, and not just in the FCO.

In the TCI work continues to restore the principles of good governance, sound public financial management and sustainable development to the territory. In December 2010 Mr Bellingham and the Minister of State at DFID, Alan Duncan, announced the milestones that would need to be met before elections could once again take place (*Hansard*, 2010b). Reaching the milestones will require care, time and hard work. The milestones identified do not include everything that will have to be done before elections can take place. The UK government will have to be satisfied that the necessary reforms have been put in place to address the issues raised by the Commission of Inquiry, to prevent such maladministration being repeated. It is our intention to hold elections in 2012 if there has been sufficient progress against the milestones.

Work is well underway on the milestones. For example, the Minister of State at DFID announced in a Written Statement at the end of February 2011 that DFID had finalised a loan guarantee to provide the TCI government with access to a maximum capital amount of $260 million over the next five years (*Hansard*, 2011a). This will enable TCI to make progress on establishing a stable economic environment and strengthening its capacity to manage its public finances (which is one of the milestones). In support of another milestone, a draft constitution was published in March and a FCO team visited the TCI to undertake a process of public consultations. The end result was a new constitution (see chapter 4) which will underpin good governance and sound public financial management in the territory (Turks and Caicos Islands Constitution Order 2011).

Turning to another of the territories, the new government soon made its position on the Falkland Islands clear, i.e. that it would continue to defend robustly the Falkland islanders' right to self-determination; and that there could be no negotiation on sovereignty unless and until the Falkland islanders so wished. The government also made clear that it was wholeheartedly committed to the Falkland islanders' right to develop their economy, including a hydrocarbons industry within their waters. The UK government has also been taking work forward on wider issues. It is fully aware of the importance of environmental issues in the territories, as demonstrated by our cross-Whitehall approach to maximise the assistance to the territories and in particular to help with challenges posed by climate change.

On 10 March 2011, in a written Statement to Parliament, the Foreign Secretary further demonstrated the government's commitment to the territories by announcing additional funding from the FCO to help rectify some of the budgetary weaknesses which had emerged in some territories in recent years (*Hansard*, 2011b). These funds went to the British Indian Ocean Territory Administration, South Georgia and the South Sandwich Islands, and the British Antarctic Territory and Ascension Island. A further £6.6 million went to reimburse the costs incurred in the previous 12 months pursuing corruption and violent crime in TCI. This was for the Special Investigation and Prosecution Team; related civil recovery work; and the Royal Turks and Caicos Islands Police. In his statement the Foreign Secretary also set out some further principles behind the new approach to the territories. He said:

> We will continue vigorously to uphold the principle of self-determination and to ensure the continued security of all the Overseas Territories. We set this commitment out clearly in the Strategic Defence and Security Review. We want to help the Territories plan their future in a competitive and unpredictable world. We will help Territories that are struggling economically to avoid unnecessary financial dependence on the UK. We will help Territories that now rely on UK financial support to reduce their dependence and pursue the path towards economic sustainability. We will ensure a sustained and robust British presence in our uninhabited Territories to protect them for future generations. We are determined that the situation we have found in the Turks and Caicos Islands is not repeated, there or elsewhere. We therefore want to work with Territories to make sure the right controls are in place to ensure good governance and sound management of public finances (*Hansard*, 2011b).

The Foreign Secretary also announced that he planned to bring all aspects of the government's policies on the OTs together in a new White Paper in the course of the year ahead; and said that we would want to consult widely on this. He confirmed that the FCO was working with other government Departments on a new strategy to underpin the government's approach to the territories; and that he intended to seek agreement on this strategy across government through the National Security Council, the Coalition government's new initiative to enhance cross-government working. Mr Bellingham had discussed the emerging thinking on the strategy with territory leaders at the Consultative Council meeting in November. He then wrote to the leaders encouraging further input.

Over the course of 2010 and 2011, the FCO and colleagues from DFID have been working more closely with other government departments, nearly all of whom are doing, or have done, work with the Territories. For example, the Department of Health produced a booklet in 2010 on what they were doing to help the territories. The FCO is encouraging other government departments to do likewise. There has been a long-standing understanding that the territories are a cross-government responsibility, but this needs to be formalised. In some ways this is not a great time to be asking other government departments to step up their engagement with the territories – many have suffered cuts of between 20 and 40 per cent in their budgets – but what the FCO and the territories are looking for is often just technical expertise. The FCO hopes to be able to make an announcement about cross-government working on the OTs in the near future. But that will not be the end of the process. The FCO will soon start working on the White Paper, which is expected to be issued sometime in early/mid 2012. Ministers are keen that we consult widely in the preparation of this, and for the White Paper to be a definitive collection of the government's policies towards the OTs.

I have already mentioned that Ministers believe that the territories are part of the British family. By extension they are also part of the European family. The EU therefore has an important role to play. The government will continue to engage with the territories, and with France, the Netherlands and Denmark; as well as the Commission, as the re-negotiation of the Overseas Association Decision proceeds (for further details see chapter 7).

References

The Anguillan (2010) 'Overseas Territories "A Huge Asset to Britain" says Henry Bellingham MP', 24 Sept. Available at www.anguillian.com/article/articleview/8809/ (accessed 9 Nov. 2011).

Conservative Party (2009) *One World Conservatism – A Conservative Agenda for International Development*, Policy Green Paper No. 11, July. Available at http://m.conservatives.com/Policy/Responsibility_Agenda.aspx (accessed 9 Nov. 2011).

Foreign Affairs Committee (2011) *Developments in UK Foreign Policy*, Oral and Written Evidence, HC 438 i, 20 January (London: The Stationery Office).

Hansard (2010a) Written ministerial answer – British Overseas Territories, Column 471W, *Hansard*, 16 June. Available at www.publications. parliament.uk/pa/cm201011/cmhansrd/cm100616/text/100616w0010. htm#100616103000023 (accessed 9 Nov. 2011).

— (2010b) Written ministerial statement – Turks and Caicos Islands, Columns 40–1WS, *Hansard*, 9 December. Available at www. publications.parliament.uk/pa/cm201011/cmhansrd/cm101209/ wmstext/101209m0001.htm (accessed 9 Nov. 2011).

— (2011a) Written ministerial statement – Turks and Caicos Islands, Column 14WS, *Hansard*, 28 February. Available at www. publications.parliament.uk/pa/cm201011/cmhansrd/cm110228/ wmstext/110228m0001.htm (accessed 9 Nov. 2011).

— (2011b) Written ministerial statement – Overseas Territories, Columns 76–7WS, *Hansard*, 10 March. Available at www.publications.parliament. uk/pa/cm201011/cmhansrd/cm110310/wmstext/110310m0001. htm#11031040000005 (accessed 9 Nov. 2011).

HM government (2010) *Securing Britain in an Age of Uncertainty: The Strategic Defence and Security Review*, CM7948, October (London: The Stationery Office).

Turks and Caicos Islands Commission of Inquiry (2009) *Turks and Caicos Islands Commission of Inquiry (2008–2009)*, Report of the Commissioner The Right Honourable Sir Robin Auld. Available at www.fco.gov.uk/ en/newsroom/latest-news/?view=News&id=20700728 (accessed 9 Nov. 2011).

Turks and Caicos Constitution Order 2011 (2011) Statutory Instruments No. 1681: The Turks and Caicos Constitution Order 2011, 13 July. Available at www.legislation.gov.uk/uksi/2011/1681/introduction/made (accessed 9 Nov. 2011).

Foreign &
Commonwealth
Written Ministerial Statement

10 March 2011

OVERSEAS TERRITORIES: UPDATE AND ADDITIONAL FUNDING

The Secretary of State for Foreign and Commonwealth Affairs (William Hague):

Our overall vision is for our Territories to be vibrant and flourishing communities, proudly retaining aspects of their British identity and generating wider opportunities for their people. We want to cherish the rich environmental assets for which, together, we are responsible.

We will continue vigorously to uphold the principle of self-determination and to ensure the continued security of all the Overseas Territories. We set this commitment out clearly in the Strategic Defence and Security Review. We want to help the Territories plan their future in a competitive and unpredictable world. We will help Territories that are struggling economically to avoid unnecessary financial dependence on the UK. We will help Territories that now rely on UK financial support to reduce their dependence and pursue the path towards economic sustainability. We will ensure a sustained and robust British presence in our uninhabited Territories to protect them for future generations.

We are determined that the situation we have found in the Turks and Caicos Islands is not repeated, there or elsewhere. We therefore want to work with Territories to make sure the right controls are in place to ensure good governance and sound management of public finances.

I am clear that, as well as seeking greater engagement with the Territories from all Government departments, the FCO must increase the resources allocated to this important work. Despite our challenging Spending Review settlement I have ensured that this is so. As I informed Parliament on 1 February, I have decided to increase the Overseas Territories Programme Fund to £7m per year. I have ensured the resources available to run the Overseas Territories network are maintained at a level which will permit the upgrading of a number of Governorships which were downgraded in recent years. This will help ensure that we are able to recruit Governors with the skills and experience to do these unusual and challenging jobs.

In addition I have reallocated resources in the current financial year to help rectify some of the budgetary weaknesses which have emerged in some territories in recent years.

Most importantly, and mindful of the recommendations of the Foreign Affairs Committee, I have approved a discretionary grant of £6.6m to the Turks and Caicos Islands Government to reimburse the costs incurred in the past year pursuing corruption and violent crime. This is for the Special Investigation and Prosecution Team; related civil recovery work; and the Royal Turks and Caicos Islands Police. My officials have coordinated this carefully with DFID's work to underpin the Territory's public finances.

This is an exceptional case. Our basic principle remains that it is an integral part of good governance for a Territory government to ensure that the criminal justice system is properly funded. Territories should not look to the UK to fund criminal investigations or prosecutions that they are reluctant to pursue themselves. But the burden in this case has been exceptional. The fiscal rescue package put in place by DFID should enable future costs to be met from the Turks and Caicos Islands Government public purse in the normal way.

I have also approved the following smaller grants.

- £1m to the British Indian Ocean Territory (BIOT) Administration to strengthen the Territory's reserves. This is necessary in the face of rising costs of operating the BIOT Patrol Vessel. These funds will also enable the Administration to support new measures to help Chagossians visit the Territory for humanitarian purposes and to contribute to environmental work in the Territory. In this context I would also like to inform the Committee that the BIOT Administration has concluded an agreement with the Blue Foundation and the Bertorelli Foundation by which the Bertorelli Foundation will donate £3.5m over the next 5 years to offset the loss of fisheries revenue which has flowed from the establishment of a full no-take Marine Protected Area. I am most grateful to these Foundations for their generous support.

- £1m to the Government of South Georgia and South Sandwich Islands to strengthen their reserves in the face of recent reductions in fisheries revenue.

- £100,000 to the Government of the British Antarctic Territory to enable them to grant a similar amount to the Antarctic Heritage Trust. This grant will be used to support the Trust's work repairing and maintaining heritage sites in the British Antarctic Territory, as we prepare to mark the many forthcoming centenaries of the heroic age of exploration. Maintaining British heritage sites is part and parcel of demonstrating UK sovereignty in Antarctica.

- £1m in capital grant to the Ascension Island Government to enable them to replace the harbour crane – a critical piece of infrastructure. This grant will facilitate the restructuring of AIG's public finances which is necessary to put them on a sustainable footing for the future.

I also plan to bring all aspects of the Government's policies on the Overseas Territories together in a new White Paper in the course of the year ahead. We will want to consult widely on this. I am working with relevant Departments on a new strategy to underpin this Government's approach to the Territories. I intend to seek agreement to this strategy across Government through the National Security Council and will update the House further once this is complete.

I will inform Parliament of the outcome of discussions in the NSC in due course.

Chapter 4

Recent constitutional developments in the UK Overseas Territories

Ian Hendry

Introduction

Between 2006 and 2010 new constitutions were negotiated and enacted for Gibraltar, the Turks and Caicos Islands, the British Virgin Islands, the Falkland Islands, the Cayman Islands, St Helena, Ascension and Tristan da Cunha, the Pitcairn Islands and Montserrat.[1] Before that period, important changes had been made to the Constitution of Bermuda in 2001 and 2003,[2] and a new constitutional instrument had been made for the British Indian Ocean Territory in 2004.[3]

Thus, of the 14 British Overseas Territories (OTs), only Anguilla, the British Antarctic Territory, South Georgia and the South Sandwich Islands and the Sovereign Base Areas of Akrotiri and Dhekelia remain unaffected by this constitutional reform programme. But preliminary discussions on constitutional reform in Anguilla were held between the UK and Anguilla governments in 2009 and 2010, which may in due course lead to proper negotiations. And in the Sovereign Base Areas a Human Rights Ordinance was enacted in 2004,[4] a significant constitutional development in itself.

---

1   See Gibraltar Constitution Order 2006 (published in SI 2006, III, p. 11503); Turks and Caicos Islands Constitution Order 2006 (SI 2006/1913); Virgin Islands Constitution Order 2007 (SI 2007/1678); Falkland Islands Constitution Order 2008 (SI 2008/2846); Cayman Islands Constitution Order 2009 (SI 2009/1379); St Helena, Ascension and Tristan da Cunha Constitution Order 2009 (SI 2009/1751); Pitcairn Constitution Order 2010 (SI 2010/244); Montserrat Constitution Order 2010 (SI 2010/2474).
2   See Bermuda Constitution (Amendment) Orders 2001 and 2003 (SI 2001/2579 and SI 2003/456).
3   British Indian Ocean Territory (Constitution) Order 2004 (published in the (2004) 36(1) BIOT Official Gazette).
4   Laws of the Sovereign Base Areas, Ordinance 9 of 2004.

In August 2009 considerable parts of the Constitution of the Turks and Caicos Islands were amended[5] so that ministerial government and the local legislative body, the House of Assembly, were suspended, after a judicial Commission of Inquiry had concluded that there was a high probability of systemic corruption in government and the legislature and among public officers in the islands.[6] A new constitution was enacted by Order in Council on 13 July 2011,[7] but is unlikely to be brought into force until late 2012. The main features of this constitution are described later in this chapter.

Background

The extraordinary intensity of constitutional development in recent years has its origin in the British government White Paper of 1999 entitled 'Partnership for progress and prosperity: Britain and the Overseas Territories'.[8] Paragraph 2.7 of this White Paper stated:

> The link between the UK and the Overseas Territories is enshrined in the constitution of each territory. The Overseas Territories believe that their constitutions need to be kept up to date and where necessary modernised. Each Overseas Territory is unique and needs a constitutional framework to suit its own circumstances. Suggestions from Overseas Territory governments for specific proposals for constitutional change will be considered carefully.

Thus the British government put the ball into the court of each territory government, and promised to consider carefully any proposals for constitutional change they might advance. Several territory governments took up this offer, but in differing ways.

In Bermuda, the elected Progressive Labour Party government proposed amendments to establish the office of Ombudsman and, even more importantly, the revision of the electoral system to establish single member, in place of dual member, constituencies. This was entirely government-driven, and the electoral proposal proved highly controversial in Bermuda. It was eventually achieved in 2003 following a Constituency Boundary Commission which made recommendations for 36 single-member constituencies and their boundaries. In Bermuda there has so far been no movement to seek more far-reaching changes to the constitution, which by any standards is an advanced

---

5   See Turks and Caicos Islands Constitution (Interim Amendment) Order 2009 (SI 2009/701, as amended by SI 2010/2966).
6   Turks and Caicos Islands Commission of Inquiry (2009) Report of the Commissioner The Right Honourable Sir Robin Auld; see also chapter 2.
7   See Turks and Caicos Islands Constitution Order 2011 (SI 2011/1681).
8   Cm 4264.

one in terms of internal self-government.[9] However, the fundamental rights chapter of the constitution, which was drafted in 1968, is in need of updating, and this is currently under consideration.

By contrast with Bermuda, several territories set in hand a process of considering the radical overhaul of their constitutions. In Gibraltar, the Falkland Islands and St Helena this task was undertaken by the local legislative body. In Anguilla, the British Virgin Islands, the Cayman Islands, Montserrat, and the Turks and Caicos Islands, local constitutional reform commissions were established, consisting of a variety of local people. The task of these commissions was to review the territory constitution, educate and consult the local people, and make recommendations for constitutional change. All produced reports in due course, which were wide-ranging and well-reasoned, and which in most cases served as a useful basis for the negotiations between the territories and the British government that followed. The one exception is Anguilla, where the local Constitutional and Electoral Reform Commission issued a comprehensive report in 2006 but the government of Anguilla has yet to agree to the opening of formal negotiations.

Process

The process of recent constitutional reform in the British OTs was, with only two exceptions, marked by painstaking negotiations between representatives of the territories and the British government. The British government representatives were a team of officials from the Foreign and Commonwealth Office (FCO) with, in some cases, a Minister chairing the final concluding session. The territory representatives varied. In the Falkland Islands, St Helena and Montserrat all the members of the local legislative body participated. In Ascension, Tristan da Cunha and Pitcairn the texts were discussed and agreed with their respective Island Councils. In Bermuda, the British Virgin Islands, the Cayman Islands and Gibraltar selected members of the local legislature from both government and opposition represented the territory. In the Turks and Caicos Islands, separate meetings had to be held with members of the government and members of the opposition, because they would not sit down together, and the Opposition boycotted the final session in London. The British Virgin Islands and the Cayman Islands also included some representatives of civil society in their negotiating teams. In all cases except Gibraltar the Governor of the territory participated in the negotiations, but in a 'cross-bench' capacity rather than as part of either delegation.

In all of these negotiations every word of the proposed new constitution (or in the case of Bermuda the constitutional amendments) had to be agreed

---

9   The Bermuda Constitution is set out in the Bermuda Constitution Order 1968 (SI 1968/182, as amended by SI 1968/463, SI 1968/726, SI 1973/233, SI 1979/452, SI 1979/1310, SI 1989/151, SI 2001/2579, SI 2003/456).

in negotiation. In Tristan da Cunha the members of the local Island Council were taken through the draft provisions by the Administrator of the island and agreed them. For Pitcairn several teleconferences were held linking members of the Island Council and other local people on Pitcairn with officials in London and the Governor in Wellington, and the draft constitution was negotiated by that extraordinary means. In all other cases face-to-face negotiations were held, mostly in the territories concerned but in some cases with a final session in London. In the Cayman Islands, St Helena, Ascension and Montserrat members of the British government team took part in public meetings and media events to explain the process and answer questions while the negotiations proceeded.

Once agreement had been reached on a draft text, there followed a process of public consultation. The draft constitution was published and discussed in the media and at public meetings. In Gibraltar and the Cayman Islands a referendum was held amongst locally registered voters, resulting in direct public approval of the proposed new constitution. In the Turks and Caicos Islands, the British Virgin Islands, the Falkland Islands and Montserrat the proposed new constitution was debated and approved by the local legislature. In St Helena the new constitution was approved by a majority of local legislative councillors, and in Ascension, Tristan da Cunha and Pitcairn by their respective Island Councils.

In the United Kingdom (UK), meanwhile, the draft constitutions were submitted to the Foreign Affairs Committee of the House of Commons for consideration, in accordance with a political arrangement made in 2002 between Jack Straw, when Foreign Secretary, and the Chairman of that Committee.[10] Final political approval was given to the new constitutions by FCO Ministers, and they were formally made law by Order in Council by Her Majesty the Queen in the Privy Council.

As noted earlier, there were two exceptions to this process of negotiation, public consultation and agreement. One was the British Indian Ocean Territory (Constitution) Order 2004, and the other was the Order in Council suspending parts of the Turks and Caicos Islands Constitution.[11] For different reasons, these constitutional instruments were 'imposed' by the British government, essentially so that closer control could be taken of these two territories. Unsurprisingly, each case provoked challenge in the English courts by way of judicial review, but in each case the lawfulness of the action taken was upheld.[12]

---

10 See House of Commons Foreign Affairs Committee Seventh Report, Session 2007–8, HC 147–1, para 29.

11 See note 5 above.

12 See R (Bancoult) v Secretary of State for Foreign and Commonwealth Affairs (No 2) [2008] UKHL 61, [2009] 1 AC 453 (HL); R (Misick) v Secretary of State for Foreign and Commonwealth Affairs [2009] EWHC 1039; [2009] EWCA Civ 1549.

Substance

The substance of the recent constitutional review negotiations resulting in new constitutions for Gibraltar, the Falkland Islands, the Cayman Islands, the British Virgin Islands, the Turks and Caicos Islands, Montserrat, St Helena, Ascension, Tristan da Cunha and Pitcairn followed a similar pattern. Each territory was keen to increase local autonomy and to reduce the reserved powers of the Governor and the UK. The outcome in each case marked an advance in local self-government. The reserved powers, in both the legislative and the executive fields, were reduced to those that were considered necessary and sufficient to ensure that the Governor and the UK government could discharge their responsibilities. A revised balance of powers was achieved that both sides could accept and that better suited modern conditions.[13]

At the same time, it was clearly stated British government policy that it would not agree to a new territory constitution which did not contain a fundamental rights chapter, and its objective was to ensure that any new or updated chapter should give effect to the European Convention on Human Rights[14] and the International Covenant on Civil and Political Rights[15] to the extent that constitutional legislation was considered necessary. Accordingly, the new constitutions of the British Virgin Islands, the Cayman Islands, St Helena, Ascension and Tristan da Cunha, and Pitcairn contain for the first time a fundamental rights chapter enforceable in the territory courts with final appeal to the Judicial Committee of the Privy Council.[16] The constitutions of Gibraltar, the Falkland Islands, Montserrat, and the Turks and Caicos Islands,[17] all of whose previous constitutions had fundamental rights chapters, contain updated chapters.[18] Each of these chapters meets the British government's stated objective, and some in fact go beyond it, including additional rights such as children's rights, a right to lawful administrative action, and the protection of the environment.[19] The strengthening of constitutional human

---

13 The exceptional step taken in 2009 to suspend parts of the Turks and Caicos Islands Constitution resulted not from the distribution of powers made by that constitution but from the local abuse of powers.

14 UKTS No 71 (1953); Cmd 8969.

15 UKTS No 6 (1977); Cmd 6702.

16 Virgin Islands Constitution, Chapter 2; Cayman Islands Constitution, Part I; St Helena, Ascension and Tristan da Cunha Constitution, Chapter 1, Part 2, Chapter 2, Part 2, and Chapter 3, Part 2; Pitcairn Constitution, Part 2.

17 With the sole exception of the right to trial by jury, the fundamental rights chapter of the Turks and Caicos Islands Constitution was not suspended in 2009.

18 Gibraltar Constitution, Chapter I; Falkland Islands Constitution, Chapter I; Montserrat Constitution, Part I; Turks and Caicos Islands Constitution, Part I.

19 See, for example, Cayman Islands Constitution, ss 17, 18 and 19.

rights protection in these eight territories is clearly an important outcome of the constitutional reform process.

A further important development was the strengthening of the regulation and control of public finance at the constitutional level in several territories, in some of which there had previously been no constitutional provisions dealing with this matter.[20] Even Tristan da Cunha and Pitcairn now have constitutional provisions dealing with the independent audit of public accounts.[21]

Apart from a rebalancing of powers, enhanced human rights protection and strengthened control of public finance, the new constitutions include some symbolic changes which the territories concerned regarded as important. In Gibraltar the House of Assembly was renamed the Gibraltar Parliament. In the British Virgin Islands and the Turks and Caicos Islands the Legislative Council was renamed the House of Assembly, and in the Falkland Islands and Montserrat it was renamed the Legislative Assembly. In the British Virgin Islands, Montserrat and the Turks and Caicos Islands the title of Chief Minister was changed to Premier and the Executive Council was renamed the Cabinet. The latter change had earlier been made in the Cayman Islands, but in the 2009 Constitution the title of Leader of Government Business was changed to Premier.

There are some novel institutional provisions in the new constitutions. In the Falkland Islands and St Helena there is constitutional provision for a Public Accounts Committee with a potentially wide remit, consisting of members drawn from both within and outside the legislative body.[22] This was an important development in these two territories where there are no political parties and thus no formal political opposition. The Public Accounts Committees were deliberately designed to help hold the elected governments to account. National Security Councils were established in the British Virgin Islands and the Cayman Islands, and a National Advisory Council in Montserrat, to advise the Governor on internal security and police matters.[23] This helps to involve some elected Ministers of these territories in issues of local political sensitivity. Politically independent Judicial Service Commissions were established in Gibraltar, the Cayman Islands, the British Virgin Islands,

---

20 See Gibraltar Constitution, Chapter VII; Virgin Islands Constitution, Chapter 8; Falkland Islands Constitution, Chapter VI; Montserrat Constitution, Part VIII; St Helena, Ascension and Tristan da Cunha Constitution, Chapter 1, Part 8 (St Helena) and Chapter 2, Part 8 (Ascension).

21 St Helena, Ascension and Tristan da Cunha Constitution, Chapter 3, Part 8; Pitcairn Constitution, s 58.

22 Falkland Islands Constitution, s 81; St Helena, Ascension and Tristan da Cunha Constitution, s 69.

23 Virgin Islands Constitution, s 57; Cayman Islands Constitution, s 58; Montserrat Constitution, s 45.

the Turks and Caicos Islands, St Helena, and Ascension.[24] A new, politically independent, office of Director of Public Prosecutions was established in the British Virgin Islands, the Cayman Islands and Montserrat.[25] The Cayman Islands and British Virgin Islands constitutions provide for a Human Rights Commission, and the Montserrat Constitution provides for a Complaints Commission.[26] In the Cayman Islands the new constitution also set up a Commission for Standards in Public Life and a Constitutional Commission.[27] All of these new bodies were designed to contribute to good government and to enhance local involvement in that effort.

The constitutions of the British Virgin Islands, the Cayman Islands, Montserrat and St Helena, Ascension and Tristan da Cunha include preambles, mostly drafted locally, that express something of the history, culture and aspirations of the people of the territory concerned. This was an innovation, and helps to give some local 'ownership' to the constitution that governs the territory. The Gibraltar Constitution Order 2006 contains an important preamble, repeating the assurances concerning British sovereignty and self-determination set out in the 1969 Gibraltar Constitution Order, but going on to recall the referendum approving the new constitution 'which gives the people of Gibraltar that degree of self-government which is compatible with British sovereignty of Gibraltar and with the fact that the UK remains fully responsible for Gibraltar's external relations'.[28] A further innovation is that the new Constitution of St Helena, Ascension and Tristan da Cunha sets out a list of 'partnership values' which form the basis of the partnership between each island and the UK and of the relationship between the three islands. The values include good faith, the rule of law, good government, sound financial management, the impartial administration of justice and the impartiality of the public service. Each organ of local government is obliged to give effect to the values, and the Governor has powers to ensure this.[29] Similar provisions are included in the new Pitcairn Constitution.[30] Indeed, it might be fairly said that these two constitutions marked the most dramatic and important constitutional developments among the British overseas territories. These

24 Gibraltar Constitution, s 57; Cayman Islands Constitution, s 105; Virgin Islands Constitution, s 94; Turks and Caicos Islands Constitution, s 81; St Helena, Ascension and Tristan da Cunha Constitution, ss 94 and 162.
25 Virgin Islands Constitution, s 59; Cayman Islands Constitution, s 57; Montserrat Constitution, s 46.
26 Cayman Islands Constitution, s 116; Virgin Islands Constitution, s 34; Montserrat Constitution, s 105.
27 Cayman Islands Constitution, ss 117 and 118.
28 Gibraltar Constitution, Preamble
29 St Helena, Ascension and Tristan da Cunha Constitution, ss 2, 3, 4, 43(5)–(8), 74(3)(a), 121 and 186.
30 Pitcairn Constitution, s 1.

remote and sparsely populated islands previously had inadequate and outdated constitutional arrangements, and their modernisation and improvement were long overdue. In particular, Ascension and Tristan da Cunha ceased to be dependencies of St Helena and now have constitutional arrangements of their own, while remaining within a single territorial grouping with St Helena. For its part, Pitcairn now has a proper constitution, replacing the skeletal provisions of the Pitcairn Order 1970.[31]

The Turks and Caicos Islands

It would be incomplete to conclude without saying something about the particular case of the Turks and Caicos Islands. Constitutionally, this territory is now in a state of transition. Since August 2009, when major parts of the 2006 Constitution were suspended, the Governor has been invested with sole legislative and executive power, subject to instructions from London and the reserved power of Her Majesty to legislate by Order in Council. In place of the previous Cabinet and House of Assembly there is an appointed Advisory Council to advise the Governor in the executive field and an appointed Consultative Forum to advise the Governor in the legislative field. But the Governor is not bound by the advice of these bodies.[32] These arrangements are temporary, while steps are taken to re-establish good government and sound financial management, and to prepare a new constitution and pave the way for a general election to a revived House of Assembly. The ultimate objective is the restoration of representative government, with a ministerial system answerable to an elected legislative body, governed by a new constitution with enhanced checks and balances and reserved powers for the Governor and the UK.

The process of public consultation in the Islands about a new constitution began in 2010, and a draft constitution was published there in March 2011. There followed a series of public meetings on the six most populated islands in May, and a final negotiation between the British government and a representative delegation of Turks and Caicos Islanders in June. The new constitution was made by Her Majesty in Council in July 2011, and is set out in the Turks and Caicos Islands Constitution Order 2011.[33] The Order provides for the Governor to bring the constitution into force by proclamation published in the local *Gazette*, and for a general election to the House of Assembly to be held within 30 days thereafter.[34] The timing of the commencement of the constitution, and thus of the next general election, cannot yet be predicted, but it is likely to be in 2012.

31 SI 1970/1434.
32 See note 5 above.
33 SI 2011/1681.
34 See ss 1(2), 4 and 8 of Order.

When brought into force, the new constitution will restore representative government to the Islands, with a House of Assembly consisting of 15 elected members, four appointed members and the Attorney General. Of the elected members, ten will be elected from single-member constituencies and five from the territory at large.[35] A Premier and up to six other Ministers will be appointed from among the elected or appointed members of the House.[36] As before the 2009 suspension of ministerial government, most matters in the executive field will be assigned to Ministers, with the Governor retaining special responsibility for defence, external affairs, internal security including the police, the regulation of international financial services and public service matters.[37]

But there are several provisions designed to enhance the accountability of executive government. First, all organs of government will be obliged to give effect to a 'Statement of Governance Principles', which will be formulated by the Secretary of State after consultation with the House of Assembly and the Turks and Caicos Islands government. The Governor will also have powers to act contrary to Cabinet advice, or even exceptionally to enact legislation, to ensure compliance with the Statement of Governance Principles.[38] Secondly, the political independence of the judiciary and the public service is strengthened.[39] Thirdly, a number of politically independent 'institutions protecting good governance' will be given constitutional status, with a variety of powers, namely an Auditor General and a National Audit Office, a Complaints Commissioner, a Director of Public Prosecutions, a Human Rights Commission, an Integrity Commission, and a Supervisor of Elections.[40] Fourthly, the new constitution includes a detailed chapter regulating public financial management. As well as establishing general principles designed to enhance sound financial management and transparency, this regulates the budgetary process, gives the House of Assembly and a Public Accounts Committee a crucial role in holding the government to account, regulates government borrowing and lending, and provides for the regular and independent audit of public accounts.[41]

In the legislative field, the controls exercisable by the Governor and the Secretary of State at the stage of assent to locally enacted bills are enhanced, as is the exceptional power of the Governor to legislate without reference to the House of Assembly.[42] The reserved power of Her Majesty to legislate for the territory by Order in Council is also retained.[43]

---

35 See ss 43 and 45 of Constitution.
36 See s 31 of Constitution.
37 See ss 36 and 37 of Constitution.
38 See ss 28, 29 and 72 of Constitution.
39 See ss 83, 84, 88 and 92 of Constitution.
40 See ss 97–105 of Constitution.
41 See ss 109–126 of Constitution.
42 See ss 72 and 73 of Constitution.
43 See s 14 of Order.

Conclusion

Happily, the experience of the Turks and Caicos Islands is exceptional. In the case of the other territories, constitutional reform, in terms of both process and substance, has proved beneficial. Their new constitutional arrangements are certainly stronger and more suited to modern conditions, and show every sign of working well. Only time will tell if the new Constitution of the Turks and Caicos Islands marks a brighter and more stable future for that troubled territory. As with all of these constitutions, the key will be whether it is operated in good faith by all concerned, for the benefit of the people whose lives it governs.

Chapter 5

Reformation of the Kingdom of the Netherlands: what are the stakes?

Lammert de Jong and Ron van der Veer

Introduction

On 10 October 2010 (10.10.10) a significant reform of the Dutch Caribbean was formalised. The Kingdom of the Netherlands, comprising three countries (the Netherlands, the Netherlands Antilles[1] and Aruba), was overhauled. The Netherlands Antilles ceased to exist as a separate country; a country, which up to 10.10.10, consisted of five islands: Curaçao, Sint Maarten, Bonaire, Saba and Sint Eustatius (Statia). Two of these islands – the largest, Curaçao and Sint Maarten – acquired a separate country status within the Kingdom, while the other three islands were integrated into the Netherlands. The population of the five islands of the Netherlands Antilles is approximately 197,000 and Aruba's population is 103,000.

When formed in 1954, the Netherlands Antilles consisted of six islands. In 1986 Aruba seceded and obtained a separate country status within the Kingdom of the Netherlands. The remaining five islands continued to be called the Netherlands Antilles. In 2010 the disintegration of the Netherlands Antilles continued when Curaçao and Sint Maarten also acquired a separate country status. The islands of Bonaire, Sint Eustatius and Saba, the so-called BES islands, were integrated into the Netherlands as public authorities (*openbare lichamen*); as such, the BES islands are now administered by the Netherlands while still retaining local government functions (more or less like municipalities in the Netherlands).

---

1   The Netherlands Antilles stands for the Dutch statehood term Het Land De Nederlandse Antillen, which means the country called the Netherlands Antilles. This is distinct from 'the Netherlands Antilles' (de Nederlandse Antillen), which refers to the collection of islands in the Dutch Caribbean that are part of the Kingdom of the Netherlands.

In some quarters of the Kingdom, this re-configuration has been lauded as a 'new beginning', yet in others it is perceived as the 'beginning of the end', the penultimate moment before the Kingdom retracts to being a single country: the Netherlands in Europe with some minuscule overseas BES territories in the Caribbean, with a population of less than 20,000, referred to as *Caraibisch Nederland*. If that does happen, the experimental postcolonial formation of a Kingdom that overarched several autonomous countries on an equal footing, one on the European continent and the others in the Southern Hemisphere, will have come to an end. The period of Dutch decolonisation that began after World War II will then definitely have reached its conclusion. Yet, the option of a 'New Beginning' must not be excluded, as high stakes are involved in the Kingdom's overseas realm, in particular for the 300,000 Dutch citizens still living in the Caribbean.

In this chapter we shall sketch the post-colonial trajectory of the Kingdom of the Netherlands, culminating in the implosion of the Netherlands Antilles on 10.10.10, and review the checks and balances of the Kingdom of the Netherlands in the Dutch Caribbean. A divergence of interests and agendas brought the partners of the Kingdom of the Netherlands together. Curaçao and Sint Maarten wanted autonomy, the BES islands wanted security, and the Netherlands wanted to safeguard good governance in the Dutch Caribbean. The question is raised as to how sustainable the intricate new structure of the Kingdom of the Netherlands will turn out to be, especially in view of intrinsic cross pressures between the Netherlands and the Caribbean islands? Will the 10.10.10 institutional reform produce a long-term and dependable stability, in particular in view of the stakes involved for the Dutch citizens in the Caribbean? Or must the partners be braced once more for a twist of those ubiquitous forces in opposite directions, i.e. local-political autonomy on the one hand, and metropolitan control on the other? And if so, will this lack of a collective mission bring the Kingdom-as-is to an end? Or will there be some kind of accommodation keeping this historically tangled statehood configuration together by default as no better option is at hand? In other words, the quintessential challenge of the Kingdom of the Netherlands may well be to protect vested Dutch citizenship for the Caribbean *rijksgenoten* (compatriot citizens) against a lack of interest on the mainland ('sell them on eBay') and a disregard in the Caribbean for the Kingdom's influence in the islands. But can this be done?

A snapshot of Dutch decolonisation

At the end of World War II, when the outlines of a post-colonial order were being drawn, the Netherlands did not distinguish between its different colonised territories, which included the immense Indonesian archipelago in the East, as well as the small territories in the western hemisphere: Suriname and the Dutch

West Indies. In the initial process of decolonisation all the territories were simply lumped together (Klinkers, 1999). After World War II ended and Japan had capitulated, Indonesia declared itself independent, an act that stunned the Netherlands. The unilateral declaration of Indonesian independence was forcibly resisted by the Dutch. Those relatively new to world power, particularly the United States, did not support this resistance and eventually forced the Dutch to negotiate with the Indonesian nationalists. The Netherlands attempted to keep Indonesia within the Kingdom by proposing a form of postcolonial federal union – a Dutch Commonwealth. It was thought that a free association of autonomous states could pacify the ambitions of the independence movement. The Indonesian nationalists, however, did not compromise and after four years of wars and several roundtable conferences the government of the Netherlands formally accepted the inevitable. The strength and appeal of Indonesia's independence movement had been misread by the Dutch and could not be contained within a liberal postcolonial Charter that aimed to keep Indonesia within the Kingdom. Indonesia's independence marked the end of the Dutch empire.

After Indonesia pulled out of the Kingdom, Suriname and the Netherlands Antilles reaped the fruits of the Netherlands' attempts to keep Indonesia on board. The arrangements that were then conceived had not been meant for these much smaller territories. The Caribbean territories, however, would not budge on the concept of a free association of autonomous states as the heir to the colonial Kingdom and stuck to the Charter of the Kingdom-to-be's original liberal terms and philosophy. The Caribbean countries claimed autonomy, not independence. They aimed to be partners on an equal footing with the Netherlands and succeeded, at least on paper, when on 15 December 1954 a new Charter of the Kingdom was enacted.

The Charter of 1954 proclaimed a voluntary constitutional partnership, bestowing a country status on a collection of islands; some were close together, some over 900 kilometres apart. As a consequence, it was an artificial construct, and not a nation rooted in local aspirations. Indeed, more than an element of truth is contained in the Antillean maxim: 'The Netherlands Antilles only exists in the Netherlands'. In retrospect, the concept of an Antillean nation-state, stringing six islands together, offered the Netherlands an easy way out of its postcolonial plight in the Dutch Caribbean. This configuration provided the offices of the Kingdom in faraway Europe with a Caribbean intermediary, the Netherlands Antilles, to govern six islands that were very different in size, character and outlook.

Het Statuut voor het Koninkrijk, the Constitution of the Kingdom of the Netherlands, designated the Kingdom as a federal state, comprising three autonomous countries, the Netherlands in Europe, and two countries in the Caribbean, Suriname and The Netherlands Antilles, albeit with a rather asymmetrical internal structure. As Hirsch Ballin described:

> The Netherlands Antilles, Aruba and the Netherlands have their own
> parliaments, governments, judicial structures and constitutions, with
> responsibilities at federal level (or 'Kingdom level' as it is called in
> the Netherlands) being limited to foreign policy, defence, nationality,
> safeguarding human rights and good governance, and a few other
> areas (2001: 25–6).

The Netherlands Antilles and Suriname became autonomous countries of the
Kingdom of the Netherlands, with a high degree of internal self-government.
The Kingdom's role in the Caribbean was never meant to be dominant. The
designers of the Charter purposefully limited its authority. The Charter was
a landmark document concluding the colonial period. Suriname and the
Netherlands Antilles would, as autonomous countries, take care of their own
business; neither the Kingdom as a whole nor the Netherlands as an equal
partner would have a say in local affairs such as government finance, social and
economic development, cultural affairs and education. The founding fathers
of the Charter defined the Kingdom essentially as a federal institution whose
formal authority was limited mainly to foreign affairs, defence and nationality.
The Kingdom's Charter was seen first and foremost as a document enshrining
the autonomy of the Caribbean territories (Hirsch Ballin, 2005: 10); yet the
Kingdom was assigned to ultimately safeguard good governance in the Dutch
Caribbean.

The Charter included the clause that any constitutional change (other
than independence of a former colony) required the unanimous consent of
the parties involved. This clause became a major obstacle later on when the
Netherlands wanted change. However, in 1954 the Netherlands gave in to the
aspirations of these small states, believing that there was little to gain or lose.
The empire was already gone. Moreover, the Charter was not meant to last for
ever since the Caribbean countries would become independent one day. But
that was not how things developed.

A permanent transatlantic LAT[2] affair

For a long time the interaction between the Netherlands and the Caribbean
countries was infrequent, mostly out of the public eye and mainly related to
government affairs; the relationship was not of great concern to either side.
In the early days, not much was known about the *rijksgenoten* (compatriot
citizens) in the Caribbean and a benign perception of overseas Dutch citizens
prevailed in the Netherlands during this period. Well-educated students,
speaking charmingly accented Dutch, hard-working and well-mannered
nurses, fun-loving carnival dancers, friendly sailors, all of whom stood out
because of their exotic colour; these images dominated the Dutch view of the

2   Living Apart Together.

Nederlanders in the Caribbean (Hulst, 2003: 24; Oostindie, 1997: 235–6). Curiosity, rather than a sense of shared identity or common interest, set the tone in those days. Initially the Roman Catholic Church and a range of Dutch and local charity organisations helped with social needs, mainly education and healthcare. Later on the Netherlands government provided generous public handouts for development cooperation so that these countries could eventually stand on their own. In those days, Suriname and the Netherlands Antilles did not claim much attention in Dutch politics and public interest. All parties were happy with a Kingdom-lite.

For Suriname the day of independence came in November 1975. On the crest of a strong wave of nationalism in the territory, and a Netherlands' political correctitude that viewed decolonisation as a historic must, Suriname left the Kingdom, though with a majority of only one vote in the Surinamese Parliament and without a public referendum. Suriname's independence triggered a major emigration to the Netherlands, which robbed the new nation-state of a substantial part of its human capital.

In 1986 Aruba succeeded in liberating itself from Curaçao's over-lordship and seceded from the Netherlands Antilles when obtaining a long-coveted *status aparte*. Yet, since Aruba wanted to remain part of the Kingdom as a separate country, it did not opt for independence. In the early 1990s a broad transatlantic political consensus emerged that the Dutch Caribbean islands would be better off remaining part of the Kingdom of the Netherlands. For the Netherlands, considerations of safeguarding good governance in the Caribbean were paramount in changing the tides of opinion. On the Antillean and Aruban side, independence had always been more intellectual wish-fulfilment than something to attain in actuality; even more so after having watched the decline of independent Suriname. Independence should therefore be held at bay. For the islands of the Netherlands Antilles and Aruba, Independence Day was never to be a real objective, rather it served as a useful rallying cry on Caribbean political platforms and agendas.

After the reality of a Kingdom with partners in the Caribbean region had rather surreptitiously become a permanent LAT phenomenon, the Charter's original definition of limited authority and regulation was not reviewed. Running their own affairs had always been of principal interest in Antillean politics; autonomy was here to stay, both now and in any future permanent relationship. At a Future of the Kingdom Conference in 1993 (*Toekomstconferentie*) the Netherlands attempted to reach agreement on changing institutional rules and regulations to empower a good governance agenda in the Caribbean region. This over-confident initiative was roundly rejected: conference documents were literally torn up in the face of the Netherlands Prime Minister who led the Dutch delegation at that time.

Caribbean disagreement notwithstanding, the winds had definitely changed. The unbearable lightness of the Kingdom (Jong, 2005a) and the allure and illusion of Antillean autonomy had to be addressed in terms that transcended the essentialist principles *en vogue* during the period of decolonisation (Jong, 2005b: 193). Unable to put mutually agreed-upon new regulation in place, the Netherlands applied its financial clout to pursue good governance. Technical Assistance (TA) from the Netherlands to the Caribbean islands increased significantly, focusing on areas of justice and law enforcement, administrative assistance and reform, and public finance.

During the 1980s and early 1990s the Kingdom operated essentially as a development aid shelter in anticipation of future independence. When all partners tacitly agreed that the Kingdom was going to stay in the Caribbean, proposals to reform the Kingdom as a permanent structure by adding new Kingdom regulations could not be agreed upon. For the Netherlands, the idea of a Kingdom-lite had become outdated. Autonomy was simply seen as a failure: huge budget deficits, poor education, social degradation and flawed law enforcement. If relations with the Caribbean islands were going to become a permanent affair, the balance of power within the Kingdom had to be reviewed, which would impact on the holy grail of Antillean autonomy.

Implosion of the Netherlands Antilles

For many politicians, both in the Netherlands and in the Antilles, Aruba's *status aparte* in 1986 meant the end of a workable Antillean nation-state. Since Aruba's exit, the government structure of the Netherlands Antilles has been in a permanent state of restructuring (*herstructurering*): one day more centralised, another more decentralised, or split up into two countries, one composed of Sint Maarten, Saba and Sint Eustatius, and the other of Curaçao and Bonaire. The postcolonial construct of the Antillean nation-state was in trouble.

Most significant in turning the tide was the spillover of Antillean problems to the Netherlands homeland – through migration of youngsters with a criminal background or no education, and drug trafficking – resulting in high levels of Antillean crime in the metropole. In 2002, the Antillean percentage of crime suspects (5.6) in the Netherlands was six times higher than for *autochthons* (0.9 per cent) and more than double the average for other immigrant populations (2.2 per cent). Moreover, the Kingdom's constitutional safeguards in the Dutch Caribbean were failing in a wide range of areas. Prison conditions were unacceptable; the deleterious air pollution (from Curaçao's refinery) was intolerable; and the deepening social disintegration of more and more neighbourhoods in Curaçao cast a worrisome doubt on the competence of the Antillean as well as the Kingdom's public authorities. The degree of violence – Curaçao's homicide rate in 2003 was 30 times higher (per 100,000) than in the Netherlands – was alarming (Jong, 2009: 32). The United Nations reported heavy drug trafficking – in 2004 some 60 per cent of all cocaine seized in the Caribbean was seized in the Dutch Caribbean (United Nations, 2007).

These statistics all contributed to the Netherlands Antilles having a failed state image, while making a mockery of the Kingdom's promise to safeguard good governance in the Dutch Caribbean. Metropolitan homeland interests, social deterioration, and serious law and order problems made it self-evident that the Kingdom's crisis-management mode was no longer fit for purpose.

At the same time politicians on both Sint Maarten and Curaçao passionately pursued a separate country status. For Sint Maarten the impetus was driven by a desire to distance itself from Curaçao. Similarly, Curaçao was determined to free itself from any responsibility for the much smaller islands of Bonaire, Saba and Sint Eustatius. Indeed, the latter had lost all trust in the governing capacity of the Netherlands Antilles, not least because of its poor fiscal management. After a series of referenda on the islands of the Netherlands Antilles, agreement was reached on a package deal concerning the needs and interests of the different parties involved. The dominating issues were: 1) the interests of Curaçao and Sint Maarten in obtaining country status; 2) the Netherlands' ultimate aim of empowering the Kingdom in safeguarding good governance and the rule of law in the Dutch Caribbean.

Finally, in 2005, all parties agreed that the Netherlands Antilles had failed to resolve the many problems the islands continued to face (*Hoofdlijnenakkoord*, 2005). For more than 20 years the viability of the nation-state of the Netherlands Antilles had been questioned. Now all parties decided that the Netherlands Antilles must go. The constitutional compact was up for amendment as all partners pushed for change, though each with its own agenda. Another five years would be needed, however, to iron out the practicalities of the 10.10.10 transformation.

Autonomy versus sustainability

For the Dutch Caribbean, the dissolution of the Netherlands Antilles and the creation of a new status for the islands implied a political change of paramount importance. In the political imaginary of Curaçao and Sint Maarten, the separate country status translated as having achieved autonomy. From now on they were autonomous countries within the realm of the Kingdom of the Netherlands. Not having opted for integration, this country status might politically be conceived as being only one step away from independence, maybe not something to go for in reality, but serving as an emergent theoretical option for the future.

On the part of the Netherlands, 10.10.10 was an attempt to put the Kingdom's house in the Dutch Caribbean in order. In recent years the Kingdom's operations had been ill-defined, opposed, ineffective, ridiculed and characterised as day-to-day crisis management. A populist True Dutch tide in the Netherlands in favour of getting rid of the Kingdom's *Absurdistan* had reinforced this negativity. However, with regard to 10.10.10 the Netherlands government insisted on putting regulation and ordinance in place to buttress the realm of the Kingdom in the Dutch Caribbean. Debt relief was a condition for establishing this new beginning, as well as the 'takeover' of the smaller islands of Bonaire, Sint Eustatius and Saba by the Netherlands. The islands were considered to be unsustainable on their own, and were ultimately abandoned by Curaçao and Sint Maarten. These dependencies preferred – out of necessity, and guided by the Netherlands Antillean experience – to be incorporated into the Netherlands.

The Netherlands had agreed to the dissolution of the Netherlands Antilles with conditions that strengthened the operational hand of the Kingdom in the Caribbean. For the Netherlands, 10.10.10 was driven by a management mission to sustain the Kingdom in the long run. On the part of Curaçao and Sint Maarten, the separate country status was framed in terms of autonomy and imagined – by some – as a stepping-stone towards the ultimate dream of independence sometime in the future.

10.10.10: Major operation! Major implications?

There is no doubt that from a political point of view the constitutional reform of the Kingdom of the Netherlands was a major operation. It was a mammoth undertaking for the legal and law making professionals and, from a global perspective, a country splitting up peacefully was a truly notable event. On 10.10.10 the country of the Netherlands Antilles ceased to exist. This date, 10 October 2010, came to define the transformation of the Kingdom of the Netherlands. But it also symbolised the political clock that was ticking in the Netherlands. The deal that had been concluded in 2005 faced more and more political opposition in the Netherlands during the years that followed, for several reasons. The financial and economic crisis of 2007–9 made it extremely difficult to provide generous debt relief. Opinion polls gave cause for concern with the Coalition government losing support at the expense of the opposition parties, including those of the far right. A political crisis over the Netherlands military presence in Afghanistan led to the government resigning in February 2010. A new Parliament was elected in June 2010 and political parties on the right and the left gained seats. They did not approve of the deal with the Caribbean islands, and so opposition against plans for generous debt relief grew. A new Dutch centre-right coalition government took office on 14 October 2010, just four days after 10.10.10. But by then it was too late to re-negotiate the terms of the transformation.

Once the principal agreement had been reached in 2005, it was necessary to make a major effort to translate the political agreements into formal arrangements and legal language. At first most politicians and civil servants in the Netherlands expected this to be a relatively straightforward and technical process that could be dealt with by civil servants and lawyers. But at the Caribbean end, this process was loaded with political implications. The ongoing negotiation rounds caused the transition date to be postponed several times from the date initially set of 1 July 2007, and – more seriously – slowed the momentum of change in all parts of the Kingdom. Hundreds of civil servants, legal advisors and consultants were involved, most of them flown in from the Netherlands. These large numbers increased misgivings and fears of being overruled among members of the islands' political circuits. This, in turn, caused the inflow of even more expertise to counter these suspicions. Royal Dutch KLM and some major hotels in The Hague and Willemstad were fully booked for years. In the process, the Council of State (an advisory body which consists of members of the royal family and Crown-appointed members) repeatedly warned that focusing on legal structures should not become an end in itself: the wellbeing of all citizens in the entire Kingdom should be the directive of this operation (Council of State, 2007: 84).

Since 1986 when Aruba gained its separate status within the Kingdom, the political climate in the Netherlands had changed considerably. The Caribbean islands no longer received favourable treatment because they were 'victims of colonialism'. The Netherlands government and a critical Parliament in The Hague wanted to make sure that public finances and law enforcement were strengthened once and for all. So in the process some major complications had to be negotiated in both political terms and legal detail.

First, The Netherlands Antilles had accumulated an enormous debt of over two billion Euros. The Netherlands agreed to facilitate a new financial beginning by redeeming a large part of the debt: €1.7 billion. In exchange for that generosity, The Hague demanded that a College of Financial Supervision (*College financieel toezicht – Cft*) be put in place. Secondly, the Netherlands aimed to secure good governance in the Caribbean countries. Numerous complaints on the functioning of the island police forces, a dysfunctional prison system, and a weak public prosecutor's office had been testimony to a flawed law enforcement process. Therefore the Dutch insisted that a Council for Law Enforcement (*Raad voor de Rechtshandhaving*) be set up to oversee law enforcement.

Both institutions now advise the governments of Curaçao and Sint Maarten (and the Dutch government for the BES islands). In addition, they also counsel the Kingdom government on any measures they think necessary. The *Cft* works with very detailed instructions as to how a budget should be prepared and executed. Indeed, the *Cft* has already justified its existence by encouraging a previously unknown financial discipline on the island governments. No longer can money be spent that is not budgeted for, or by politicians or public servants who are not authorised to do so. The Council for Law Enforcement reports on a regular basis on the entire chain of law enforcement (public prosecutor, police and prison system, but also on customs and other law enforcement departments). Only the Dutch Caribbean Combined Court of Justice (working for all six islands) is not subject to scrutiny by the Council for Law Enforcement.[3]

For the Netherlands, the transition of the BES islands was a major operation. They had to be integrated into the Netherlands departmental and regional architecture as public entities (*openbare lichamen*); as such, the BES islands were going to be administered by the Netherlands while retaining local government functions. Regardless of the small population of the islands (less than 20,000 altogether), this constitutional transition was a significant undertaking. The Netherlands government transition manager counted 401 government tasks that had to be transferred from the Netherlands Antilles to the Netherlands; divided over 14 Dutch ministries. In order to effect a smooth transition, the three small BES islands were inundated with reconnaissance missions. In 2007, every other day a departmental delegation from The Hague (180 in total, not counting special advisors, consultants, parliamentarians, municipal and provincial delegations) visited these islands to see for themselves the condition of the public services that would eventually be added to their portfolios (Jong, 2009: 177). As a result the KLM airline expanded its World Business Class on this transatlantic route. Those who wanted to get rid of the Kingdom's *Absurdistan* ridiculed the size of this operation and its epic manpower input.

In terms of nationality, 10.10.10 did not make amendments. The inhabitants of the three (now Dutch) islands Bonaire, Sint Eustatius and Saba already had Dutch nationality (as do the citizens of Aruba, Curaçao and Sint Maarten). But what did change is that the Netherlands Constitution (*Grondwet*) is now the constitution of those 20,000 Caribbean Dutch nationals. The first article of the constitution is all about equal treatment in equal cases,[4] giving rise to a highly politicised debate concerning what this constitutional equality really means in the three BES islands. What about Dutch law and the regulation of the minimum wage, taxes, gay marriage, abortion, euthanasia and the liberal policies on soft drugs, just to mention a few of the sensitive topics? Confusion reached a climax when in the summer of 2010 the Dutch Parliament instructed the Dutch government to impose, within a year, legislation on abortion, euthanasia and same sex marriage on the BES islands. The amendment was

3   The decisions of the Combined Court of Justice can be appealed at the Hoge Raad der Nederlanden, which is the Supreme Court of the Kingdom for civil, criminal and tax law.

4   Article 1: 'Allen die zich in Nederland bevinden, worden in gelijke gevallen gelijk behandeld. Discriminatie wegens godsdienst, levensovertuiging, politieke gezindheid, ras, geslacht of op welke grond dan ook, is niet toegestaan.' (All those who are in the Netherlands will be treated equally in equal cases. Discrimination for reasons of religion, the way people want to live, political views, race, sex or on any other grounds is not permitted).

voted for in the Second Chamber of Parliament, basically against the wishes of the Dutch government, and without any consultation of the islands. A combination of left and liberal parties formed a unique and short-lived union just to enforce some of the Dutch liberal crown jewels on islands that never asked for such a present in the first place. The islands were shocked.

For their part, the islands wondered why the same equality was not applied when it came to the issue of social security which is much higher in the Netherlands. In this case, however, The Hague emphasised that the enormous social-economic differences between the European and Caribbean parts of the Kingdom stood in the way. The debate on equality of cases and treatment will surely return to the agenda and will be an important topic when the experiences of the BES islands are evaluated in 2015.

It would seem that the renovated Kingdom of the Netherlands is all about change. Surely, the image of a wholesale changeover is supported by the disappearance of one country and the birth of five new public entities (two of them being new countries). On the other hand it may be helpful to demonstrate what actually stays the same. And that – surprisingly – is quite a lot. To the outside world the Kingdom basically still looks the way it has done since 1975 when Suriname became independent. Nothing has changed in the world of foreign affairs and defence. Foreign policy was and remains a so-called Kingdom affair, which actually means that The Hague is in charge. The same is true for all other pre-existing Kingdom responsibilities.

Although the three BES islands are now integrated into the Netherlands, they are not integrated into the European Union (EU). This issue was considered too complex to be solved on 10.10.10 and was therefore postponed for at least another four years. Thus a person living in Bonaire, Statia or Saba is in fact living in the Netherlands but not inside the EU or Schengen area. The *acquis communautaire* of the EU is effective in the Netherlands but not in the BES islands. This differs from the French islands like Martinique, Guadeloupe, and St Martin (see chapter 6). These are integrated in the French Republic as overseas departments, and fully integrated in the EU as well. For the Dutch BES islands, it is not yet clear if they will eventually end up with a status like the French overseas departments, or that another constitutional position will be found.

10.10.10: Checks and balances of the Kingdom

How will the transformation of the Dutch Caribbean affect the functioning of the Kingdom and the good governance performance of the Caribbean member countries? During the transformation process, a legalistic debate on new structures, tasks and responsibilities assumed central importance. No analysis had been conducted on the provisions of the existing Charter to maintain good governance in the Caribbean: why had they not been applied when called for?

All partners were more interested in negotiating new institutional conditions instead of reviewing the roots of the existing good governance problems. The Council of State said on several occasions that an analysis should be made first of the existing checks and balances within the Kingdom before embarking on a new design (Council of State, 2010: 83). However, none of the negotiating parties wanted to risk (further) delays in the process by evaluating the Kingdom's troubled past. At the same time, a critical analysis of the raison d'être of the Kingdom was missing: why is it there, what should its mission be, and what is its practical use to citizens on the islands and in the Netherlands? All partners (tacitly) agreed that such an exercise would open a Pandora's Box that could forestall 10.10.10 for many years.

The checks and balances in the updated Kingdom are essentially similar to the old ones (for a review of the old ones, see Borman, 2005). The new provisions on financial supervision and law enforcement (both only for Curaçao and Sint Maarten, on a temporary basis, to be evaluated in five years' time) are largely revisions of clauses contained in the pre-existing Charter. For instance, the growth of the enormous debt built up in the past could easily have been defined as a severe case of bad governance (*onbehoorlijk bestuur*). This would have entitled the Kingdom to intervene; yet no effective action was taken at that time. The political will was lacking since a decision whether something is a severe case of bad governance (more or less structural, or endemic) is – in the end – a political one.

All parties have agreed that the Netherlands Antilles has not functioned effectively since 2005, but the question of who was to blame for this malfunctioning remained obscured. What about the functioning of the Kingdom itself and its laxity in applying the Charter's provisions to set things right? The key article outlining the Charter's checks and balances is number 43. It states that the individual countries within the Kingdom are responsible themselves for upholding the rule of law and good governance (including respect for human rights). The second part of article 43 defines the Kingdom's responsibility: it must ensure and guarantee that the countries do what the article's first part requires them to do. The requirements in this second part have never been carried out. Only on two occasions since 1954 has the Kingdom imposed some form of higher supervision (most recently on Sint Maarten in 1992), but another legal basis was used.[5] Article 43 (and the related article 51, which authorises the Kingdom to give instructions, or even take over specific government functions) remained in the closet as some sort of nuclear deterrent, preferably never to be used.[6]

---

5   The government of Sint Maarten was accused of incompetence, undemocratic practices and widescale corruption. The legality of the intervention was based on the *Staatsregeling Nederlandse Antillen*, the Constitution of the Netherlands Antilles.
6   Articles 43 and 51 of the Kingdom Charter (in Dutch):

The following steps must be taken before this authority can be applied (Borman, 2005). Firstly, the Kingdom must conclude that the rule of law and/ or good governance is gravely violated, and that this violation is more or less on a structural basis (not one nasty incident, but a number of them). Secondly, the Kingdom must come to the conclusion that the country (or countries) involved are not capable themselves of adjusting the situation. Thirdly, and as an ultimate resort, the Kingdom must act to restore the rule of law or good governance as quickly as possible. Furthermore, the Charter implicitly states that the island authorities must first have had a chance to fix the problem themselves. Basically, all this requires political judgement, for nowhere does the Charter indicate when such a situation occurs.

So in the end the Kingdom government in The Hague decides upon the use of the Kingdom's higher supervision, which can be imposed against the will of the island(s) concerned. The Council of State of the Kingdom reviews such a measure (as is done with all law proposals). The Council particularly checks the rationale: does the measure have the right motivation, is it proportionate, is it accurately addressing the problem, and so on. Yet, even without positive advice from the Council, the measure can be forced upon an island when the Dutch Parliament agrees to do so. This was the procedure before 10.10.10 and it still is today. An appeal procedure may in the future be added to this intervention process.[7]

Emotional and political arguments have always stood in the way when considering higher supervision according to the Charter's articles 43 and 51. Its use would mean active intervention by the former colonial power; the Netherlands would actually become fully responsible (again). Another reservation is embedded in the question, what is to be done if higher supervision

---

Article 43.1: *Elk der landen draagt zorg voor de verwezenlijking van de fundamentele menselijke rechten en vrijheden, de rechtszekerheid en de deugdelijkheid van bestuur.*
Article 43.2: *Het waarborgen van deze rechten, vrijheden, rechtszekerheid en deugdelijkheid van bestuur is aangelegenheid van het Koninkrijk.*
Article 51: *Wanneer een orgaan in Aruba, Curaçao of Sint Maarten niet of niet voldoende voorziet in hetgeen het ingevolge het Statuut, een internationale regeling, een rijkswet of een algemene maatregel van rijksbestuur moet verrichten, kan, onder aanwijzing van de rechtsgronden en de beweegredenen, waarop hij berust, een algemene maatregel van rijksbestuur bepalen op welke wijze hierin wordt voorzien.*

7   The new Kingdom Charter contains two articles (12a and 38a) to deal with conflicts that may arise in future. Such an arrangement for resolving conflicts was missing in the previous version of the Charter. It is not yet clear how this will be formalised. Some (for instance, a large section of Aruba's parliament) are of the opinion that the Supreme Court (Hoge Raad) should fulfil this function, while others suggest that the Council of State (Raad van State) becomes the arbiter, as it already does when disagreements arise in terms of financial supervision. Others advocate a new institution.

does not work out in the way it was planned? Despite these reservations, the Kingdom has had the authority all along to redress governance in the Dutch Caribbean. These checks and balances have always existed within the Kingdom but have been rarely applied in the past. Therefore the question remains whether the 10.10.10 redefinition of the Kingdom was necessary? In the 10.10.10 transformation process much emphasis was placed on the creation of separate countries, while little attention was given to the functioning of the Kingdom itself.

Will the Kingdom act differently in the future? Maybe! On 10.10.10 the Kingdom gained operational strength by setting up monitoring bodies for public finance and law enforcement, in sharp contrast to the crisis management mode of earlier days when the Kingdom Council of Ministers had to be involved every so often. Also, the direct interaction between Kingdom and individual Caribbean countries, without the intermediary of the Netherlands Antilles, facilitates the Kingdom's operation. The Netherlands Antilles can no longer be told that it must act first before the Kingdom exercises its responsibility, and so serve as an excuse for the Kingdom doing nothing. And the Caribbean countries can no longer blame the Netherlands Antilles for lapses in good governance in their islands: since 10.10.10 the island authorities themselves are directly responsible.

For the Caribbean countries the question is how their responsibility to uphold the rule of law and good governance will be effectuated. For the Kingdom the question is how dedicated it will be in safeguarding good governance as the essential condition of Netherlands citizenship in the Caribbean. These questions cannot be answered at present. One can only wonder, firstly, whether or not 10.10.10 has recharged the good governance mission of the newly minted Caribbean countries and, secondly, whether the Kingdom's commitment has been reinforced to provide the essential backstop in case a country's good governance mission fails. The 10.10.10 winning lottery ticket has yet to be drawn.

New beginning, more of the same, or the beginning of the end?

In the Caribbean the new order was welcomed with balloons and banners – 10.10.10 was warmly celebrated. But in the shadows some people were unhappy. 'My country has been taken away,' cried one Antillean citizen. Born on Bonaire, having lived for decades in Curaçao, and now in retirement in Sint Maarten, she had lost her bearings.[8] Others grumbled, in particular politicians on Curaçao, that the trade-off for the separate status had been too high, considering the heavier hand of the Kingdom in local affairs, especially in relation to public finances and law enforcement.

8   Interview on Sint Maarten, October 2010.

But overall a state of jubilance marked the day. Proudly counting their blessings, Curaçao and Sint Maarten declared themselves autonomous countries, which was not completely beside the point: they were no longer twinned together in a communal form of statehood, nor were they any longer the benefactors of small dependent Antillean islands. In these respects Curaçao and Sint Maarten had indeed become autonomous. Yet when the matter of autonomy is weighed on the scales of the Kingdom, both Curaçao and Sint Maarten had lost. In that context, the new countries had sacrificed some degree of self-government as public finance and law enforcement were now brought under day-to-day Kingdom monitoring (for an initial period of five years). Curaçao and Sint Maarten are now less autonomous than the Netherlands Antilles was previously. Notwithstanding the plusses and minuses in the various worlds where autonomy plays out, Sint Maarten and Curaçao were branded with the status of autonomous countries.

Visions of the Kingdom

The institutional reform of 10.10.10 was not grounded in a communal mission of the Kingdom, or accompanied with a vision that placed its operations in the Caribbean in a new perspective. In other words, a new corporate mission statement was lacking because it was considered a waste of time – a route to nowhere – in view of the intimidating question of how to achieve agreement amongst the partners before the clock struck 10.10.10. The Hague had not forgotten the shredded-papers failure of the conference on 'The Future of the Kingdom' in 1993.

In a surprising twist, however, the Dutch Minister for Kingdom Relations emphasised – in June 2011 half a year after the 10.10.10 celebratory bells had rung – that a vision must now be developed to substantiate its raison d'être as well as the operations of the refurbished Kingdom.[9] Against the backdrop of the Kingdom's troubling past of crises, quarrels and legalistic simplifications, a new outlook had to be defined. The Minister for Kingdom Relations stated in particular that the Kingdom's safeguards should not be seen as a substitute for a Caribbean country's own due course and cause, but must be applied only in a case of ultimate redress. The Caribbean counterparts themselves must uphold democratic law and financial order in their respective countries. These countries must rigorously live by these public standards, not because of a stand-by Kingdom as a supervising guard, but because of their own focus and direction. In this view, the Kingdom does not hold the key to Caribbean good

---

9   See www.rijksoverheid.nl/onderwerpen/caribische-deel-van-het-koninkrijk/
    documenten-en-publicaties/toespraken/2011/05/23/toespraak-minister-donner-
    tijdens-de-bijeenkomst-van-de-vereniging-antilliaans-netwerk-op-20-mei-2011-in-
    amsterdam.html.

governance. In other words, the Kingdom must not be identified as a European superintendent in the Caribbean region.

The Minister for Kingdom Relations urged his partners in the Dutch Caribbean to come forward with their visions. To that end a Kingdom conference was planned for the autumn of 2011. The initial reaction of Aruba was positive, but the governments of Sint Maarten and Curaçao indicated that they had more important business to deal with, particularly the transition from Antillean statehood to running their autonomous countries. Further, the urgency of a substantive long-term vision for the Kingdom may well be undermined in time by possible independence ambitions sparked by Curaçao and Sint Maarten becoming autonomous countries. So the articulation of a substantive vision for the Kingdom could be overtaken by events.

The Netherlands quest for Dutch interests

With this new beginning, the Netherlands government once more began a search for Dutch interests that are served by the Kingdom of the Netherlands still having a presence in the Caribbean. The lack of cultural, linguistic and institutional commonality among the countries of the Kingdom works against its permanence in the Caribbean: what do they have in common that still might bind them together? What interests do they share? On a practical level, the Caribbean interests can easily be defined in terms of standards of living, rule of law, good governance and entitlement to a Kingdom of the Netherlands passport that gives unrestricted access to the Netherlands, Europe and a much wider world. But what are the Netherlands' interests? Trying to answer this raises other, more awkward questions. At a workshop on Sint Maarten, Denicio Brison challenged: 'Why are the Dutch still here, please explain?' in his presentation 'The Kingdom's Charter: Fifty years in the wilderness'. Brison had not found a satisfactory answer:

> I have never been able to figure out what exactly keeps Holland
> hanging on. The answer I have been able to distil from several Dutch
> authors is mostly a colonial hangover that they do not know how to
> cure (Brison, 2005: 69–84).

In a previous informal setting in 2003 a former Governor-General of the Netherlands Antilles urged that the Netherlands articulate its practical interest in retaining a presence in the Caribbean; such would help balance the relationship. In reply, a former minister for Kingdom Relations suggested that it was better not to even raise this question in the first place, as it was doubtful that any convincing argument could be found.

After 10.10.10 had been inaugurated, the current Minister for Kingdom Relations publicly raised the issue of the 'Dutch stake' in the Caribbean. He argued that the Netherlands overseas presence can no longer be justified by the shadows of Dutch colonial history. According to his view, the Kingdom will inevitably be forced to renege on its constitutional ties with the Dutch Caribbean countries in the absence of Dutch interests. Instead of looking backwards, some modern-day interests must galvanise the mission of an updated transatlantic Kingdom. Only then will the Dutch come to realise that 'we' (the European Dutch) are losing out when cutting the Caribbean ties. Thus spoke the Minister for Kingdom Relations, half a year after the institutional transformation of 10.10.10.[10]

Various interests should be explored, according to the Minister for Kingdom Relations: the gloss of cultural diversity within the Kingdom, for example, but, more importantly, economic and strategic advantages. Dutch economic interest could be served by trade and cooperation, for instance in the area of sustainable energy. Moreover, Dutch trade with Latin America could make use of the so-called 'hub function' of the Dutch Caribbean. This 'hub function', which also applies to joint ventures between Dutch and Caribbean companies, has been advertised time and again, though with little result. The KLM airline has tried to do business with the *Antilliaanse Luchtvaart Maatschappij* (Antillean Airlines, ALM) and so, too, did PTT-Telecom with telephone companies overseas. Both failed because *autonomistas* in Curaçao and Sint Maarten framed these endeavours in terms of a Dutch intrusion of *Nos Patrimonio Nashonal* (Jong, 2002: 60–7). Some ventures have worked well, and still do, for instance between the port authorities of Curaçao and Rotterdam. But overall, Dutch corporations do not seem thrilled about doing business with or via the Dutch Caribbean. Moreover, a Caribbean 'hub' has been superseded by online connections, while multinationals like Philips and Royal Dutch Shell do not need a 'hub' when doing business overseas.

Strategic Dutch interests, according to the Minister in 2011, might be served by Caribbean public security and the war on drugs in the Caribbean. Instead of tightening the security in the (air) ports of Rotterdam and Amsterdam, the trade in drugs can be better stopped by a Coast Guard of the Kingdom in Caribbean waters, which cooperates with the British, French and US Coast Guard.[11] Another Dutch strategic interest in the region is the new reality that the Netherlands after 10.10.10 has become a Caribbean country, whose approximately 20,000 nationals depend on neighbouring stability and good inter-island connections, especially for health care, energy, drinking water and travel. As a neighbouring country the Netherlands now has a particular interest in the state of public affairs of Sint Maarten (the support link for Saba and Sint Eustatius) and Curaçao (for Bonaire), and in the Caribbean region as a whole as well as neighbouring Venezuela.

10 De eilanden op drift. Television interview with Piet Hein Donner, Amsterdam, De Balie, 20 May 2011.

11 The co-operation is formalised in the Joint Interagency Task Force South, situated in Key West, Florida, US.

This new strategic Netherlands interest is flawed as it makes a fateful difference between Dutch citizens who live on Netherlands territory in the Caribbean (*Caraibisch Nederland*), and Dutch citizens who live on Sint Maarten and Curaçao, separate countries, yet part of the Kingdom of the Netherlands. All along – including the time when the Netherlands Antilles still existed – the Kingdom of the Netherlands had a strategic interest in the Caribbean region. The Netherlands in Europe and the Caribbean countries have not had separate Dutch nationality since 1954. Does the recent change of the Netherlands having become a Caribbean country with 20,000 inhabitants justify a major change in strategic interest?

None of these specific interests, or the total sum of them, looks convincing when assessed against the forceful imagination of a populist Dutch *Absurdistan*. In the Netherlands, the presence of the Kingdom in the Caribbean is facing ridicule and denigration; the Dutch Caribbean has lost political currency – a majority of the Dutch public no longer seems to support a constituency in the Caribbean region. The strength of such opinion does not bend in the face of so-called Dutch interests, and even more so as these interests appear flawed on closer inspection. These make-believe 'interests' are easily swayed by adverse opinions; they will not turn the tide.

What is the Dutch interest then? The Kingdom of the Netherlands is to uphold the paramount significance of Dutch nationality and citizenship in the Caribbean, which is a right that should not crumble under the whims of opinion polls and adverse political agendas in the metropole or the Caribbean countries. Dutch citizenship in the Caribbean stands as a right on its own, which does not need to be rationalised by Dutch interests nor excused because of dark pages in Dutch history (Welie, 2008). The principal feature of the Kingdom of the Netherlands having a presence in the Caribbean is contingent upon the island residents having Dutch citizenship, which cannot be taken away by an obvious lack of Dutch economic or strategic interest. Indeed, the *Nederlanders* in the Caribbean are compatriots, who on occasion have a super sensitive antenna when their right of Dutch nationality is encroached upon. For them, Netherlands citizenship is not a lottery ticket. Thus in the Dutch Caribbean the stakes are high.

What are the stakes?

The Dutch Caribbean shares the pains and pleasures of other non-independent Caribbean entities in balancing the advantages of metropolitan alignment, be it with the Netherlands, France, the UK or the USA, that is, with the missing link of independence.[12] Compared to the islands that surfed the wave of

12   France – St Martin, Guadeloupe, Martinique; UK – Anguilla, British Virgin Islands, Cayman Islands, Montserrat and Turks and Caicos Islands; the USA – Puerto Rico and US Virgin Islands.

independence in the 1960s and 1970s, the non-independent Caribbean islands are much better off. Study after study enumerates the differences. Per capita GDP in the non-independent Caribbean is almost twice the size of per capita GDP in sovereign Caribbean independent states. They have the best of both worlds (Sutton, 2008: 4), and demonstrate a 'happy picture':

> They possess urban economies that are closely tied to the metropolitan government through subsidies or commerce; and have benefited from the extension of developmental upsurge experienced by their respective metropolis during the last forty years. In addition, (these) territories have social and economic indicators that reveal high life expectancy, high income and educational levels, and low levels of disease (Ramos, 2001: xiv–xv).

In addition, freedom of movement in a world that has become increasingly restrictive has become a highly prized asset of being constitutionally allied to the metropole (Hintjens, 1995: 18). USA passports for Puerto Ricans and European passports for the Dutch, French and British Caribbean provide unrestricted access where others do not. Having a Kingdom of the Netherlands passport is for many residents of the Dutch Caribbean the ultimate prize of being a Dutch citizen and, from the point of view of economics, 'a dependent constitutional status is assiduously preserved, partly because of its attractiveness to international investors' (Hintjens, 1997: 540). All in all the preservation of metropolitan ties has proven to be rather beneficial, in the Dutch Caribbean too, so much so that for most people the option of independence is not a realistic one.

Even so, the nomenclature used to describe the status quo of these islands speaks volumes. One of the books on the non-independent Caribbean lists various titles which point at the dark clouds overhanging these islands' destinies: 'Fifty years of assimilation', 'The construction of dependency', 'The recolonisation of Aruba', 'Eternal Empire: Britain's Caribbean colonies in the global arena' (Ramos and Rivera, 2001). Over and again, the question is raised: 'can cultural dignity be preserved in the absence of political sovereignty?' (Miles, 2001: 57). All in all, it is generally believed that the positive assets of metropolitan guardianship have come at a questionable price for the non-independent Caribbean: they have forfeited independent statehood and acquiesced to some degree of autonomy.

Precisely this condition is at the root of the Caribbean territories' unending battle of testing metropolitan rule to its limits up to but not including a demand for independence. Being Dutch in the Caribbean paradoxically entails that several degrees of separation from the Dutch must be maintained (Guadeloupe, 2005, 2006). The *autonomistas* on Curacao call upon the island's historical *Nos Patriminio Nashonal* to invigorate visceral autochthonous drives, especially when dealing with the Dutch. Instead of becoming integrated the *autonomistas* harbour a strong sense of *Nos Patriminio Nashonal,* asserting that they never will be Dutch. Over and over again the relations with the metropole have soured over how much and which areas of government will be left to autonomous Caribbean rule, and to what extent Caribbean island government affairs can be kept free from metropolitan interference. Constitutional status is dealt with as a matter of principle. This is not surprising as such status is historically related to the former colonial plight of a territory and its people. What is even more significant is the equation of independence with individual self-respect, self-determination and human rights. Consequently the peoples and territories that did not choose to become independent had to find meaningful answers for themselves to these fundamental identity issues. One way of dealing with a non-independent status is to underline the territory's free choice or autonomy. Puerto Rico accentuates that its association with the USA is a free association (Duany, 2002); the Netherlands Antilles and Aruba, and now Curaçao and Sint Maarten, claim that they are autonomous countries in the Kingdom of the Netherlands; the *Départements d'Outre-Mer* emphasise that they have chosen to be part of France.

In the case of the Dutch Caribbean, autonomy is engraved in stone, serving as a constant point of contention when dealing with The Hague. Only recently, in early 2011, a battle flared up over metropolitan monitoring of public finances in Sint Maarten. However balanced Paul Sutton's qualification 'the best of both worlds' may be, in day-to-day relationships a different language testifies to disparaging sentiments. For some Dutch citizens in the Caribbean, separation and distinction from metropolitan *Nederland* is a better deal. *Autonomistas* on Curaçao place their hopes in finding offshore oil to become rich and so escape from being forever held by the Dutch.[13] The Olympic Committee of the Netherlands Antilles prided itself on forestalling a worst-case scenario of Antillean men and women having to participate under the Netherlands banner.[14] A former Aruban resident-representative in the Netherlands captioned his election pamphlet, 'More Europe means less Holland', when running in Aruba for a seat in the European Parliament election of 2009 and, moreover, on a metropolitan Dutch Christian-Democrat political party ticket.[15]

Greater or better autonomy is promoted to salvage the non-independent linkage (Sutton, 2008: 16). Yet even under the best of circumstances, the non-independent Caribbean has to balance irreconcilable stakes, which causes bewilderment at best, but often denigration and disrespect, occasionally culminating in pure hatred. Dutch political parties on the far right express loudly and clearly: 'Sell them on eBay, hand them over to Venezuela', intending to get rid of the Kingdom's *Absurdistan*. Some more considerate metropolitan partners may not speak out so blatantly but their behaviour does reflect that

13 Antillean (online) News Bulletin, 6 May 2009.
14 Remco Tevreden, 'NAOC in sportpolitiek vaarwater', in Antilliaanse Nieuwsbrief, p. 11, Jaargang 50, March/April 2009.
15 E-mail Aruba Observer, Eerst registreren, dan pas stemmen, 1 April 2009.

centuries ago these Caribbean islands were labelled *Islas Inutiles*. Instead of the Best of Both Worlds, the non-independent Dutch Caribbean faces a challenge of squaring the circle: having Netherlands citizenship without becoming Dutch burghers (Guadeloupe, 2005) and running their 'autonomous' countries under metropolitan control. Those are the stakes, not only for these Caribbean islands, but also for the metropolitan power – The Hague – that recognises a vested interest in Dutch citizenship in the small-scale world of the Dutch Caribbean.

As long as its citizenry does not steer the Caribbean countries into independence, the Kingdom's mission is to uphold their Dutch citizenship, *à tort et à travers*. This citizenship embraces individual rights and privileges, as well as democratic and good governance standards. According to the Charter, every country is in principle itself responsible for upholding fundamental human rights and freedoms, the rule of law and good governance. The Kingdom's mission is to safeguard this. If not, the Kingdom must act to bring a Caribbean country government back on course, due to the agreement that Caribbean compatriots are included in a vested Netherlands citizenship. That is why Bonaire, Saba and Sint Eustatius are now integrated in the Netherlands. That is why the other islands have chosen to be part of the Kingdom as separate countries. That is why the Kingdom must be on alert and act whenever called upon, now more diligently than before, because of the Kingdom's promise-renewed to Dutch nationals in the Caribbean.

The institutional transformation of 10.10.10 can be qualified as a confirmation of the Kingdom's mandate to safeguard democratic law and order as the indispensable conditions of Dutch citizenship in the Caribbean – of course, only as long as Dutch nationality is appreciated. To that end the Kingdom must act, and apply its authority and powers when democratic governance standards are challenged there. Contrary to what may have been believed, the momentum of 10.10.10 is not a relaxation of the Kingdom's presence but instead the beginning of a hands-on operation in the Dutch Caribbean. Indeed, the Kingdom's mission is to serve Dutch citizenship in the Caribbean countries; 10.10.10 must be conceived as an institutional expression of such an agreed-upon mission. On occasion this will disrupt the Kingdom, sometimes on the mainland, other times in the Caribbean; no doubt about that. On the other hand, it is naïve to expect that the 10.10.10 transformation would produce a tranquil set of relations with so much at stake, so many competing interests, and so many conflicting views on what matters in the Kingdom.

References

C. Borman (2005) *Het Statuut voor het Koninkrijk* (Deventer: Uitgeverij Kluwer BV).

D. Brison (2005) 'The Kingdom's Charter (Het Statuut): fifty years in the wilderness', in L. de Jong and D. Boersema (eds.), *The Kingdom of the Netherlands in the Caribbean: 1954–2004. What Next?*, pp. 35–43 (Amsterdam: Rozenberg).

Council of State (2007) *Jaarverslag (Annual Report) 2006*, The Hague.

— (2010) *Jaarverslag (Annual Report) 2009*, The Hague.

J. Daniel (2002) 'Development policies in the French Caribbean: from state centrality to competitive polycentrism', in A.M. Bissessar (ed.), *Policy Transfers, New Public Management and Globalization. Mexico and the Caribbean*, pp. 97–113 (Lanham: University Press of America).

— (2005) 'Département d'outre mer. Guadeloupe and Martinique', in L. de Jong (ed.), *Extended Statehood in the Caribbean. Paradoxes of Quasi Colonialism, Local Autonomy and Extended Statehood in the USA, French, Dutch and British Caribbean*, pp. 59–123 (Amsterdam: Rozenberg).

J.L Dietz (1986) *Economic History of Puerto Rico: Institutional Change and Capitalist Development* (New Jersey: Princeton University Press).

J. Duany (2002) *The Puerto Rican Nation on the Move: Identities on the Island and in the United States* (Chapel Hill and London: University of North Carolina Press).

F. Guadeloupe (2005) 'Introducing an anti-national pragmatist on Saint Martin & Sint Maarten', in L. de Jong (ed.), *Extended Statehood in the Caribbean. Paradoxes of Quasi Colonialism, Local Autonomy and Extended Statehood in the USA, French, Dutch and British Caribbean*, pp. 157–75 (Amsterdam: Rozenberg).

— (2006) *Chanting Down the New Jerusalem: The Politics of Belonging on Saint Martin & Sint Maarten* (Amsterdam: Rozenberg).

H.M. Hintjens (1995) *Alternatives to Independence: Explorations in Post-Colonial Relations* (Aldershot: Dartmouth).

— (1997) 'Governance options in Europe's Caribbean dependencies: the end of independence', *The Round Table* 344, pp. 533–47.

E.M.H. Hirsch Ballin (2002) 'The constitutional relationship between the Caribbean Overseas Countries and Territories and their mother countries', *Conference Report: The Economic Development of the Caribbean Overseas Countries and Territories: The Role of their European Partners*, The Hague: Ministry for the Interior and Kingdom Relations, June 2001.

— (2005) Introduction, in L. de Jong and D. Boersema (eds.), *The Kingdom of the Netherlands in the Caribbean: 1954–2004. What Next?*, pp. 9–13 (Amsterdam: Rozenberg).

Hoofdlijnenakkoord tussen de Nederlandse Antillen, Nederland, Curaçao, Sint Maarten, Bonaire, Sint Eustatius en Saba, Ministry of the Interior and Kingdom Relations, 22 October. Available at www.rijksoverheid. nl/onderwerpen/caribische-deel-van-het-koninkrijk/documenten-en-publicaties/convenanten/2005/10/22/antillen-hoofdlijnenakkoord.html (accessed 10 Nov. 2011).

H. van Hulst (2003) *Geen snelle recepten. Gezichtspunten en bouwstenen voor een andere aanpak van Antilliaanse jongeren* (Amsterdam: Aksant).

L. de Jong (2002) *De werkvloer van het Koninkrijk: Over de samenwerking van Nederland met de Nederlandse Antillen en Aruba* (Amsterdam: Rozenberg).

— (2005a) 'De ondraaglijke lichtheid van het Koninkrijk', in A.G. Broek (ed.), *Antillen/Aruba uit de gunst*, Christen Democratische Verkenningen (CDV), pp. 76–86 (Amsterdam: Boom Tijdschriften).

— (2005b) 'Comparing notes on extended statehood in the Caribbean', in L. de Jong (ed.), *Extended Statehood in the Caribbean. Paradoxes of Quasi Colonialism, Local Autonomy and Extended Statehood in the USA, French, Dutch and British Caribbean*, pp. 177–203 (Amsterdam: Rozenberg).

– (2009) 'The implosion of the Netherlands Antilles', in P. Clegg and E. Pantojas-Garcia (eds.), *Governance in the Non-Independent Caribbean, Challenges and Opportunities in the Twenty-First Century*, pp. 24–44 (Kingston and Miami: Ian Randle).

— (2010) *Being Dutch, More or Less. In a Comparative Perspective of USA and Caribbean Practices* (Amsterdam: Rozenberg).

I. Klinkers (1999) *De weg naar het Statuut: Het Nederlandse dekolonisatiebeleid in de Caraïben (1940–1945) in vergelijkend perspectief* (Utrecht: University of Utrecht).

J. McElroy and K. de Albuquerque (1995) 'The social and economic propensity for political dependence in the insular Caribbean', *Social and Economic Studies* 44 (2 & 3), pp. 167–93.

W.S. Miles (2001) 'Fifty years of "assimilation": assessing France's experience of Caribbean decolonisation through administrative reform', in A.G. Ramos & A. Rivera (eds.), *Islands at the Crossroads. Politics in the Non-Independent Caribbean*, pp. 45–60 (Kingston: Ian Randle/Boulder: Lynne Rienner).

G. Oostindie (1997) *Het paradijs overzee: De 'Nederlandse' Caraïben in Nederland* (Amsterdam: Bert Bakker).

— (2009) 'Migration paradoxes of non-sovereignty. A comparative perspective on the Dutch Caribbean', in P. Clegg and E. Pantojas-Garcia (eds.), *Governance in the Non-Independent Caribbean. Challenges and Opportunities in the Twenty-First Century*, pp. 163–81 (Kingston and Miami: Ian Randle).

A.G. Ramos and A. Rivera (eds.) (2001) *Islands at the Crossroads. Politics in the Non-Independent Caribbean* (Kingston: Ian Randle/Boulder: Lynne Rienner).

A.G. Ramos (2001) 'Caribbean territories at the crossroads', in A.G. Ramos and A. Rivera (eds.), *Islands at the Crossroads. Politics in the Non-Independent Caribbean*, pp. xii–xxi (Kingston: Ian Randle/Boulder: Lynne Rienner).

A. Rivera (2001) 'Conclusion: rethinking politics in the non-independent territories, in A.G. Ramos and A. Rivera (eds.), *Islands at the Crossroads. Politics in the Non-Independent Caribbean*, pp. 160–79 (Kingston: Ian Randle/Boulder: Lynne Rienner).

A. Rodriguez Jr (2000) 'On being Puerto Rican: report from the Eastern Front', *CENTRO Journal* XI (2), 95–100.

P. Sutton (2008) '"The best of both worlds": autonomy and decolonisation in the Caribbean', London Metropolitan University, Caribbean Studies Working Paper No. 2, Aug.

United Nations (2007) 'Drug trafficking and the Netherlands Antilles', in *Crime, Violence, and Development: Trends, Costs, and Policy Options in the Caribbean*, chapter 7. Joint report by the United Nations Office on Drugs and Crime and the Latin American and Caribbean Region of the World Bank.

R. van Welie (2008) 'Slave trading and slavery in the Dutch Colonial Empire: a global comparison', *New West Indian Guide* 82 (1 & 2), pp. 47–96.

WODC (2007) *Georganiseerde Criminaliteit en Rechtshandhaving op St. Maarten*, Wetenschappelijk Onderzoek en Documentatie Centrum, The Hague.

World Bank (2001) *Netherlands Antilles: Elements of a Strategy for Economic Recovery and Sustainable Growth*, interim report, World Bank Mission, Latin America and the Caribbean Region, Dec.

Chapter 6

The French Overseas Territories in transition

Nathalie Mrgudovic

Introduction

France declared 2011 '*Année des outre-mer*' (the Year of the Overseas) in recognition that each of the French Overseas Territories (or FOTs) had reached a milestone in its relations with France. Having passed from colonies (or protectorates) to French Overseas Territories or Overseas *Départements* in 1946, they have evolved progressively at different speeds and degrees. If the initial changes suggested by the United Nations (UN) were mostly justified on political and ideological grounds (the right to independence, self-determination and sovereignty), the current changes, this time encouraged by France, in the main appear to be an attempt to alleviate economic dependency.

At the 2004 conference on the United Kingdom Overseas Territories (UKOTs), organised by and held at the Institute of Commonwealth Studies in London, I presented an analysis of the FOTs and the evolution of their statuses since the origins of this 'Overseas France'.[1] I will therefore give only a brief overview here of these territories and the main characteristics of their statuses in order to focus on the constitutional and institutional developments that took place, mostly in 2003 and 2008. I will also consider the statutory amendments adopted in July 2011 by the French Parliament to address the political instability that had recently emerged in two of the French territories in the South Pacific. Finally, in the light of these recent developments in the FOTs, I will question their institutional evolution. However, given the complexity of this subject, this chapter will simply sketch out the main points worthy of deeper reflection.

Immediately after the Second World War, and in a context of decolonisation promoted by the UN, the four oldest French colonies

---

1   See Mrgudovic, in Killingray and Taylor (2005), pp. 65–86.

of Martinique, Guadeloupe, Guyane and la Réunion became, in 1946,[2] four *Départements d'Outre-Mer* (DOMs or Overseas Departments). Their status was characterised by a legislative regime identical (with some minor adaptations taking into account their remoteness and tropical island status or territory) to the one applied to the *départements* in mainland France. They were organised around a local council (*Conseil Général*) and municipalities, and a *Préfet* representing the State. The DOMs were all represented in the French Parliament by locally elected *députés* and *sénateurs*. However, this DOM status contained an intrinsic flaw, only addressed quite recently, in that identical status had been bestowed on the four overseas entities with no real attempt to adapt it to their own specificities and needs. Guyane, in particular, located between Brazil and Suriname and both covered and surrounded by rain forest, was the DOM that suffered most from this uniform status.[3]

A few months after the law on integration (*loi de départementalisation*) was passed, the Constitution of 1946, implementing the Fourth Republic, was adopted. In the rest of the French Empire, with some exceptions, the colonies were transformed into French *Territoires d'Outre-mer* (TOMs or Overseas Territories). However after 12 years of constant governmental instability, the Fourth Republic collapsed. A referendum was organised in September 1958 to adopt the new French Constitution that was to establish the Fifth Republic. The inhabitants of the TOMs (therefore excluding the four DOMs) could choose either to remain within the Republic or to become independent. Only Guinea chose independence. All the other TOMs adopted the first solution and had then to opt for one of the three following options: they could choose either legislative integration and thus become a DOM, or they could decide to become a State in free association with France, a solution adopted by all the African TOMs. This was a non-official but understood transitional and peaceful evolution towards independence. Or they could remain a TOM, characterised by their legislative specificity – the French Parliament had to stipulate if a law was (and still is) applicable to one, some, or all TOMs. Besides this legislative distinction, there were two other major differences between a DOM and a TOM. First, each TOM was given a tailor-made status that would take into account its characteristics and needs and allow some degree of autonomy,[4] reflected in the nature of its institutions and local powers. Second, the TOMs

---

2   Law no. 46–451 19 March 1946.

3   Deforestation, illegal immigration, illegal exploitation of gold, are three examples of what Guyane, and especially its indigenous populations, continue to endure partly as a result of being given a status not specifically designed to allow Guyane to better address these issues.

4   Although this degree of autonomy was seriously reduced in 1958 compared to what the 1956 Defferre Law had offered. See Mrgudovic (2005).

were given the right of 'free-determination' as enshrined in the Preamble to the Constitution of 1958.[5]

By 1962, and after the wave of independence in Africa, 11 French overseas territories remained;[6] four DOMs (Martinique, Guadeloupe, Guyane and Réunion) and seven TOMs: New-Caledonia, French Polynesia, Wallis and Futuna in the South Pacific, the Comoros Islands, French Somaliland,[7] the TAAF (*Terres australes et antarctiques françaises*/Austral and Antarctic French Lands) in the Indian and Antarctic Oceans, and St Pierre et Miquelon in the North Atlantic.[8] Finally, the common and important result was that these overseas populations had all become French citizens, with the same legal status as any other French citizen (i.e. from metropolitan France)[9] and in due course as any other European citizen.[10]

Besides these two categories of overseas collectivities, recognised in the 1958 Constitution, new statuses have developed since the 1970s. The Comoros Islands, as any TOM was entitled to, used its right to self-determination, held a referendum and gained its independence in 1975. However, of the four islands of the archipelago, Mayotte decided to remain French, and from then on it would never cease proclaiming its wish to become a DOM. In 1976 this island became a *Collectivité Territoriale d'Outre-mer* (CTOM), a status mid-way between a DOM and a TOM, and so, in 1985, did St Pierre et Miquelon solely for economic reasons.[11] New Caledonia and French Polynesia have also

---

5   As yet another sign of France's desire to distinguish itself from the rest of the world, the constitution's preamble spoke of 'libre-détermination' (free-determination), as if it defiantly wanted to avoid using the official expression of 'auto-détermination' ('self-determination') used by the international community.

6   The year 1962 is selected, instead of 1958, because Wallis and Futuna had exceptionally remained a Protectorate until 1961 and, in 1962, was the last French possession to become a TOM. For an analysis of this delay, see Allison (2010).

7   Côte des Somalis, renamed the French Territory of the Afars and the Issas in 1967 before its independence in 1977 when the name was changed to the Republic of Djibouti.

8   St Pierre et Miquelon, whose economy relied heavily on fisheries, saw its status changed over the years mainly because of the European fisheries policy. It became a DOM in 1976 and then, in 1985, a French Overseas Territorial Collectivité or CTOM, a hybrid status that allowed the FOT to keep all the benefits of integration while being exempt from the European fisheries regulations.

9   With regard to some social benefits, the populations from the FOTs and the DOMs, in particular, have not benefited automatically from the same level of benefits as their compatriots living in the metropole.

10 As implemented by the Maastricht Treaty in 1992 and the Amsterdam Treaty of 1997.

11 Mayotte has been requesting its 'départementalisation' since 1975 in order to secure its future within the French Republic for economic reasons, but also to be protected from the new Republic of Comoros that never accepted its secession. In the case

experimented with an evolution in their respective statuses as TOMs, gaining more and more autonomy from the late 1980s. However, this occurred in two totally different contexts: one through violence – in New Caledonia a near civil war erupted in the mid 1980s between pro- and anti-independence groups; the other, mostly due to political lobbying – the role and ambition of Gaston Flosse, who became the 'President of French Polynesia', was crucial in this. Because of these two different contexts, the statuses have led to two different perspectives: New Caledonia is now heading toward a referendum on self-determination whereas French Polynesia is not.[12]

Concerning the DOMs, two important constitutional reforms were introduced in 2003 and 2008 that addressed the evolution of the 'collectivités territoriales' (or 'territorial collectivity'), both overseas and in mainland France. A territorial collectivity, an elected local council, benefits from a certain degree of power in administering the collectivity in question. Initially, the 1958 French Constitution listed as territorial collectivities the communes (municipalities), départements (counties) and territoires d'outre-mer (overseas territories). In the first constitutional reform on decentralisation in 1982, the regions were then added to this list and granted specific powers.[13] In 2003, the second phase of the reform on decentralisation impacted on both the TOMs and DOMs. The former were to be replaced by two categories: the collectivities with a specific status (collectivités à statut particulier, although New Caledonia was already designated as such since 1999) and the Overseas Collectivities ('Collectivités d'Outre-Mer' or COMs) covered by a reformulated Article 74 of the Constitution. The DOMs, covered by the revised Article 73, were encouraged to implement a simplification in their administration.

Although the reform of 2008 seemed more focused on the DOMs, the reforms or acts of 2003 and 2008 concerned all the FOTs (except New Caledonia which had a special status) and revolved around the key notions of self-determination and autonomy. The status of the now 12 FOTs[14] has therefore evolved since 1958, as has the constitution. The principal object of this chapter will be to demonstrate that the recent constitutional or institutional developments in the FOTs highlight the fact that the relationship France has

---

of St Pierre et Miquelon – TOM, then DOM – France changed its status again in order to avoid the strict fisheries policy developed by the European Community that applied to the DOMs (and all Outermost Regions).

12 Although New Caledonia's situation and status is of course more complicated. See Mrgudovic (2003) and (2005).

13 A Département is in charge mainly of the social welfare issues, whereas the Région is more focused on economic and cultural development.

14 The Comoros is no longer a FOT, whereas St Martin and St Barthélemy became two new ones when they decided not to be administered any longer by Guadeloupe and became COMs.

developed with its overseas territories since 1946 might well have reached a new level.

2000–3: decentralisation, phase 2

Besides reformulating Articles 73 and 74 of the constitution (concerning the FOTs), the second phase of decentralisation implemented in 2003 introduced a new element: the possibility for the FOTs to organise a local referendum that would lead to a change in their status. This is particularly interesting for the DOMs as they could consider a status of autonomy. However, in 2000, as a precursor to the second phase of decentralisation, such a possibility had already been open to the DOMs.

Self-determination in 2000: too early for the DOMs?

In 1997, Article 227-2 of the Treaty establishing the European Community had been amended in accordance with the Amsterdam Treaty of June 1997. In France, the award decree (*décret d'attribution* no. 97-721 of 16/06/1997) had then redefined the objectives of the Ministry for Overseas Territories as split between a mission of sovereignty development, on the one hand, and a mission of economic and social development, on the other. This is what inspired the *Loi d'Orientation pour l'Outre-mer* (LOOM) (Overseas Act) of 2000 (Faberon and Ziller, 2007: 59; Belorgey, 2002: 87–8; Mrgudovic, 2005). This Act had two objectives: to increase decentralisation, and to open up new perspectives of institutional evolution for the DOMs.

The second objective led to the creation, in each DOM,[15] of an ad hoc consultative body, a *Congrès*, composed of all regional and departmental councillors that would meet to discuss the institutional evolution of the territory. They could adopt a proposal to be submitted to the Prime Minister who would then decide whether or not to submit it to Parliament. This institution would then pass a law (or not) to authorise a local referendum on the proposed new status, which could include independence.[16] Whatever the result of this consultation, it is the Constitutional Council that would have (and still has) the last word on whether to adopt any proposed new status.

This LOOM was the first encouragement made to all DOMs to consider a change in their old and somewhat inappropriate status. In initiating the LOOM, the then Prime Minister, Socialist Lionel Jospin, in a time of cohabitation under Conservative President Chirac, had given the DOMs, for the first time since their creation, the possibility to consider some evolution in their status including independence (see below). However, this attempt drew a blank due to a combination of two factors: first, the slowness of local councillors to agree

15 Réunion, however, would always refuse to consider any change to its status.
16 Although this option is not very popular in the DOMs (Gay, 2003).

upon a common proposal; and second, the objection of the populations of the DOMs to any change in their status which was perceived as a threat to the level of subventions received from the French State. Therefore, although in Martinique, for example, a pro-independence leader Alfred Marie-Jeanne has regularly been re-elected mayor, deputy and President of the Regional Council,[17] independence was never the way forward for a large majority of Martinicans, for whom Marie-Jeanne's personality and integrity were the main reasons for his popularity (see Yang-Ting, 2000).

However, could the LOOM really have led to independence? Jurists such as Jean-Yves Faberon and Jacques Ziller did not consider independence as a possibility and, although they described the LOOM as a new perspective on the evolution of the DOMs' institutions, they limited this evolution to Article 73 (Faberon and Ziller, 2007: 60), i.e. with the exception of independence. I disagree, as Article 62 of the LOOM is very imprecise when it evokes 'any proposal of institutional evolution' without setting a limit (LOOM, 2000, Art. 62). To me, this 'loose' formulation was intentional, as Prime Minister Jospin did not want to exclude the possibility of the DOMs considering independence (Mrgudovic, 2005). However, within such a perspective, there were two major obstacles to overcome: first, this proposal had to be supported by the Prime Minister, then by the Parliament, and finally endorsed by the Constitutional Council; and second and most importantly, the DOMs' representatives did not react quickly enough to submit any kind of proposal before the forthcoming presidential elections, which, in a way, demonstrated their lack of enthusiasm for a change in status. However, later, in 2003, the victory of the conservatives at the 2002 presidential election led to some modifications to the LOOM and in particular clarified the possible options open to the DOMs.

2003: decentralisation or recentralisation?

When the first reform on decentralisation was introduced in 1982, and with it the creation of the region as a new territorial collectivity, a problem emerged with regard to the DOMs. A region was supposed to geographically encompass a few *départements*. However, in the case of the DOMs, geography was one major problem in this division of duties and powers as the new overseas regions (ROMs or *Régions d'Outre-Mer*) were to gather under their umbrella only one department each. The Regional Council and the Departmental Council were therefore to share the same electorate and the same geography. The proposal to create for each of these four DOMs a single collectivity that would incorporate the responsibilities of the department and the region was

---

17 Alfred Marie-Jeanne was the President of the Regional Council between 1998 and 2010 and has been Député at the French National Assembly since 1997. He was also the Mayor of Rivière-Pilote between 1971 and 2000.

rejected by the Constitutional Council for it was perceived as a violation of the principle of equality (with the metropolitan collectivities). This is why the four DOMs also had to become four ROMs (that in turn constituted four DROMs: *Départements et Régions d'Outre-Mer*). This new quite peculiar double status was in a way even more in contradiction with what existed in mainland France. This did not appear, however, to be the view of the Constitutional Council.

In 2003, the introduction of a second phase of the decentralisation policy established in 1982 led to changes to the French Constitution, particularly with regard to the Overseas Collectivities. This new Constitutional Reform on Decentralisation (to be applied at national level) aimed to create a better, more coherent, and more responsible administrative and political management of the regions, *départements* and municipalities. It was aimed at reorganising the FOTs into two new administrative categories. For this purpose, two 'new' Articles and a new Chapter were introduced into the constitution, dedicated to the 'Overseas Collectivities' (COMs) ruled by the new Article 74 (with a regime of autonomy and legislative specificity); the collectivities ruled by Article 73 (corresponding to the legislative identity of the DOMs-ROMs); and the collectivities with a special status (New Caledonia and Corsica). New Caledonia also benefited from a chapter in the constitution (chapter XII) entirely dedicated to its current status and its progressive evolution towards self-determination.

This reform also introduced the possibility of administrative 'experimentation' in two respects. First, the reform opened the possibility to all FOTs to swap status and adopt legislative identity (Article 73) or legislative specificity and autonomy (Article 74), although this second option differed from the previous TOM status as it did not give the right to hold a referendum on independence. This right had been solely maintained for the 'old' TOMs, French Polynesia, and Wallis and Futuna. It should be noted that New Caledonia had not been a TOM since 1999, its current status having been created to provide for and guarantee the best conditions to organise a referendum on self-determination (with the possibility of independence) between 2014 and 2018. Second, within Article 73, although the legislative identity that characterised the DROMs had been maintained, it was now possible to create a new *Collectivité* (with a new Council) to replace the department and the region (although this option was rejected by the Constitutional Council in 1982). Article 73 could also be used to create a single council while retaining the two collectivities (DOM and ROM).

Following this constitutional reform, councillors of Martinique and Guadeloupe submitted proposals and a referendum was organised in both DOMs, on 7 December 2003, to consider a single territorial collectivity. In both cases, the populations agreed with their councillors' enthusiasm and rejected that possibility (in Martinique with 51 per cent and in Guadeloupe with 73 per cent). In Guyane the lack of consensus between the elected representatives did not permit the organisation of such a referendum. Finally, in order to take into account the strong opposition of Réunion to any change to its status, a 'third' option had then to be considered for the DROMs, the status quo.

Although Martinicans and Guadeloupeans refused any change to their status (as did, in a way, Guyane and la Réunion), the two islands administered by Guadeloupe, St Martin and St Barthélemy, also had the opportunity to organise a referendum in December 2003, this being on whether to become a COM (*Collectivité d'Outre-Mer*). Being ruled by Article 74 meant 'emancipation' from Guadeloupe, to administer themselves and improve their economic development in an autonomous way. While St Martin wanted, among other things, to be able to tackle the problem of immigration from its Dutch neighbour Sint Maarten, St Barthélemy wanted to be able to manage, develop and benefit more directly from its lucrative tourist activities.[18] The results in both islands were overwhelmingly in favour of the new status (76 per cent in St Martin and 96 per cent in St Barthélemy). The two organic Laws of 21 February 2007 recognised this change and established the new statuses, allowing the two new COMs to develop, for example, their own taxation policy in accordance with French Law.

This reform has therefore empowered the DOMs, in particular, with the opportunity to be less dependent on the central authorities and entitled them to test their own capacities to initiate new means of political and economic development. If St Martin and St Barthélemy have been keen to embrace this opportunity, the ambiguous attitude of the four DOMs towards this option is far less understandable and might explain why the French government keeps trying to incite them in that direction.

The 2008 Reform: towards more autonomy?

The 2008 project of territorial reform introduced by President Nicolas Sarkozy, and adopted on 16 December 2010, concerns all territorial collectivities (regions, departments, municipalities), and aims at 'simplifying' the administration of the various types of collectivities, in mainland and overseas France. It considers the evolution of the DOMs, in particular, wishing to prevent dysfunctions such as damaging political rivalry between the regions and departments and their elected councils. President Sarkozy wanted the territorial collectivities and the DOMs, in particular, to gain more political and economic responsibility in order to promote good governance and also to generate more of their own incomes. As Sarkozy stated: 'There is a strong aspiration for improvement that translates into the current claim for an endogenous economic model capable of generating incomes and local employment' (Sarkozy, 2009).[19]

18 St Barthélemy is renowned for 'jet set' tourism.
19 'Il y a une aspiration puissante à un mieux être que traduit aujourd'hui la revendication d'un modèle économique endogène susceptible de favoriser la création de richesses et d'emplois locaux.'

The socio-economic crisis in the DOMs

This 'strong aspiration' refers directly to the social crisis that erupted at the end of 2008 in Guadeloupe and spread to the rest of the DOMs over the ensuing few months[20] in the context of a global economic crisis that had translated into yet another increase in the price of petrol (already higher in the FOTs due to the distribution monopolies that prevail there). It then developed into a protest movement against 'la vie chère' (the high cost of living) with the 'Alliance Against Profiteering' (in creole: Lyannaj Kont Pwofitasyon or LKP) becoming the driving force of the protest.[21] The denunciation of the 'colonial' (in the sense of exploitative) economic system and price-making policy in Guadeloupe, and in the rest of the DOMs, led to massive strikes that lasted much longer than expected – 44 days in Guadeloupe, 38 days in Martinique, 15 days in Guyane and eight days in Réunion. The LKP accused the richest families, usually descendants of colonial families, of holding and maintaining monopolies, with the silent support of the Republic, in the key economic sectors such as the import-export and the supermarket sectors in particular.[22] The notions of 'pigmentocratie' and 'ethnoclasses', often used by some prominent figures in local politics or literature to describe the situation in the French Antilles,[23] underlay the LKP's discourse.

After vigorous negotiations, the response of the government was first to agree upon a salary increment of €200 for those on low salaries in the public and private sectors, and also to organise the 'États Généraux de l'Outre-Mer': a general discussion, via the internet and local meetings, on Overseas Territories involving the populations and elected authorities of the FOTs and the rest of France. This was followed by the organisation of an Inter-Ministerial Committee on the Overseas Territories, a general meeting with President Sarkozy, the Ministers directly involved with the FOTs and local representatives and actors, to identify the sectors or issues, shared or specific to each FOT that needed reform or renewed support. The crisis, and the following États Généraux and Inter-ministerial Committee, reinforced the determination of the government to 'encourage' the FOTs to adopt a more coherent and responsible attitude towards their political, social and economic situation.

The 2008 reform, first promoted in the DOMs, represents what President Sarkozy also wishes to achieve in mainland France. Therefore, as with

---

20 On this crisis see my chapter, 'Guadeloupe 2009: Issues politiques à une crise sociale?' in Reno (2011).

21 This movement brought together nearly 40 unions, political parties and movements.

22 In Martinique for instance the 'Béké' (white colonial rich) families own 52 per cent of the land and control 40 per cent of the economy, while representing only one per cent of the population.

23 The writer Raphaël Confiant and the President (socialist) of the Regional Council of Guadeloupe, Victorin Lurel

Decentralisation in 1982, the DOMs could again appear as a sort of institutional laboratory for the Republic. This territorial reform must be implemented by the collectivities by 2014. This could explain the significant encouragement, presented as a response to the 2009 crisis, from the President (and the Ministry for Overseas Territories) to the DOMs to adopt, by January 2010, the status of Article 74, or at least prepare the implementation of article 73 according to the 2003 (and 2008) reforms on collectivities. While Martinique and Guyane decided upon a new single collectivity (and a single territorial council), Guadeloupe's elected councillors are still debating the characteristics of a single 'Assembly' and have submitted a Bill proposal to the National Assembly. In December 2010 the Parliament decided that, when the reform is implemented in 2014, Guadeloupe should have 45 councillors in one territorial Assembly. However, the current councillors are questioning the competences of this 'Territorial Assembly' and its legality (as it should not be allowed to deliberate without the approval of the Guadeloupeans by referendum). The Bill also asks for an increase in the number of councillors to 65.[24]

Towards more responsibility

The main objectives of this reform are greater economic self-reliance and better governance (with greater political involvement of the populations). One indicator is the balance of trade, where imports largely outweigh exports, except in the case of New Caledonia (Thiou, 2010), and therefore there is a high level of dependency on funds from Paris (which reached €12.7 billion in 2009) (Performance Publique, 2010). The government considers that improved economic self-reliance could be achieved in part through the politics of regional integration of the FOTs. Promoted by France over the last decade, first in its South Pacific Territories, the government is now encouraging the rest of the FOTs to more economic insertion and regional cooperation, hence reinforcing their capabilities of endogenous economic development (and reducing their dependence on public funding). The *États Généraux de l'Outre-Mer* and the *Comité Interministériel de l'Outre-mer* represent important initiatives to encourage the DOMs in that direction.

One could therefore summarise the reform of 2008, and the subsequent governmental initiatives, as an official attempt to put an end to the vicious cycle of dependency that can take two forms: a dependency cultivated by France and for France and the local elites to preserve economic control; and a dependency claimed by the overseas populations (as they do not want

---

24 Bill proposal no. 3585 to adapt the reform on collectivity to Guadeloupe's characterictics and constraints. Submitted by Victorin Lurel to the National Assembly on 22 June 2011, www.assemblee-nationale.fr/13/propositions/pion3585.asp (accessed 18 Jan. 2012)

to give up a standard of living that has been kept artificially high). This dependency, in both forms, could explain the reluctance of the DOMs to move towards emancipation. This could also be illustrated by the fact that, with the new Article 73, the DOMs have been granted more freedom to adapt laws and regulations passed by the French Parliament, but in reality they have so far made very little use of this new power (Cointat and Frimat, 2011b).

What framework for the evolution of the FOTs?

As for a possible simplification of statuses implied by the constitutional reforms of 2003 and 2008, this did not take place. Today there are as many statuses as there are FOTs: Réunion (DROM, Art.73);[25] Mayotte (in evolution towards full integration, Art.73); Martinique; Guyane (Art. 73, soon to become two single collectivities,[26] each of them managed by a single council); Guadeloupe (Art. 73, has opted to retain its two collectivities with one single council); St Pierre & Miquelon (Art. 74 with some adaptations); St Barthélemy and St Martin (two COMs Art. 74, new regime); French Polynesia and Wallis & Futuna (Art. 74 'old regime' as they retain the possibility to ask for a referendum on self-determination that could include independence); the TAAF (still considered a TOM); and last New Caledonia (Special Collectivity).

Already in 2000, at the time of the first attempt to allow the DOMs to adapt or change their status, President Jacques Chirac had acknowledged that 'uniform statuses are over and each overseas collectivity should evolve, if it so wishes, toward a somehow tailored status'.[27] Nicolas Sarkozy, following on from Chirac's declaration of 2000, confirmed this in his speech of November 2009 where he stated that '[t]he unity of the Republic does not imply a uniformity of its institutions'.[28] He repeated it in his speech of January 2010 in Réunion: 'I see nothing shocking in considering that each of the overseas territories would endorse an organisation adapted to its own characteristics as long as this does

---

25 Réunion will remain a DROM Art.73, until the deadline of 2014 for the implementation of the 2008 general reform on collectivities (although the next President, if Sarkozy is not re-elected in 2012, could decide otherwise).

26 There is still no agreement on the date of this implementation. The year agreed upon for the rest of the collectivities is 2014, but 2012 is the government's preferred date (i.e. before the presidential elections, which would complete the 2008 reform programme).

27 Jacques Chirac, (Martinique, 11 March 2000): 'Les statuts uniformes ont vécu et chaque collectivité d'outre-mer doit pouvoir désormais, si elle le souhaite, évoluer vers un statut différencié, en quelque sorte un statut sur mesure'.

28 'L'unité de la République n'est pas l'uniformité de ses institutions.'

not affect the principle of unity of the Republic.'[29] Therefore, whatever the option chosen, a FOT under Article 73 or 74 could not evolve outside the Republic. In his speech in Réunion in January 2010, Sarkozy recalled to that effect, '[w]e have equipped ourselves with a Constitution that allows for great flexibility that I intend to use (...) with one red line (...) independence. The overseas territories are French and will remain French.'[30] So is it correct to say that the FOTs are prisoners of the Republic? The populations and their representatives have, since 2000, demonstrated that independence is not the issue. Therefore such a declaration (by President Sarkozy) could appear needlessly conservative. Self-determination should be left accessible to all FOTs and not only to the old TOMs.

This right to self-determination, and the very large degree of autonomy enjoyed by the three French territories of the Pacific, does not however exclude a possible intervention of the state if it becomes necessary, as the situations in French Polynesia and New Caledonia recently illustrated. Indeed, French Polynesia's 'wide autonomy' (as described in its status) has not helped to prevent a high level of political instability in the territory. Since its last status conferred in 2004 that granted Tahiti even more autonomy than the status it was given in 1996 (in external relations and in legislative power for example), the territory has experienced no fewer than 12 governments. This has been caused by governments with small majorities and a fractious, opportunistic and self-serving Parliament (Al Wardi, 2008). This is why Sarkozy in his New Year speech in January 2011 declared to the French Polynesian politicians that, although the intention was to give them a maximum of responsibilities, the state would not hesitate to intervene if the political situation got out of control and the local institutions failed to perform as they should. In response, in July 2011, the Parliament amended the 2004 status of French Polynesia in order to regulate the use of the motion of no-confidence and therefore guarantee a more stable political, and consequently economic and social, situation in the archipelago (Quentin, 2011).

The necessary intervention of the State in the domestic policy of French Polynesia has highlighted the fragility of this 'wide autonomy'. However this should not deter the rest of the FOTs from considering this option as the way forward even though the large choice of possible statuses is guaranteed by the constitution.

29 'Je ne vois pas ce qu'il y a de choquant à considérer que chaque territoire ultramarin puisse se doter d'une organisation adaptée à ses caractéristiques propres, à condition que cela ne remette pas en cause le principe d'unité de la République'. Sarkozy repeated this in a speech in Guadeloupe in January 2011.
30 'Nous nous sommes dotés d'une Constitution qui nous permet beaucoup de souplesse. Je compte en faire usage (...) avec une seule ligne rouge (...) l'indépendance. L'outre-mer est français et restera français'.

New Caledonia and Mayotte: an evolving institutional spectrum for the FOTs

With its amendments of 1998 and 2008, the French Constitution now presents a large panel of possible options to accommodate the particular situation of each FOT within the Republic. The examples of New Caledonia and Mayotte present the two opposite situations characteristic of the new face of this 'Overseas France'. One wants (or has agreed) to consider independence while the other has never stopped claiming more integration.

New Caledonia: on a rocky path to self-determination?

The *Accords de Matignon-Oudinot*, signed in 1988 to defuse the threat of civil war between the pro-independence Kanak[31] and the loyalist Caldoches, organised a ten-year period of political, social, cultural and economic compensation (*rééquilibrage*) in favour of the Kanak, and was to end with a referendum on self-determination. However in 1998, both actors, with the agreement of the State, agreed in the Nouméa Accord that, in order to securely construct a 'shared future' (*un avenir commun*), a further period of 15 to 20 years was needed. This new agreement was established to further experiment with and then consolidate the elements of a 'shared sovereignty'[32] with a progressive and definitive handing over of most political, administrative and legislative powers from the State to the territory's authorities. However, the State would retain its five '*pouvoirs régaliens*' or 'sovereign powers' (defence, foreign policy, currency, justice and public order) until the next referendum. As set out in the Nouméa Agreement, the Parliament of New Caledonia (the *Congrès*) must, before 2014, set a date for the referendum on self-determination some time between 2014 and 2018. The citizens of New Caledonia[33] will then decide whether to maintain – and the form this will take – their relations with France. They will have to decide on the transfer of the five '*pouvoirs régaliens*' to New Caledonia, which in turn will impact on the organisation of citizenship, nationality and international status.[34]

---

31 The Melanesian Kanak population represent about 40 per cent of the total population (250,000) of New Caledonia, while the Caldoches (the European descendants of the colons and convicts established in New Caledonia since the 1850s), together with most of the rest of the population, today represent the majority and are generally opposed to independence.

32 Preamble, Nouméa Accord, 1998.

33 Those who voted in the referendum in 1988, and those who reach 18 in the meantime, will be entitled to take part in this referendum on self-determination. This is another demonstration of the will of the French state as well as of the major actors in New Caledonia to allow the Kanak population, or more exactly the pro-independence Caledonians, to express their will in the most favourable conditions.

34 Article 5, Nouméa Accord 1998.

Since 1998, the population and authorities of New Caledonia have been encouraged to develop their own attributes of sovereignty (motto, anthem, bank notes and flag) (Nouméa Accord, 1998). In April 2008, a motto was officially announced: 'Land of word, land of sharing' ('*Terre de parole, terre de partage*'), as well as an anthem 'Let us be united, let us become brothers' ('*Soyons unis, devenons frères*').[35] Later that year, the national *Conseil d'État* recognised the validity of these two markers of identity (*signes identitaires*) and, in August 2010, the *Congrès* of New Caledonia voted to endorse the motto, the anthem and the proposals regarding the design of the bank notes. However, in 2011, New Caledonia was shaken from within its own government when the then President Philippe Gomes opposed flying the pro-independence flag of the independentist group FLNKS (Socialist and Kanak Front of National Liberation) alongside the national flag, claiming this was in opposition to the spirit of the Nouméa Accords and a threat to the political stability established by the Matignon and Nouméa Accords (Cointat and Frimat), 2011b: 11–12). The display of the two flags had, however, become commonplace since 1988 (even in non-independentist towns with the exception of La Foa, Moindou and Bourail), and this had also become common practice in French Polynesia since 1984 without causing any significant opposition. This controversy resulted in the resignations of two political groups (first the pro-independence *Union Calédonienne*, then Gomes' loyalist *Calédonie Ensemble*) from the coalition government. But it was the three successive resignations from government of the President's own group that clearly appeared to be a deliberate act intended to provoke an early general election by overthrowing the *Congrès* (the institution that constitutes the heart of Caledonian politics). This was the first time this political tool (the collective demission of a group within the government), established in the Organic Law that implemented the Nouméa Accord, was deliberately used to block Caledonian institutions and threatened to jeopardise the so-far rather peaceful process towards self-determination. Exceptionally, the *Congrès* then decided to ask the State (and Parliament) to amend the article in the organic law that concerned the collective demission of part of the government, in order to prevent an abuse of this instrument in the future and therefore guarantee the return of a peaceful and stable political transition towards the referendum on self-determination.[36]

It is surprising that such an event took place at the initiative of the President and his political group when, as was well known at the time, pro-France voters constituted the majority of the electorate in New Caledonia. This can be explained by the growing division amongst loyalist groups and some of their leaders who, in a more peaceful context (in front of pro-independence

---

35 Several proposals were considered for the bank notes.
36 A delay of 18 months between two possible collective resignations has now been introduced to the Organic Law of 1999.

representatives entirely focused on the quest for the best option for a sovereign New Caledonia), have let personal ambitions prevail over the general interest. Since Gomes' eviction from power previous President Harold Martin (loyalist) has been re-installed in his position as President of the government. More open and more respected across the whole political spectrum, his return might be a guarantee of stability although, as the pressure increases with the referendum deadline approaching, violence could erupt again.

Mayotte: a 'DOM' at last!

After more than 30 years, the small island of Mayotte, in the Indian Ocean, finally managed to obtain what it had been claiming since its secession from the Comoros islands in 1975. Mayotte, initially autonomous (when it was part of the TOM of French Comoros) became an 'Overseas Territorial Collectivity' in 1976 and an 'Overseas Departmental Collectivity' in 2000, despite Mayotte having claimed to be 'assimilated' in the French Republic since 1975. France therefore appears to have created these special statuses to accommodate a request it did not want to satisfy. These French citizens had been asking for a referendum on 'self-determination' to opt for the opposite option than the one usually associated with this sort of referendum. After nearly 30 years of 'hesitation', France eventually agreed to hold two referenda in Mayotte, the first in 2000 on the status of CDOM[37] being a preparatory stage of the second held in 2009 on self-determination.[38]

The outcome was an overwhelming majority (96 per cent) in favour of Article 73 (and legislative identity). The long reluctance of France to undergo this statutory change could be explained by the fact that Mayotte is 98 per cent Muslim and its population's fluency in French is not what one would expect from a French territory. The people of Mayotte have always enjoyed 'special treatment' particularly when it comes to language and secularism. Two main languages are spoken there alongside French, which often remains relegated to schools, administration and the media. Besides, Mayotte was ruled by Islamic religious law until 2011,[39] an exception to the secular rule in the Republic that could have been accommodated in the status of a TOM or even a CTOM (and their legislative specificity), but not any longer under a regime based on legislative identity with mainland France. Therefore, from 2000, the common law had to be extended progressively to this territory's population. The delay

---

37 In CDOM and CTOM the C stands for 'Collectivity'.

38 In 2000, 73 per cent of the Mahorese declared themselves in favour of the new status that was supposed to facilitate their move towards 'départementalisation' and, in 2009, 96 per cent of the Mahoreses decided to become the 'Département de Mayotte'.

39 Although some changes, such as banning polygamy, have been progressively introduced since 2000 in preparation for the likelihood of integration.

in acceding to Mayotte's wish could also be understood in terms of France not wanting to provoke the Comoros, who continue to oppose the secession of Mayotte and are very active in expressing their view, and the UN, which never endorsed France's decision to split the result of the referendum of 1975 between the four islands.

In March 2011 Mayotte became the 101st French *Département*, although it is not per se a DOM as it has become (ahead of any others) a new 'single collectivity' ruled by Article 73. Designated as 'Le département de Mayotte', its combined competences are those of a *département* and of a region managed by a single council. Despite its new status, it will not immediately enjoy all the social and economic benefits given to the rest of the DOMs. The French central authorities can put forward two main reasons for the 25-year delay. First, Mayotte's economic situation is challenged by a series of impediments such as a very young and fast-growing population (200,000 and counting) and a very low generated income (mainly from horticulture). Second, progressive '*départementalisation*' was carried out in an attempt to limit the extremely high level of immigration mostly from the neighbouring Comoros islands. To raise the level of public financial support immediately would have subjected Mayotte to an even higher level of illegal immigration, jeopardising Mayotte's chance of a successful transition. This is why full social and economic advantages will be granted progressively so as to allow the Mahorese to adapt to the major cultural and economic changes they will now have to face.[40]

Finally, a last point concerning the FOTs' change of statuses is the impact these alterations will have on their European status. For example, St Barthélemy and St Martin's adoption of a status that allows more autonomy has also led to a change in their European treatment. In January 2012, St Barthélemy is scheduled to give up its outermost region status to enter the OCTs category (Overseas Countries and Territories). This means reduced financial support from Europe, but also less constraint. On the other hand, Mayotte in becoming a DOM should soon see its European status 'upgraded' from OCT to an outermost region in 2014.

Conclusion

Despite 'encouragement' from the French government and the President, autonomy does not seem to be an attractive option for the populations of the DOMs, who have repeatedly demonstrated their preference for the status quo. The referenda of 2003 and 2008 could be described as failed attempts to simplify the overseas statuses. But is this what matters? In point of fact, the efficiency and dynamism of the local leaders and of the populations is what is really at stake. In the former TOMs, now COMs, self-determination,

---

40   See Mrgudovic (2005) for a more detailed report on this situation.

a right maintained for French Polynesia and Wallis and Futuna, does not seem to be the main concern of the populations. Even in French Polynesia, the political instability that has been present since 2004 does not incline the population to claim independence, nor even more autonomy, but rather a better managed 'country'.[41] This claim is therefore aimed more at local politicians in the overseas territories, rather than at the French State, and is not at the institutional level but at the political one. Lastly, New Caledonia, the territory with the strongest claim for independence, seems to become more and more hesitant and cautious. If we simply consider the figures, there is no means by which independence could ever be a democratic option. However, to guarantee peace and development the pro-independence component of the population and its various political representatives have to be recognised and granted power based not on figures but on principles and ideals. This is what was sought with the status of 1988 and 1999. These encompass dignity, the ability of all Caledonians to decide for themselves on their destiny and the degree of association they want with France. This last point will largely depend on their ability to support themselves financially. And that is exactly the policy President Sarkozy has tried to develop in the rest of the FOTs as well, with one nuance however: they will have to develop their financial autonomy while remaining within the boundaries of the *République*. If the latter does not seem to cause much concern, the former might prove more challenging to establish. But it will require patience, determination (from the overseas elected representatives) and courage (from most of the FOTs populations) to recognise that eventually autonomy will be the only way forward for the FOTs.

References

L. Allison (2010) *Wallis et Futuna 1958–1962. Une approche de la politique gaulliste dans le Pacifique* (Editions Universitaires Européennes).

S. Al Wardi (2008) *Tahiti Nui ou les dérives de l'autonomie* (Paris: L'Harmattan).

G. Belorgey (2002) 'Le Ministère de l'outre-mer: les raisons de la permanence et les besoins de réforme', *Revue française d'administration publique* 2002/1 (101), pp. 83–96.

L. Blériot (2005) 'Les Départements et Régions d'Outre-Mer: un statut à la carte', *Pouvoirs* 2005/2 (113), pp. 59–72.

J. Chirac (2000) Official Address, Martinique, 11 March 2000. Available on http://discours.vie-publique.fr/notices/007000112.html (accessed 18 Sept. 2011).

41 At Flosse's request, the 2004 status allowed French Polynesia to be called a 'country'. Although it has no legal application, this appellation remains symbolically important for Flosse which insisted on using this as evidence of apparent sovereignty.

C. Cointat and B. Frimat (2011a) *Rapport au Sénat on Saint Pierre et Miquelon*, Sénat 308, 15 Feb., p. 79.

— (2011b) *Rapport au Sénat sur la Martinique, la Guadeloupe et la Guyane et l'article 73*, Sénat 410, 6 April, p. 91.

C. Cointat (2011) *Rapport au Sénat sur la Martinique et la Guyane et l'application de l'article 73 de la Constitution*, Sénat 467, 27 April, p. 402.

S. Diémert (2005) 'Le droit de l'Outre-Mer', *Pouvoirs* 2005/2 (113), pp. 101–12.

J.Y. Faberon and J. Ziller (2007) *Droit des Collectivités d'Outre-mer*, Paris, Librairie Générale de Droit et de Jurisprudence, EJA.

J.C. Gay (2003) *L'outre-mer français en mouvement*, Paris, La Documentation Française.

P. Gosselin (2011) *Official Reports to the Assemblée Nationale on Martinique and on Guyane on the application of article 73 of the Constitution*, nos. 3554 and 3555, 22 June, p. 345.

B. Hopquin (2011) 'Mayotte devient le 101ème département de France', *Le Monde*, 30 March.

J. Jorda (2004) 'Les Collectivités Territoriales Outre-Mer et la revision de la Constitution', *Revue Française de Droit Constitutionnel* 2003/2004 (56), pp. 697–723.

C-L. Lise (2009) 'Avis nº 105 sur le projet de loi de finances pour 2010, Adopté par l'Assemblée nationale', 19 Nov., Sénat, Paris.

Loi de Finances Pour 2011, 'Loi nº 2010–1657 du 29 décembre 2010'. Available at: www.assemblee-nationale.fr/13/projets/pl2824.asp (accessed 18 Sept. 2011).

Loi d'Orientation Pour l'Outre-Mer (LOOM), 'Loi 2000–1207', 13 Dec. 2000, www.outre-mer.gouv.fr.

A. Lotti (2010) *Wallis et Futuna 1958–1962. Une approche de la politique gaulliste dans le Pacifique* (Editions Universitaires Européennes).

Ministry for Overseas Territories, www.outre-mer.gouv.fr.

A. Moyrand and O.A.H. Angelo (1999) 'International law perspectives on the evolution in status of the French Overseas Territories', *Revue Juridique de Polynésie* 5, pp. 49–69.

N. Mrgudovic (2003) 'New Caledonia's struggle for independence. A regional perspective', *The New Pacific Review* 2 (1), pp. 105–25.

— (2005) 'The French Overseas Territories in change', in D. Killingray and D. Taylor (eds.) *The United Kingdom Overseas Territories: Past, Present and Future*, pp. 65–86 (University of London).

— (2011) 'Guadeloupe 2009: Issues politiques à une crise sociale?', in F. Reno (ed.), *Le Mouvement social de janvier 2009*. To be published in 2012.

M.L. Penchard (2011) 'Toward a statut à la carte for each DOM', interview, *L'Express*, 20–26 April 2011.

Performance Publique, www.performance-publique.budget.gouv.fr.

D. Quentin (2011) *Le fonctionnement des institutions de la Polynésie français*, Report no. 3556, Assemblée nationale, 22 June.

N. Sarkozy (2009) Official address, Inter-Ministerial Council for the Overseas Territories, Elysée Palace, Paris, 6 Nov. Available at www.elysee. fr/president/les-dossiers/outre-mer/outre-mer.8080.html (accessed 18 Sept. 2011).

— (2010) Official address, 'New Year wishes to Overseas France', St Denis de la Réunion, 19 Jan. Available at www.elysee.fr/president/les-dossiers/ outre-mer/outre-mer.8080.html (accessed 18 Sept. 2011).

— (2011) Official address, Pointe à Pitre, Guadeloupe, Jan. 2011. Available at: www.elysee.fr/president/les-dossiers/outre-mer/outre-mer.8080.html (accessed 18 Sept. 2011).

E. Thiou (2010) 'Commerce extérieur: Reprise des importations et hausse des exportations', Paris, INSEE. Available at http://insee.fr/fr/themes/ document.asp?reg_id=25&ref_id=17660 (accessed 18 Sept. 2011).

J. Yang-Ting (2000) *Le Mouvement indépendantiste martiniquais: essai de présentation du 'Marie-Jeannisme'*, Petit-Bourg.

Chapter 7

The European Union and its Overseas Countries and Territories: the search for a new relationship

Paul Sutton

Introduction

The European Union (EU) has had a special relationship with its Overseas Countries and Territories (OCTs) since the original founding Treaty of Rome in 1957. In that treaty the European Economic Community (EEC) defined its objectives to the OCT in Part Four, which set out the arrangements for an association of the OCT and defined the purpose of association as: 'To promote the economic and social development of the countries and territories and to establish close economic relations between them and the Community as a whole' (Article 131). The OCTs listed then included colonies, overseas territories and overseas departments of France, the Netherlands, Belgium and Italy. In the 1960s many of these gained independence which meant they were no longer covered by these arrangements, although with the accession of the United Kingdom (UK) in 1973 some others were added. The current association arrangement, adopted in November 2001, governs relations with 25 OCT countries: 11 British (Anguilla, British Virgin Islands, Cayman Islands, Montserrat, Turks and Caicos Islands, St Helena and Dependencies, Falkland Islands, South Georgia and South Sandwich islands, British Antarctic Territories, British Indian Ocean Territories, and Pitcairn; six French (French Polynesia, New Caledonia and Dependencies, Wallis and Futuna Islands, Mayotte, Saint Pierre and Miquelon, and French Southern and Antarctic Territories); six Dutch (Aruba, Bonaire, Curaçao, Saba, Sint Eustatius and Sint Maarten) and one Danish (Greenland).[1]

---

1   Bermuda at its own request has never had an association agreement with the EU. Greenland became an OCT in 1986. The Netherlands Antilles was counted as a single OCT until it fragmented into five separate entities on 10 November 2010: Curacao, Sint Maarten, Bonaire, Sint Eustatius and Saba.

In June 2008 the European Commission (EC) released a Green Paper on 'Future relations between the EU and the Overseas Countries and Territories' (Commission of the European Communities, 2008a) setting out the case for a new and distinctive relationship between the EU and the OCTs. It also launched a public consultation process and later drew on this to set out further proposals in 'Elements for a new partnership between the EU and the Overseas Countries and Territories' in November 2009 (Commission of the European Communities, 2009). The collective response of the OCTs and their respective EU member states was made in a Joint Position Paper presented to the Overseas Countries and Territories Ministerial Conference in New Caledonia in February 2011 (Joint Position Paper, 2011). The release of these documents, the various negotiations and discussions around them by the OCTs and their member governments (Denmark, France, the Netherlands and the UK), and the engagement of the EC and the OCTs in the Overseas Countries and Territories Association is likely to deliver a different relationship between the EU and the OCTs than in the past, with the new relationship to take effect no later than 1 January 2014. This chapter traces these developments to date (July 2011) with a particular focus on the involvement of the UK OCTs.

OCT Association: a brief history

The association system promoted two key elements of development cooperation: the gradual freeing of trade between the associates and the EEC member states, and the provision of financial aid by member states to the associates through the European Development Fund (EDF). Following independence these provisions were carried forward in a slightly modified form for ex-colonies in Africa and the Indian Ocean in a parallel but distinct set of arrangements embodied in the First and then the Second Yaoundé Conventions of 1964 and 1969. In January 1973 the UK joined the EEC and in 1975 the Lomé Convention was agreed between 46 African, Caribbean and Pacific states, including now 22 ex-colonies of the UK. The Lomé Convention was widely recognised as an innovative framework for development which brought in many new features of development cooperation, as well as modifying some existing provisions, for example the abandonment of reciprocity in trade relations between the EEC member states and the developing countries signatory to the Yaoundé Conventions. It also significantly increased the financial assistance available under the EDF. In all, these agreements provided the most privileged relationship in terms of aid and trade between any group of independent developing countries and the EU and, while they were subsequently renegotiated on a regular basis, they included an ever larger number of African, Caribbean and Pacific (ACP) states, reaching 79 in the successor Cotonou Agreement of 2000. During this time the EU increased to 27 member states with further enlargement in 2007.

The arrangements governing relations between the OCT and the EU have been set out since 1964 in successive 'Overseas Association Decisions' made by the European Council, initially for five-year periods then increasing to ten years from 1991. Until 1991 the development cooperation delivered by these arrangements followed those negotiated in the Yaoundé and Lomé Conventions. The OCTs were able to export the majority of their products to the EU on a non-reciprocal trade basis as from 1976. They were also able to access EDF funds in a special envelope set aside for their exclusive use, given in block grants to France, the Netherlands and the UK and allocated through national and regional cooperation programmes and other financial assistance provisions set out in the various Conventions. It is noteworthy that the sums given for national programmes to the British, Dutch and French OCTs were identical in the Fifth EDF (1980–5) at 20 million ecu each but varied thereafter: in the Sixth EDF (1985–90) the Dutch and French were given 26.5 million ecu but the British only 10.5 million ecu and in the Seventh EDF (1990–5) the French were allocated 40.2 million ecu, the Dutch 30.3 million ecu and the British 15.5 million ecu.[2] The total EU allocations to the OCTs in those years, including modest provision from the European Investment Bank (EIB), were 109 million ecu (Fifth EDF), 120 million ecu (Sixth EDF) and 165 million ecu (Seventh EDF). The Eighth EDF (1995–2000) allocated 200 million ecu in total, of which 50.3 million were for national programmes in the French OCTs, 35.3 million ecus for the Dutch and 19.2 million ecus for the British (Commission of the European Communities, 1999).

The Council Decision of 25 July 1991, on the association of the OCTs with the EU, continued the established practice of introducing, into the new Association Decision, changes to the Lomé Convention which had been agreed in the Fourth Convention in 1990. However, the 1991 decision also went further and in several areas departed from the principle of 'parallelism'. For example, all products originating in the OCT were to have free and unlimited access to the EU and special provisions for cumulation (the importation and processing of products from ACP countries and their onward delivery to the EU free of import duties and quantitative restrictions) were permitted. This immediately led to difficulties in 1992 when the EU claimed it was being 'flooded by' rice and sugar products imported from the ACP via some Caribbean OCTs with minimal processing (Hillebrink 2008: 304–7). In 1993, and again in 1996 and 1997, the EU adopted 'safeguard measures' to first limit such trade and then from 1997 enacted new regulations to control it. The 1991 Decision also set a number of 'objectives' for the OCTs in various policy areas and introduced a new institutional aspect to EU-OCT relations by proposing a three-way dialogue in relations, including for the first time

---

2   The ecu is the European Currency Unit with a rate of exchange to one US$ of 1.116 (1981) and 0.763 (1985).

separate OCT participation alongside EU and member state participation. The National Indicative programmes for individual OCTs in the Seventh EDF, for example, were signed by an OCT representative as well as by representatives from the EU and the relevant 'metropolitan' member state.

The next significant change in OCT-EU relations came with the adoption of the Treaty of Amsterdam in October 1997 and the mid-term review of the Association Decision the following month. In Declaration 36, on the OCTs, the EU recognised that the original association arrangements had been 'designed for countries and territories that were numerous, covered vast areas and had large populations', whereas today there are 'only 20 OCTs and they are extremely scattered island territories with a total population of approximately 900,000'. It also noted that 'the arrangements have changed little since 1957' and that 'most OCTs lag far behind in structural terms, a fact linked to their particularly severe geographical and economic handicaps. In these circumstances, the special arrangements for association as they were conceived in 1957 can no longer deal effectively with the challenges of OCT development'. The EU therefore proposed a review of the association arrangements by February 2000 to promote their economic and social development, improve the effectiveness of aid, develop economic relations between the OCT and the EU, and 'take greater account of the diversity and specific characteristics of the individual OCTs' (EU, Treaty of Amsterdam, 1997). In anticipation of such changes the EU introduced, via the 1997 Association Decision, the possibility of the OCT accessing a limited number of EU programmes open to EU citizens on the grounds that many of the inhabitants of the OCT were citizens of the EU and therefore eligible to benefit from them. These included programmes covering education and training, culture and the audio-visual sector, research and development, and industrial cooperation (Commission of the European Communities, 1999a). While this move was modest it further added to a distinction now being drawn between the ACP and the OCT and carried forward in the 2001 Association Decision.

The Council Decision on association of 27 November 2001 governs the current relations between the OCT and the EU.[3] It was the subject, in the words of the EU Commissioner most directly involved, Poul Nielson, 'of long, and sometimes difficult, negotiations' (cited in Sutton, 2002: 19) which were extended on two occasions before final agreement was reached. Negotiations were particularly problematic on trade issues given the experience of the application of 'safeguard' procedures noted earlier (some aspects of which were then still under challenge in the European Court of Justice). They were also informed by a more active involvement of the OCTs who were for the first time directly consulted by the EC and brought together in a meeting in April 1999

3   The Decision was updated and slightly amended in 2007, primarily to extend it to December 2013 to coincide with the dates of the Tenth EDF.

to discuss the issues and make suggestions, some of which were adopted. The key elements of the Decision built on existing practice. It confirmed preferential trade arrangements, widened access to EU budget lines, and provided for greater involvement in EDF funding decisions, with allocations now made directly to individual OCTs rather than through the decision of the member states. It also allowed for recognition of the special needs of the most isolated and least developed OCTs. The funding for the Ninth EDF (2000–7) was fixed at 175 million euros and subsequently at 286 million euros for the Tenth EDF (2008–13). Not all OCTs were allocated funds due to their relatively high per capita incomes, i.e. above the EU average, although they remained eligible for funds under regional programmes. The amounts allocated under the Tenth EDF for the national indicative programmes of the UK OCTs were: Anguilla (11.7 million euros); Falkland Islands (4.66 million euros); Montserrat (15.66 million euros); Pitcairn (3 million euros); St Helena and Dependencies (16.63 million euros); and Turks and Caicos Islands (11.85 million euros). The sum total for individual UK territories was 63.5 million euros, the Dutch 32.88 million euros and the French 99.75 million euros (all figures calculated from Commission of the European Communities, 2008/b: Annex II).

In summary, the OCTs have gradually moved to a more distinctive issue area within EU relations. The early 'parallelism', whereby arrangements for the OCT mirrored those of the ACP, have been modified somewhat although the ACP impress continues to be seen even in the 2001 Association Decision. The EU acknowledged this in its Green Paper where, notwithstanding the changes made since 1991, it stated that 'the overall approach to the OCTs remained nevertheless closely inspired by the ACP-EC Partnership Agreement and its classic development cooperation logic based on the fight against poverty, despite the mismatch between such an approach and the OCTs' contemporary situation' (Commission of the European Communities, 2008a: 5). The need for fundamental change, first identified in the Treaty of Amsterdam, had therefore not been fully followed through, but was now becoming pressing, particularly with questions being asked within the EU about the association arrangements by new member states following enlargement in May 2004. Additionally, the OCTs had themselves become more active and vocal, particularly within the Overseas Countries and Territories Association (OCTA), and were seeking a new approach covering all aspects of the relationship.

Developing a voice in Europe: the OCTs and OCTA

The voice of the OCTs in the EU has taken three principal forms: individual representation by the OCT within the EU and/or within their respective metropoles; regular structured dialogue with the EU through the medium of trilateral meetings in Brussels and annual 'partnership forums'; and the coordination of positions within OCTA.

The individual OCTs, of course, are not sovereign states and therefore operate under some limitations within the international system, particularly in respect of the advancement of their interests through recognition and formal diplomatic representation. At the same time they have been part of a growing movement in the last decade or so which has seen sub-national island jurisdictions foster their autonomy from their metropolitan states and use it to promote a vigorous 'para-diplomacy', which has significantly advanced their economic development (Baldacchino, 2010). Within Europe examples of such 'para-diplomacy', defined as 'a field of international activity which simulates or approximates official and conventional international relations' (Bartmann, 2009: 56) have increased in recent years, involving at the margin not only the OCTs but also other jurisdictions with a measure of autonomy such as the Faroe Islands and the UK Crown Dependencies of Jersey, Guernsey and the Isle of Man.

Greenland is now the only OCT with representatives stationed in Brussels since French Polynesia recently closed its office there. The result is that the key resource for most OCTs for diplomacy with the EU has been their representation in the metropole. For the Dutch this has been The Hague and, for the French, Paris (although Wallis and Futuna are represented in Brussels through Eurodom, a specialist consultancy). For all the UK OCTs, it is London. Within the latter, policy towards the EU has rarely been a major interest for officials unless they have had a specific task, for example, the recent short-term chairmanship of OCTA by the representative of St Helena. The OCT officials concerned have therefore had to travel to Brussels for regular meetings and may, because of other commitments, miss important ones. They may also have to cover areas in which they are not necessarily well-briefed or very familiar. In recognition of this problem, two 'technical' Partnership Working Groups, on Trade and Regional Integration and on Financial Services, were established in 2005. These were later supplemented by two more on the Environment and the Revision of the Decision. However, several have run into difficulties and have functioned ad hoc since 2008, a situation which has been attributed in part to the lack of commitment of resources by the OCTs and the EU to fund technical experts' full participation in them (Hannibal et al., 2011). The net effect of such 'partial' engagement is, not surprisingly, a rather 'patchy' performance by the OCTs in their regular (approximately every six weeks) tripartite meetings in Brussels involving the EC, officials from the metropolitan countries and the OCTs themselves. It also leads, according to interviews with some of the participants involved (2010/2011), to OCTs' reliance on the 'goodwill' of their respective metropoles to act in their best interest in Brussels when they are absent, a practice which is apparently not uncommon but also not unproblematic given that differences of opinion do necessarily arise.

In addition to the regular tripartite meetings in Brussels, chaired by the Commission, an annual dialogue with the EC has been instituted through the 'Partnership Forum'. To date, there have been nine Forums held in alternate years in Brussels and an OCT country (Bonaire, September 2002; Brussels, December 2003; French Polynesia, March 2005; Brussels, December 2005; Greenland, September 2006; Brussels, November 2007; Cayman Islands, September 2008; Brussels, March 2010; and New Caledonia, March 2011). The Forum is usually held over two days and involves officials from the EU (including on most occasions the Commissioner responsible for development), officials and occasionally ministers (usually a French minister) from the metropoles, and OCT officials and ministers. Generally, representation is good when the Forum is held in Brussels but more regionally skewed when it is held in an OCT. The agenda of the Forums broadly reflect the central theme in the partnership arrangements: trade and financial assistance, particularly programming and access to EDF funds on which difficulties are always reported (see, for example, Chairman's Summary of Discussions, Second OCT-EU Forum, 2003; Minutes of the Third OCT-EU Forum, 2005; Report of the Fifth OCT-EU Forum, 2006; Report of the Eighth OCT-EU Forum, 2010). Other issues reflect current themes and have covered the environment, financial regulation in offshore centres, the vulnerability of the OCTs, and the 'outermost regions' (ORs),[4] and political arrangements, particularly the proposal for a new EU-OCT relationship. Bilateral meetings 'in the wings' between representatives of a specific OCT and EU officials have now become a regular feature of recent Forums.

A common interest among the OCTs first began to take coherent shape in June 2000 when representatives of the British Virgin Islands, French Polynesia and the Netherlands Antilles began meeting to coordinate their positions towards the new Association Decision then under discussion in the EC. This action was followed up in November 2000 at the First OCT Ministerial Conference in Brussels when the governments of seven OCTs proposed the establishment of the OCTA. The organisation was formally instituted at the Second OCT Ministerial Conference in Bonaire in 2002 and membership is open only to the OCTs. It operates on the basis of a President and an executive committee elected annually at the Ministerial Conference which allows for some rotation of office. Ministerial Conferences have been held annually since 2002 to co-ordinate with and precede the OCT-EU Forum. The most important business has been the adoption of the Political Resolution which informs the common OCT approach to the subsequent Forum. As such, the

4   The term 'outermost regions' refers to special arrangements the EU has adopted in respect of the overseas French (Martinique, Guadeloupe, French Guiana, Réunion, St Barthélemy, St Martin), Spanish (the Canary Islands) and Portuguese (Azores and Madeira) territories which are classed as integral parts of the EU.

OCTs have used the Political Resolution to signal their special interests and needs and to some extent structure the agenda and subsequent discussions in the Forum. Among issues raised in political resolutions over the years have been, inter alia, a separate development fund exclusive to the OCTs, a closer approximation of the OCTs to benefits and arrangements governing the EU ORs, some involvement of the OCTs in EU negotiations with ACP countries for Economic Partnership Agreements (EPAs), greater recognition of the vulnerability of the OCTs in determining EDF and other EU financial allocations, greater economic support for environmental stewardship by the OCTs, financial support for a full time OCTA Secretariat/Bureau to be based in Brussels, and promotion within the forthcoming Association Decision of a framework coherent enough to recognise the commonality of interest of the OCTs but also flexible enough to accommodate their very different individual situations and needs (see, for example, Political Resolution, December 2003; Political Resolution, December 2005; Political Resolution, September 2006; Political Resolution, November 2007; Political Declaration, November 2008; Political Declaration, March 2010). In 2008 the OCT called for a small permanent bureau (four persons) to be established in Brussels to better promote its work and in 2011 a proposal was submitted to the EC to finance its utilisation of EDF regional funds. In November 2007 OCTA presented a detailed draft strategic plan to guide its work in the period 2008–13 in which it set out a number of objectives designed to improve cooperation, increase capacity and raise awareness of the OCTs. A revised shortened version was adopted and published in 2010 (OCTA Strategic Plan, 2010). It also publishes a newsletter and hosts a website (www.octassociation.org).

The OCTs have clearly improved their position in the EU as compared to ten years ago. However, they continue to face restrictions on account of their non-sovereignty, for example the EU resisted their proposal to be included as participants in their own right in the negotiations of the EPAs and they continue largely to be reactive in their response to the EU, in part because the OCTA Bureau has yet to be fully established. The Executive Committee is active but operates within a mandate determined by the annual Ministerial meeting which limits a more proactive approach. The collective voice of the OCTs is less developed and more muted on this account and the individual voice of an OCT correspondingly larger. Within this framework some OCTs, notably French Polynesia and New Caledonia, have championed the OCT as have some individual OCT officials, again mainly French. The British OCTs are committed players but with the exception of Clive Stanbrook of the Turks and Caicos Islands in the mid 2000s none have so far sought to be captains for any length of time. The British OCTs therefore see the EU very much as a 'distant second' compared to their relations with the UK. For example, collective positions towards OCTA are elaborated in a sub-committee of the United Kingdom Overseas Territories Association, the main organisation in

London promoting the collective interests of the UK Overseas Territories in the UK. In this strategy they are not too different from the other OCTs although in the interviews I have conducted (2010/2011) I have established that the EU relationship is not as well known 'back home' in the individual UK OCTs as it is in the French, Dutch and Danish OCTs.

Developing EU policy: the EC and the future of the OCTs

The Commission undertook its first comprehensive study of the association arrangements in 1999 (Commission of the European Communities, 1999b). The catalyst was the Treaty of Amsterdam which asked the European Council to review the association arrangements by February 2000. In its Communication to the Council the EU set out in detail the history and current basis of the association arrangements and set out 'policy options' for change to be considered when the Association Decision came up for renewal in 2001. The proposals were both technical and political. The former involved trade, financial instruments, right of establishment, currencies and the euro, and 'grey' areas such as free movement of persons, diplomas and veterinary and health rules. The latter discussed drugs and money laundering, the applicable World Trade Organisation regime and the institutional dimension of the association. In some areas the Commission proposed radical departures from the existing arrangements, such as its proposal to the Council that it should draw up policy guidelines for the future amendment to Part Four of the Treaty which would more clearly spell out the relationship of the OCTs to the EU. Such proposals proved controversial and were not adopted with the result that the eventual Association Decision built largely on existing practice, albeit adding new dimensions and depth to it.

The OCTs and the metropolitan member states were not happy with this outcome and in 2003 adopted a Joint Position Paper which called for a major review of the association arrangements. In 2005 the Commission began working on the elements of a new relationship. A small dedicated OCT Task Force was created within its Directorate General for Development to carry it forward. In November 2007 it released a concept paper on the future of the EU/OCT association for discussion at the Partnership Forum and in June 2008 the Commission published the Green Paper on 'Future relations between the EU and the Overseas Countries and Territories' (Commission of the European Communities, 2008a). At the same time it launched a public consultation process from 1 July until 17 October 2008 and organised a 'stakeholder conference' in Brussels on 3 October 2008 to discuss the Green Paper. In his address to the conference the EC Director General for Development, Stefano Manservi, asserted that the Commission had 'no pre-cooked' answers for the future shape of OCT relations with the EU (*The Courier*, 2008: 12).

The Green Paper and the accompanying Working Document (Commission of the European Communities, 2008b) provide a comprehensive overview of EU-OCT relations. They summarise the current legal basis of the 'association arrangements', provide information on the individual OCTs and detail the trade arrangements between them and the EU. The many differences between the OCTs are highlighted but the common characteristics they share are also identified, including their vulnerability as micro-island economies and their distinct position within the EU. The major aim of the Green Paper is to identify the 'challenges and opportunities' facing the OCT in order to define an 'overall philosophy that should underpin relations in the longer term' (Commission of the European Communities, 2008a: 2). This, in turn, would inform the new policy towards them to be decided by the European Council.

The main part of the Green Paper sets out 14 questions to which it sought answers in the consultation. These cover three main areas: the character of the partnership between the EU and the OCTs, which deal mainly with political issues; trade arrangements between them, which are largely framed as technical issues; and the OCTs' specific characteristics that focus on questions of sustainable development. In so doing, the Commission was clearly trying to move the discussion of the OCTs beyond the parameters of the 2001 Association Decision (European Union, 2001) which was largely technical and focused on implementation and administration, towards something which was more policy focused and which could command a new approach towards the OCT within the European Council. The last point is of some significance since the Green Paper makes it clear that there had been a mounting opposition within some EU member states to the arrangements of the Association Decision, especially those relating to development assistance.

The 32 responses the Commission received to its Green Paper were published on its website. Half of these came from governments of which 13 were OCTs and three were metropoles (the French government did not respond directly). A preliminary analysis of the comments from the OCTs has been presented by Hannibal et al. (2011: 16–20). They identify two approaches. The first invokes notions of 'solidarity' and stresses the 'right' to assistance from the EU based on 'development needs', 'moral responsibilities' and compensation for negative impacts such as climate change for which the EU is in part responsible. Essentially, Hannibal et al. claim, this approach 'insists on a continuation of the current relationship ... maintaining OCT dependency on the EU' (2011: 18). The second approach seeks a more 'equal' relationship with the EU through identifying issues in which the OCT can be of importance to the EU. Examples include the spread of European values which the OCTs share with the EU and the promotion of OCTs as 'centres of excellence' within their regions. Much of this remains ill-defined in the various responses of the OCTs leading Hannibal et al. to argue that this approach is less a departure from previous practice than might be supposed and hence simply another way of confirming 'the asymmetrical dependency relationship of the past' (2011: 20). In all, they conclude, the responses to the Green Paper will be a disappointment to the Commission who were looking for more positive examples of 'reciprocity' and 'mutual benefit' as well as other ideas as to how the OCTs 'might be of concrete value to the EU'. They also suggest 'these replies will be difficult to "sell" to the rest of the European Council in the negotiations on the next financial framework for the OCTs' (2011: 20), implying significant political difficulties ahead.

The five responses from the UK OCTs (Montserrat, Pitcairn and the Turks and Caicos Islands did not respond) were in the same vein. The principal focus of Anguilla's comments was access to European funding programmes to offset acute vulnerabilities and protect the environment. The major concern was therefore to preserve existing benefits and if possible increase them for the most vulnerable.[5] The British Virgin Islands (BVI) response was more balanced and more detailed.[6] It broadly supported the thrust of the Green Paper and provided detailed and thoughtful responses to most of the questions. It argued for special recognition from the EU in respect of trade and for additional resources to offset its many vulnerabilities. It also supported the recognition of mutual interests on matters of the environment and on global regulation of offshore financial centres, although in respect of the latter it robustly argued for a level playing field which it claimed the EU had not always provided. Indeed, the response throughout suggested the need for 'policy space', which allowed the BVI to determine its own priorities and pace of change within any future EU-OCT framework rather than be subject to the 'one-size-fits-all' approach (the phrase appears six times) which the EU had applied in the past. The Cayman Islands (CI) response was brief and did not answer any of the specific questions posed in the Green Paper. Instead it set out issues about which the CI was especially concerned – offshore finance, disaster management and 'small size', which should be taken into account in any future EU policy towards them.[7] The Falklands Islands (FI) response was similar to the BVI in

---

5   Information obtained from Government of Anguilla, 'Anguilla's response to the Green Paper', 2008, at http://ec.europa.eu/europeaid/how/public-consultation/3841 which was last available in July 2010. Anguilla's response appeared to be to a series of questions that were posed while the Green Paper was in the process of being drafted and not to the 14 questions specifically set out in the Green Paper as published.

6   Information obtained from Government of the British Virgin Islands, 'Response by the Government of the British Virgin Islands', 30 October 2008, at http:// ec.europa.eu/europeaid/how/public-consultation/3841 last available in July 2010.

7   Information obtained from Government of the Cayman Islands, 'Cayman Islands Response – Letter from Kurt Tibbets, Leader of Government Business', 14 October 2008, at http://ec.europa.eu/europeaid/how/public-consultation/3841 last available in July 2010.

providing detailed answers to questions but distinct from it in being more specific to its own case.[8] Issues of remoteness and the constraints imposed by the political conflict with Argentina were therefore prominent. So also was the importance of the relationship with the UK. Within these parameters the FI sought a closer but more nuanced arrangement with the EU which would preserve and increase its benefits, including an increased transfer of resources. In return, it could offer some advantages to the EU in terms of access to natural resources and its geographic position but little else. The issues of isolation and remoteness also featured in the response from St Helena.[9] These constituted major constraints, it claimed, which meant St Helena could offer the EU very little. At the same time it meant that its needs were very great since it lacked infrastructure, especially transport, which could make it sustainable. St Helena's response was therefore mainly concerned with how aid could be increased, simplified and made more relevant to it, including programmes and provision that recognise the differences between St Helena and its dependencies.

The responses made by the UK OCTs clearly prioritised different forms of development assistance. Most of them had nothing to say about trade. Their relationship with the EU is therefore mostly 'one-sided' and acutely 'aid-dependent'. The exceptions are the BVI and CI who have strong service sectors in finance and tourism and who receive no direct aid from the EU. The arguments put forward in the Green Paper for major changes in the relationship were viewed with some suspicion and the idea of a common position on the OCT by the EU was not supported unless it was flexible enough to accommodate the individual needs of each OCT. It is this singular territorial focus which is the paramount concern of every UK OCT in its response to the Green Paper. In itself, this is not surprising since it underlines the insularity found in nearly every small island polity in which the affairs of the island dominate politics in the island. But it does create difficulties for external agents in formulating and developing a common policy to that island and other islands which has value and meaning for all involved.

The Commission published its response to the consultation in November 2009 (Commission of the European Communities, 2009). It stated it was 'in favour of a significant change in the approach to the association of the OCTs with the EU' (Commission of the European Communities, 2009: 19). This new approach would reflect the fact that the OCTs belong to the

---

8   Information obtained from Government of the Falkland Islands, 'Letter from Mike Summers, Legislative Council and Compilation of Comments from Private Sector and Government on OAD Green Paper', 22 Sept. 2008, at http://ec.europa.eu/europeaid/how/public-consultation/3841 last available in July 2010.

9   Information obtained from Government of St Helena and Dependencies, 'Comments on the Green Paper', 2008, at http://ec.europa.eu/europeaid/how/public-consultation/3841 last available in July 2010.

same 'European family' as the member states, even though they are not part of the EU as such. The EU would recognise their 'unique relationship' with the OCTs and show solidarity towards them by promoting their 'sustainable development' but it would also expect the OCTs to promote the EU's values and standards, especially in their immediate region. The Commission 'thus believes the future relationship should be more reciprocal, based on mutual interests' (Commission of the European Communities, 2009: 4).

In terms of specific details, the Commission set out a three-part strategy as the basis of future cooperation. The first was to enhance the competitiveness of the OCTs in key areas such as education and training, information and communication technologies, macroeconomic stability, small and medium-sized enterprises and good economic and political governance. The second was to increase resilience by reducing vulnerability to economic shocks, environmental challenges, energy dependence and natural disasters. The third was to promote cooperation on economic, environmental and cultural matters between the OCTs and with relevant ACP countries and the OR territories within their respective regions. In respect of trade, the existing advantages would be maintained, although some changes would be proposed on transhipment, rules of origin and to facilitate links with ACP EPAs. The financial framework was to be radically revised. The EU would provide development aid in the future 'to a very limited number of OCTs, if any' (Commission of the European Communities, 2009: 5). Instead, new forms of financial assistance would be provided, possibly based on horizontal Community programmes that had been pioneered in the ORs.[10] In all, while these measures addressed some of the issues raised in the consultation they also repeated many of the themes set out in the Green Paper. The consultation therefore did little to radically revise the Commission's approach or introduce much new thinking. Instead it confirmed it and bound the OCT to it inasmuch as the OCTs offered no radical dissent to the EU's approach.

The Commission's proposals were approved in all essentials at the European Council on 22 December 2009. It is worthy of note that it directly quoted the section of the Commission's Communication (2009) which mentioned 'the Commission's view that "the [Union's] internal policies, and in particular its regional policy offer interesting examples"' (European Council, 2009), suggesting that the Council would consider proposals that more closely approximated the OCT to the ORs than was currently the case or had been argued by the Commission. It also asked for an interim report on activity to

---

10 Horizontal programmes are generally open only to member states of the EU and implement horizontal policies of the EU designed to advance objectives set in common by member states in broad areas such as regional development, social progress and environmental protection. Implementation is via mechanisms such as the European Regional Development Fund and the European Social Fund.

be presented to it before the end of 2010 and for 'specific proposals' to be presented to it before July 2012. The 'Roadmap' subsequently published by the Commission in 2010 (Commission of the European Communities, 2010) set out a programme of work in 2010/2011 to meet this target, including the establishment of a Steering Group within the Commission to take it forward.

The Joint Position Paper of 2011

The next major step in developing policy was the production and release of a Joint Position Paper (JPP) compiled by the four metropolitan governments and the OCTs in 2010/11 (Joint Position Paper, 2011).[11] The four metropolitan governments had initiated the process by producing a Common Document in November 2008 which set out their views on how to modernise and improve the relations between the OCTs and the EU and build on the distinctiveness of the OCTs as 'outposts of the EU' (Common Document, 2008). However, the main work of drafting the JPP fell to OCTA and in particular to Chloé Calvignac of New Caledonia, who 'shouldered the bulk of the work in producing the first drafts and collating the editing suggestions' (OCTA Newsletter, 2010), and to Keddel Worboys of St Helena, who was Acting President of OCTA during the crucial period when the document was put together. Meetings were held in London and Paris as well as in Brussels. A draft was circulated to metropolitan governments in August 2010 and the final agreed draft was adopted at the Forum in New Caledonia in March 2011 (the Cayman Islands did not sign).

The JPP is a restatement of many of the main issues in EU-OCT relations over the last ten years. It discusses trade, environmental issues and financial assistance, where the principal intention is to maintain existing benefits and achieve enhanced provision where possible, these being more effectively delivered and better calibrated to the needs of individual OCTs, including through a dedicated financial instrument solely for the OCTs. To this end, the main focus of EU-OCT relations should be to achieve the sustainable development of the OCTs by improving their competitiveness, tackling vulnerability and encouraging regional co-operation. It also discusses mutual benefits maintaining that the OCTs 'are present in all parts of the world and should be seen as assets for the EU' (Joint Position Paper, 2011: 2), particularly in their regions where the OCTs can promote EU values and standards. This requires the OCTs to be seen as 'members of the EU family' (Joint Position Paper, 2011: 2), which means that a special and privileged relationship should prevail which takes the OCTs more into account in the workings of

11 A previous Joint Position Paper on the future status of the OCTs within the EU had been released in December 2003 and responded to by the Commission in July 2004. The French government was the key force in initiating and then compiling this first paper.

the Commission internally and overseas, including more participation and greater access to EU horizontal programmes. As a result, improved partnership arrangements should be put in place with better management of the OCTs in EU regional delegations and increased opportunities for dialogue with the EU on policies directly concerning or likely to impact on the OCTs. The JPP ends with seven 'key messages' reinforcing the above points one of which reads: 'the new partnership framework should be at least as beneficial as it is under the current OAD (Overseas Association Decision) and should further improve the quality and standard of living in the OCTs while striving to reduce the difference between the OCTs and the ORs. Funding over the period after 2013 should match the ambition of the renewed OAD' (Joint Position Paper, 2011: 10).

The JPP draws on material presented in the annual political resolutions of the OCTA ministerial conferences, the reports of the various OCT-EU Forums, and the discussions around the Green Paper. It is therefore very much a compilation of existing material rather than a radical departure taking thinking on OCT-EU relations in new directions. No doubt this reflects the difficulties of achieving agreement between the OCTs which has proved problematic in the past and which is most easily overcome via the presentation of a 'shopping list' in which everyone can find something to their particular benefit, which to some extent the JPP resembles. The four metropolitan states also had to be accommodated and while the JPP incorporates many of the points made in their Common Document not all achieved what they wanted. The UK, for example, found its reference to 'value for money' removed in the final stages and the Dutch proved difficult from the beginning in discussions with the OCT, largely in relation to issues arising from the dissolution of the Netherlands Antilles. Nevertheless, OCTA made no changes to the draft JPP at their meeting in New Caledonia prior to its presentation and, on receipt, the Commission would not have been particularly surprised at its content as it was all too familiar to them from previous encounters. In accordance with protocol, Andris Piebalgs, the European Commissioner for Development, welcomed the JPP in his address to the Forum, stating that all seemed to 'share the same vision' and giving a 'personal commitment that all the ideas, proposals and views contained in the Joint Position Paper or presented during the Forum will be given full consideration' (Commission of the European Communities, 2011). The OCTA at their meeting called for 'the next forum of dialogue to take place before the end of 2011' to build on 'the existing political momentum and to ensure the maximum level of consultation between the EU, the OCTs and their MS (member states)' before the Commission submitted its proposals to the European Council in mid 2012 (Political Declaration, 2011). In seeking this, the OCTs were clearly showing some concern that any proposal by the Commission should not come as any surprise and should broadly reflect their views.

Towards a new policy for the OCT

The Commission will need to take into consideration several developments in its final recommendations. The first is the emergence of an OCT voice and presence in the EU in recent years, which has been encouraged and supported by the Commission and by the metropolitan states. This has shifted the debate around the Association Decision from a unilateral decision by EU member states in the European Council towards a negotiated agreement which needs to have the involvement of the OCTs and theoretically their consent. However, no mechanism was introduced into the Lisbon Treaty on European Union to change decision-making in respect of the Association Decision which remains based on unanimity in the European Council on a proposal submitted by the Commission. The OCTs may therefore find that arguments and recommendations put forward by them to the Commission are ignored or watered down. In reality they can do little about this since the OCTs remain politically weak in the EU. The relatively few responses by civil society to the Green Paper consultation exercise points to a very limited interest within the EU on OCT matters. This is further compounded by the low level of engagement with the European Parliament in which only one Member, Maurice Ponga from New Caledonia, takes more than a passing interest in them. The voice of the OCTs will be heard in the forthcoming Association Decision but in the present circumstances it is not one which will necessarily be acted upon.

The second consideration is a shift of emphasis away from an Association Decision informed by EU relations with ACP countries towards one informed by the EU's commitment to its ORs. The EU's special relationship with the ACP has become more attenuated in recent years as the EU has at the same time invigorated its programmes with the ORs, beginning with special measures in favour of the French ORs since 1989, and the Spanish and Portuguese since 1991. This has delivered substantial assistance to the ORs which in the period 2007–13 are allocated 7.8 billion euros (including 4.5 billion from the European Regional Development Fund and 1.3 billion from the European Social Fund). The existence of these programmes has not gone unnoticed in the OCTs, particularly the French and the Dutch, who have commissioned studies on whether a change of status to OR would be of advantage to them.[12] Additionally, the reasoning behind such special assistance by the EU has also attracted attention in the OCTs as it mirrors in many ways the arguments for assistance to them: remoteness, insularity, smallness, climate and economic dependence. Indeed the parallels and possibility of convergence become even more marked when the activities of the Commission

12 The Lisbon Treaty in Article 355 (6) permits individual Danish, Dutch and French OCTs, on the initiative of their metropolitan member state, to amend their status to OR with the unanimous consent of the European Council. The UK OCTs are not mentioned and therefore do not have this right to change their status.

in recent years are considered. These include a 'strategy paper for the ORs', a consultation exercise launched in 2007 followed by a stakeholder conference in 2008, and a Commission policy paper entitled 'The Outermost Regions: an asset for Europe' (Commission of the European Communities, 2008c) in which much of the language and many of the arguments are directly applicable to the OCTs. It is also possible to detect in the successive meetings of the OCT-EU Forum a strengthening argument in favour of adapting features from the OR 'model' into the OCT arrangements. The JPP makes this explicit with its call to 'reduce the difference between the OCTs and the ORs'. However, this is an unlikely eventuality when it is recalled that OCT financial assistance for the Tenth EDF (286 million euros) is a mere 3.66 per cent of that allocated to the ORs for a similar time period and that some EU member states have already challenged 'generous' funding for the OCTs in previous Association Decisions.

Third, metropolitan states remain paramount and decisive in EU-OCT affairs. It is inconceivable that an Association Decision would be passed against the wishes of any one of them. At the same time they have been generally supportive of the interests of their particular OCTs. The most active has been France and its Minister for Overseas Territories, Marie-Luce Penchard, who has promoted the idea of closer relations with the EU and attended recent OCT-EU Forums, including that in New Caledonia. This contrasts with the UK where no minister has ever attended a Forum and some UK OCTs believe it takes too relaxed an approach to pushing their interests in the Commission (interviews by the author 2010/2011). The Dutch and the Danish fit between these two positions, with the Dutch more active in the past and the Danish particularly supportive of the special position of Greenland with its practice of direct relations with the Commission. The metropolitan states can also act collectively together, with ad hoc meetings between officials and occasional ministerial contact as in the meeting in Paris in March 2011 between Marie-Luce Penchard and Sir Henry Bellingham, the UK Minister for the Overseas Territories, which discussed the Association Decision (Foreign and Commonwealth Office, 2011a). Ministers from the four metropolitan states did not meet collectively, however, to discuss the JPP, and negotiations were conducted by officials (Foreign and Commonwealth Office, 2011b), as is the case for most EU-OCT matters.

The Association Decision is not an easy one for the Commission to craft. In 2001 the Decision was marked by controversy and delay, and the mandate for the Commission to deliver its proposals to the European Council in July 2012, 18 months before a final decision has to be made, can be interpreted as a prudent anticipation of difficulties. This reading could also be made of the Commission's entire approach since 2005 with its various papers, consultation process and its desire to depart from 'updating' previous Association Decisions to delivering something more akin to a distinct policy. The future shape of the Decision is not yet clear but will need to be flexible enough to allow for application to individual OCTs yet also cohesive enough to warrant their treatment as a distinctive group. In the end it will need to be a compromise in the Council between those insisting on the special place of the OCTs in the EU and those who see them as the prime responsibility of the metropolitan member states. The history of EU-OCT relations in the last ten years suggests a Decision more favourable to the former than the latter and hence the institutionalisation of a stronger European dimension in individual OCT relations than has been the case in the past, particularly for the UK OCTs.

References

G. Baldacchino (2010) *Island Enclaves: Offshoring Strategies, Creative Governance and Subnational Island Jurisdictions* (Montreal and Kingston: McGill-Queen's University Press).

B. Bartmann (2009) 'In or out: sub-national island jurisdictions and the antechamber of para-diplomacy', in Godfrey Baldacchino and David Milne (eds.), *The Case for Non-Sovereignty: lessons from sub-national island jurisdictions*, pp. 53–72 (London and New York: Routledge).

Common Document (2008) *Common Document of the Governments of the Kingdom of Denmark, the French Republic, the Netherlands, the United Kingdom of Great Britain and Northern Ireland Regarding the Future Relations between the EU and the OCTs*, Nov.

Commission of the European Communities (1999a) 'The European Union and the Overseas Countries and Territories', DE 99 (Luxembourg: European Communities).

— (1999b) *The Status of OCTs Associated with the EC and Options for 'OCT 2000'*, Vol. 1. COM (1999) 163 final, Brussels, 20 May 1999.

— (2008a) 'Future relations between the EU and the Overseas Countries and Territories', (SEC (2008) 2067), Brussels, 25 June 2008 COM (2008) 383 final.

— (2008b) Commission staff working document accompanying the Green Paper 'Future relations between the EU and the Overseas Countries and Territories', (SEC (2008) 2067), Brussels, 25 June 2008 COM (2008) 383 final.

— (2008c) 'The outermost regions: an asset for Europe', COM (2008) 642 final, Brussels, 17 Oct. 2008.

— (2009) 'Elements for a new partnership between the EU and the Overseas Countries and Territories (OCTs)', Brussels, 6.11.2009 (COM) 2009 623 final.

— (2010) 'Roadmap: Proposal for Council Decision replacing Council Decision 2001/822/EC of 27 November 2001 on the association of the overseas countries and territories', DG DEV/D task force OCT, 19 Oct. 2010.

— (2011) 'The future of OCT-EU relations'. Speech by Andris Piebalgs, OCT-EU Forum, Nouméa, New Caledonia, 1 March 2011.

The Courier (2008) 'OCTs an opportunity for Europe', Brussels, Edition No. VIII (N.S.) Oct./Nov., p. 12. Available at www.acp-eucourier.info/fileadmin/issues/2008/08/TheCourier-2008-08.pdf (accessed 17 Sept. 2011).

European Union (2001) 'Council Decision of 27 November 2001 on the association of the Overseas Countries and Territories with the European Union', *Official Journal of the European Communities* L31 4/1 30.11.2001.

— (2009) 'Council conclusions on the EU's relations with the Overseas Countries and Territories (OCTs)', Brussels, 10 Dec. 16710/09.

Foreign and Commonwealth Office (2011a) Letter to the Chair of the Foreign Affairs Committee from Sir Henry Bellingham – 'Overseas Countries and Territories: Relationship with the EU', OCT 13, House of Commons Foreign Affairs Select Committee, Overseas Territories, 30 March. Available at www.publications.parliament.uk/pa/cm201012/cmselect/cmfaff/writev/overseas/ot05.htm (accessed 17 Sept. 2011).

— (2011b) Memorandum for the Foreign Affairs Committee: Overseas Countries and Territories – 'Relationship with the EU', OT 19, House of Commons Foreign Affairs Select Committee, Overseas Territories, May. Available at www.publications.parliament.uk/pa/cm201012/cmselect/cmfaff/writev/overseas/ot12.htm (accessed 17 Sept. 2011).

I. Hannibal, K. Holst, U Pram Gad and R. Adler-Nissen (2011) 'How the EU promotes OCT subjectivity – and how the OCTs use it in Brussels', draft paper presented to the conference, Micropolities in the Margins of Europe – Postcolonial Sovereignty Games, Nuuk, Greenland, 18–19 April.

S. Hillebrink (2008) *The Right to Self-determination and Post-Colonial Governance: the case of the Netherlands Antilles and Aruba* (The Hague: T.M.C. Asser Press).

Joint Position Paper (2011) 'Joint Position Paper of the Governments of the Kingdom of Denmark, the French Republic, the Kingdom of the Netherlands, the United Kingdom of Great Britain and Northern Ireland, and the Overseas Countries and Territories on the Future of Relations between the Overseas Countries and Territories and the European Union', Draft 17 Feb.

OCT-EU Forum (2003) Chairman's Summary Outcome of discussions and proposals for a follow-up, Second Forum. Available at www.octassociation.org/oldsite/oct_ministerial_conference.asp (accessed 17 Sept. 2011).

— (2005) Minutes of the Third Forum. Available at www.octassociation.org/oldsite/oct_ministerial_conference.asp (accessed 17 Sept. 2011).

— (2006) Report of the Fifth Forum. Available at www.octassociation.org/oldsite/oct_ministerial_conference.asp (accessed 17 Sept. 2011).

— (2010) Report on the Eighth Forum. Available at http://eeas.europa.eu/oct/forum/index_en.htm (accessed 25 Sept. 2011).

OCTA Newsletter (2010) *Overseas Countries and Territories Association Newsletter*, Editorial, Issue 9, Fourth Quarter, p. 1. Available at www.octassociation.org/visual%20identity%20and%20publications/Newsletter/on_9_en.pdf (accessed 17 Sept. 2011).

OCTA Strategic Plan (2010) 'Overseas Countries and Territories Association Strategic Plan' *2010*, Brussels, 24 March. Available at www.octassociation.org/visual%20identity%20and%20publications/reports/octa%20strategic%20plan%20final.pdf (accessed 17 Sept. 2011).

Political Resolution (2003) 'Final Declaration of the OCT 2003 Ministerial Conference', Brussels, 4 December. Available at www.octassociation.org/oldsite/oct_ministerial_conference.asp (accessed 17 Sept. 2011).

Political Declaration (2005) 'Final Declaration of the OCT 2005 Ministerial Conference', Brussels, 6 December. Available at www.octassociation.org/oldsite/oct_ministerial_conference.asp (accessed 17 Sept. 2011).

Political Declaration (2006) 'Final Declaration of the OCT 2006 Ministerial Conference', Nuuk, 6 September. Available at www.octassociation.org/oldsite/oct_ministerial_conference.asp (accessed 17 Sept. 2011).

Political Resolution (2007) 'Final Declaration of the 2007 Ministerial Conference', Brussels, 27 November. Available at www.octassociation.org/oldsite/oct_ministerial_conference.asp (accessed 17 Sept. 2011).

Political Declaration (2008) 'Final Declaration of the 2008 Ministerial Conference', Cayman Islands, 26 Nov. Available at www.octassociation.org/oldsite/oct_ministerial_conference.asp (accessed 17 Sept. 2011).

Political Declaration (2010) 'Final Declaration of the 2009 Ministerial Conference', Brussels, 24 March. Available at http://eeas.europa.eu/oct/forum/index_en.htm (accessed 25 Sept. 2011).

G. Sutton (2002) 'The Overseas Countries and Territories: renewed partnership with the Community', *The ACP-EU Courier*, Jan.–Feb., pp. 19–20. Available at http://ec.europa.eu/development/icenter/repository/190_ACP_EU_01_en.pdf (accessed 17 Sept. 2011).

Chapter 8

Looking for Plan B: what next for island hosts of offshore finance?[1]

Mark P. Hampton and John Christensen

Introduction

Facing sustained pressure from the US Obama Administration, the Organisation for Economic Cooperation and Development (OECD) and the European Union, the Swiss authorities look likely to abandon or significantly modify their banking secrecy laws in the near future (*International Herald Tribune*, 2009). Other tax havens are coming under similar pressure to modify their laws and treaty arrangements to improve international cooperation on tax information-sharing. In January 2010 the OECD announced that tax havens had signed more than 300 tax information exchange agreements in the preceding 12 months, signalling what they described as 'one of the big success stories of the G20' (Houlder, 2010a: 1). The European Court of Justice has also taken a lead in tackling harmful tax practices, and its landmark judgment of April 2005, the Halifax Case, ruled against transactions that have tax avoidance as their sole purpose.[2] Additionally, the British, French and other OECD governments are supporting new accounting rules that will require multinational companies to publish accounts for all subsidiaries in the countries where they operate; rules designed to reduce radically the scope for shifting profits to tax havens (Houlder, 2010a: 2).

Cumulatively these pressures seem likely to have a significant impact on small island economies hosting offshore financial centres (OFCs), some of which were already facing budgetary crises arising from other factors. For example, in September 2009 the government of the Cayman Islands, a British

---

1 This article first appeared in *The Round Table* 100 (413), pp. 169–81, April 2011. Inevitably some bibliographical details may have changed.
2 A comment on the ECJ ruling is available at www.internationaltaxreview.com/ ?Page¼10&PUBID¼35&ISS¼21603&SID¼622016&TYPE¼20.

Overseas Territory, sought emergency backing from the UK Foreign and Commonwealth Office to borrow £278m on the private markets. In response, a Foreign Office minister proposed radical reform of their tax arrangements, stating: 'I fear you will have no choice but to consider new taxes, perhaps payroll and property taxes such as in the British Virgin Islands' (Mathiason, 2009: 7). In October 2009, UK Treasury officials advised senior politicians from the British Crown Dependencies that the EU Code of Conduct Group on Business Taxation would not accept their proposed tax reforms, placing Guernsey and Jersey in potential fiscal crisis (Quérée, 2009). In February 2010, in response to a statement from the UK Secretary to the Treasury about multinational company reporting requirements,[3] the business correspondent of the *Jersey Evening Post* commented: 'It's not only banking secrecy that's dead. Tax avoidance – the industry that helped Jersey become so prosperous – now appears to be on its last legs as well', concluding that 'it would be a good idea to start planning now for this brave new world' (Body, 2010). Unlike the multilateral initiative in the 1990s against tax havens, spearheaded by the OECD, which fizzled out when the US Bush Administration withdrew its support in 2001 (Palan et al., 2010: 224), the current initiatives are being driven by three power blocs, the Group of 20 countries, the EU and the US, all of which are confronted by the deepest recessions experienced since the 1930s. Domestic budgetary pressures within these economies have played an important part in swinging the pendulum away from tax havens. In this context, preparing development strategies that reduce dependence on rent incomes from what the OECD terms 'the tax industry' (OECD, 1998) should be regarded as a priority for small islands.

Theorising island hosts: path dependence

Although there is a growing literature on small island economies (SIEs),[4] this paper focuses on one aspect, path dependence, as an analytical tool to examine SIE hosts of offshore finance. Scott (2001: 367) defines path dependence as 'systems in which early choices or actions, often determined by transient conditions, bias subsequent development in favour of particular outcomes'. Martin and Sunley (2006: 402) add, 'The past thus sets the possibilities while the present controls what possibility is to be explored'.

For small islands that are former colonies, path dependence was applied by Acemoglu et al. (2002), who discussed the 'reversal of fortune' concept; however, they were criticised by Austin (2008) for over-simplifying the lines

---

3   The speech is available at www.hm-treasury.gov.uk/speech_fst_270110.htm.
4   Approaches range from conventional neoclassical orthodoxies (World Bank, 2005; Armstrong and Read, 2006) via 'vulnerabilities' (Briguglio, 1995) to broadly political economy-type writings (Hampton and Christensen, 2002; Baldacchino, 2006).

of causation over time. Feyrer and Sacerdote (2009) examined the links between colonialism and the modern-day income of islands, pointing to an overall positive correlation between islands being colonial possessions and present national income levels. However, Bertram (2007) argues that the type of approach used (econometrics) had key flaws in its data-gathering and demonstrated a limited understanding of the specifics of SIEs.

MacKinnon et al. (2007) argue that when analysing a particular phase in a region's development it is crucial also to consider the existing social relations that shape localised practices and operational routines. This requires a focus on specific circumstances that can give rise to 'lock-in' to a particular form of development in which local economic actors pursue a course of action that may ultimately lead to an 'economic cul-de-sac'. This paper follows this line of logic, arguing that actions and decisions at certain times, in this case to allow OFC firms to 'locate' in SIEs, are likely to have 'locked-in' these jurisdictions to a development path that may indeed prove to be what MacKinnon et al. (2007) dub an 'economic cul-de-sac'.

Here this notion is developed further, and it is argued that events since 2007 and 2008, including exogenous shocks, have exacerbated this trend. According to Grabher (1993) and Hassink (2005) there are three distinct aspects of 'lock-in': functional, cognitive and political. Functional lock-in arises from the web of relations between firms, forms of production or economic activity, and the links created between customers and suppliers. Cognitive lock-in (or world view) arises from failures to interpret correctly signs of external change, and the failure of collective learning mechanisms. Finally, political lock-in refers to social relations and the power dynamics that underpin economic development, especially failures of political, business and labour leaders to adapt policy mechanisms to allow local innovation and learning. Of these three aspects, Hassink (2005) argues that cognitive and political lock-ins are closely related and, significantly, can cause outcomes that 'paralyse competition and tranquillize large industries' (Hassink, 2005: 523). An example of this can be found in the case of Swiss private banks, which, faced with mounting pressure to abolish the protective mechanism provided by that country's banking secrecy law, feel themselves unable to compete effectively at global level (Zaki, 2010). Here, we would agree with MacKinnon et al. (2007: 5), who comment that the net effect of these aspects of lock-in further leads to 'collective myopia', that is, a legacy of inherited social infrastructures that actively discourages innovation and new business start-up. Arguably this can be observed in Jersey and many other SIE hosts of offshore finance.

Within the path dependence literature, a link can also be established to place dependence (Martin and Sunley, 2006), as despite the so-called 'end of geography' notions (O'Brien, 1992), physical location, by which we mean proximity to major financial centres such as London or New York, remains a key attraction for the largest OFCs (Hampton, 1996a; Hampton and

Christensen, 2007; Markoff, 2009). Hampton and Christensen (2002: 168) argued that SIE hosts 'have become locked into their relationships with the offshore finance industry by their dependence upon the earnings potential of predominantly imported skills and expertise, and their lack of skills and knowledge in alternative sectors. This means that any attempts at diversification into other sectors would be constrained by the need for wholesale re-skilling and the acquisition of new knowledge bases.'

Contrary to Park's argument (1982), the experiences of SIEs such as the Channel Islands, Cayman, and Turks and Caicos, demonstrate that hosting OFCs does not lead to transferable knowledge gains or increasing entrepreneurial flair because the majority of the activities located in these OFCs consists of what could be termed 'wrapper' activity, that is, creating and administering structures that give the form but not the substance of a functional presence. Even where these islands have created niche markets for themselves (e.g. securitisation in Jersey, captive insurance in Guernsey), most of the specialists working in these fields have been imported from elsewhere.

The emergence of offshore finance

Offshore finance's rise since the 1960s[5] has been detailed by Hampton (1996a), Palan (2003), Palan et al. (2010) and Sharman (2006), but here we can note certain key points. First, there has been the instrumental role played by OECD states (particularly the UK) in creating and supporting tax havens and offshore finance[6] in many small jurisdictions, especially former colonies and continuing dependencies such as the Cayman Islands in the 1960s and Vanuatu in the 1970s.

Second, this explicit support from mainland states, combined with the expansion of globalising financial capital (initially US and Canadian banks plus UK merchant banks), met the rising international demand for both specialist retail banking (asset management for wealthy individuals) and wholesale banking (Eurocurrency and Eurobond markets) for other banks and multinational corporations.

Third, such initiatives overlapped with the personal interests of key local actors such as the lawyers Vassel Johnson in Cayman and Reg Jeune in Jersey, the latter's practice going on to become a prominent member of the

---

5   Offshore finance and tax havens have earlier origins with notable and organised commercial activity from at least the 1920s (Hampton, 1996a) but significant changes in the scale and scope of activities dates from the 1960s.

6   The argument over definitions of 'tax havens' versus 'offshore finance centres' has been discussed across the literature (see, for example, Hampton, 1996a; Palan et al., 2010) and by civil society groups such as TJN who have popularised the term 'secrecy jurisdictions' (see www.secrecyjurisdictions.com).

'Offshore Magic Circle'[7] of law firms, with Jeune taking a leading political role as President of the States of Jersey's Policy and Resources Committee. These pioneer law firms were able to make sizeable profits in the new world of offshore finance as it grew in the island hosts. By the 1990s the so-called shadow economy of offshore finance was host to an estimated US$11.5 trillion of assets belonging to wealthy individuals (Tax Justice Network (TJN), 2005), and including differing types of financial structure (varieties of foundations, trusts, tax-exempt companies, international business companies, offshore funds, hedge funds, structured investment vehicles, captive insurance, etc.). After two decades of benign neglect by the international community, however, and despite ad hoc and relatively small-scale initiatives from individual countries' revenue authorities to combat the most blatant tax dodging, by the mid 1990s the international context within which tax havens operate was beginning to change. Initially the islands were able to resist most of the pressures for change. The 1998 Harmful Tax Competition initiative (OECD, 1998) – launched by the OECD at the behest of the G7 – was strongly opposed by the 35 tax havens, mostly SIEs, subsequently blacklisted in 2000 (Sanders, 2002; Vlcek, 2007). Their opposition was supported by the incoming George W. Bush administration, whose Treasury Secretary, Paul O'Neill, effectively ended the initiative when he withdrew US support in May 2001 (Palan et al., 2010: 217). Lacking the necessary political support, the OECD persevered through its Global Forum process with negotiating agreements with so-called 'cooperating jurisdictions' to remove some of their harmful tax practices. Other changes were also underway, for example the European Court of Justice ruling mentioned above, but political agreement on the need to tackle banking secrecy and strengthen international cooperation with tax information exchange was effectively stalled until April 2009, when the G20 nations, led by British Prime Minister Brown, French President Sarkozy, German Chancellor Merkel and US President Obama, launched a new initiative against tax havens, with the OECD as the prime agent (*La Tribune*, 2009).

The 2009 initiative differed in several respects from the 1998 Harmful Tax Competition programme. First, the OECD targeted a broader range of tax havens, including OECD nations such as Austria, Luxembourg and Switzerland. Crucially, by this stage amendments to Article 26 of the OECD's Model Agreement for Tax Information Exchange included a facility for overriding banking secrecy laws where evidence existed of criminal activity, including tax evasion. Second, the OECD made a distinction between cooperating

7   This description is given to themselves by the so-called leading offshore legal firms. It appears in recruitment adverts, e.g. on the www.legalweekjobs.com website. One job advert dated 22 February 2010 (US$180–210,000 'tax free') was entitled: 'Senior Structured Finance Associate—Cayman Islands—Offshore Magic Circle Client'.

jurisdictions, specifically those that had already negotiated a minimum of 12 tax information exchange agreements (the so-called White List jurisdictions), from those that had agreed to cooperate but had not achieved the minimum threshold (Grey List jurisdictions), and those that still resisted cooperation (Black List jurisdictions). Third, the public mood had also swung against tax havens, with civil society coalitions in Europe, North America and various developing countries calling for measures to close the loopholes exploited by those who use tax havens.[8] In August 2009 OECD Secretary-General Angel Curria felt sufficiently optimistic to state: 'It seems almost unbelievable, but the era of banking secrecy for tax purposes will soon be over. In tomorrow's world, there will be no more havens in which to hide funds from the taxman' (Gurria, 2009).

Critics such as the Tax Justice Network, however, have argued that the OECD initiative lacks coherence because it fails to target main players such as the UK and US (*Le Monde*, 2009). The TJN, a global civil society coalition that coordinates advocacy efforts for international cooperation on tax matters, published an alternative list of 'secrecy jurisdictions' in November 2009 that ranked the US at the top, and included the UK in the top five.[9] Critics have also argued that the bilateral tax information exchange agreements at the heart of the OECD programme are weak and ineffective at deterring the use of tax havens as centres for tax evasion (Financial Times, 2009). As an alternative they propose the automatic information exchange model adopted by the European Union in 2005 (Global Financial Integrity et al., 2009), which they claim has a stronger deterrent effect than the 'upon request' system used in the OECD Model Agreement. Importantly, the jurisdiction of the EU Savings Tax Directive (STD) extends beyond the member states to include their dependent territories such as the British Crown Dependencies and the Dutch Antilles.

With strong political pressure from France and Germany (*La Tribune*, 2009) and from powerful coalitions within the European Parliament, in early 2010 the European Commission tabled proposals that, once implemented, will strengthen the STD and extend its scope.[10] Specifically, the revised STD includes provisions requiring information exchange for trusts, foundations,

---

8   Approximately 120 civil society organisations, including development non-governmental organisations, human rights organisations, trade unions, faith groups and others, agreed by an overwhelming majority at a meeting in Paris on 12 January 2009 that tackling tax havens was the number one priority for campaigning around the April 2009 G20 summit in London. Most recently (December 2010) tax avoidance campaigners from UK Uncut targeted Topshop outlets in major UK cities. The owners of Topshop, Sir Philip Green and his wife, were heavily criticised for their use of the Monaco tax haven to avoid UK taxes on dividends (BBC, 2010).

9   See www.financialsecrecyindex.com.

10 See http://register.consilium.europa.eu/pdf/en/09/st16/st16473-re01.en09.pdf.

shell companies and other legal persons. This amendment radically transforms the activities of many SIE tax havens, which use Anglo-Saxon trust laws and nominee company directors as the principal basis for shielding clients from external investigation.

The strengthened STD is likely to be agreed in 2010 and implemented by 2012. The revised model will probably become the global standard for international information exchange, with a number of Latin American countries indicating that they would like an opportunity to pilot this standard with EU support.[11] In addition to strengthening its STD, the EU's Code of Conduct Group on Business Taxation has required the removal of tax measures deemed harmful to the Single Market. The powers of this Group have also extended to dependent territories, some of which have been required to alter radically their tax regimes to remove preferential treatments targeted at companies registered but not trading in tax havens. The British Crown Dependencies, for example, have had their domestic corporate tax regimes overturned on the basis that they 'ring-fence' preferential treatments from local investors (Houlder, 2009). EU intervention has forced Guernsey, the Isle of Man and Jersey to transform their tax regimes, with the latter facing significant structural budget deficits as it struggles to finance public spending while also retaining some attractions as a tax haven.

Unlike in 2000, tax havens are now finding it difficult to resist international pressure for reform (Palan et al., 2010). This is partly because some of them, the Cayman Islands and Jersey, for example, themselves face severe budgetary pressures. As noted earlier, the former has been required by the UK government to introduce new taxes to overcome a severe structural budget deficit (Mathiason, 2009). Attempts to coordinate a counter-attack against anti-tax haven measures have been inhibited by strong campaigns in France, Germany and the UK sparked by revelations of how banks operating from Liechtenstein and Switzerland have actively supported tax evasion by wealthy clients.[12] In the US, public opinion was mobilised during the 2008 presidential campaigns by Barack Obama's regular references to an office block in Grand Cayman that houses over 12,000 registered businesses: 'either this is the largest building in the world or the largest tax scam in the world. And I think the American people know which it is. It's the kind of tax scam that we need to end' (Evans, 2009).

11 In January 2010 the Tax Justice Network, working in partnership with the Inter-American Centre of Tax Administrations, launched a pilot project involving three Latin American countries that have indicated interest in negotiating multilateral information exchange treaties with the EU countries.

12 See civil society letter to G20 Finance Ministers on 28 October 2009 in the run-up to the G20 Saint Andrews conference, signed by Eurodad, LatinDad, TJN, CIDSE, GFI, Christian Aid, Oxfam, Action Aid and the Plateforme Paradis Fiscaux et Judiciaires.

It is unlikely that the initiatives set in motion in 2009 will cause the demise of all tax havens; but there is little doubt that the combination of measures by the OECD and EU will restrict the activities of existing actors and radically reduce their ability to resist requests for international cooperation in tackling tax evasion. As a result of international pressure, banking secrecy laws will probably be degraded to the point of being disabled within the course of the coming decade (*Financial Times*, 2009), and calls are being made for trusts and shell companies to be made more transparent (Global Financial Integrity et al., 2009). Cumulatively this will reduce the scope of many SIE tax havens that rely heavily on secrecy as their prime attraction.

It is not clear whether the islands will be able to resist the current wave of initiatives against tax evasion as they did in the early 2000s. Their successful counter-attack against the OECD Harmful Tax Competition initiative used accusations of 'fiscal colonialism' against the OECD countries, and portrayed the battle as a 'brave fight' of the small and 'powerless' against the 'cartel' of OECD countries (Mitchell, 2001; Sanders, 2002). More recently, accusations have been made about a 'witch-hunt' against Caribbean tax havens (Hutchinson-Jafar, 2009), but the inclusion of Austria, Luxembourg and Switzerland on the 2009 Grey List undermines the earlier arguments about OECD tax havens 'ganging-up' against their SIE rivals, and additionally, many of the functional SIE tax havens wish to shed their image as bolt-holes for tax evaders and consequently do not want to be seen to be publicly resisting pressures to negotiate tax information exchange agreements with third-party countries.

What happens next?

In 2005, Richard J. Hay, a London-based lawyer acting as adviser to SIE tax havens, strongly advised his clients to support the OECD's 'on request' model for information exchange, as the alternative, the EU's automatic exchange process, would significantly affect demand for offshore private wealth management (Hay, 2005). OECD countries have sought to establish the on-request model as the global standard, and the majority of tax havens listed on the OECD Grey List in April 2009 are negotiating the minimum of 12 Tax Information Exchange Agreements (TIEAs) required to secure upgrade to the White List. Meanwhile, however, the goal posts are moving rapidly. The OECD has already indicated that it regards 12 TIEAs as the absolute minimum and expects the bar to rise. It has also initiated a peer review process to monitor how effectively the tax havens are meeting their treaty obligations. At the same time political pressure in support of automatic information exchange has increased significantly since the 2009 G20 London Summit. By the end of 2010, the OECD intends to release its guidelines on country-by-country reporting by multinational companies, which will make it significantly easier for national tax authorities to detect profits shifting to tax havens. Cumulatively these pressures are eroding the secrecy space that many tax havens depend on to attract their clients (Hampton, 1996b).

In the course of the past decade several of the less functional SIE tax havens have retrenched from financial services (for example, Samoa, Vanuatu and the Cook Islands: ABC Radio Australia, 2009), or closed down their OFCs entirely (Niue, Nauru and the Marshall Islands). In the Western hemisphere, the Turks and Caicos Islands were placed under direct rule from Whitehall in 2009 after a British government Commission of Enquiry concluded that there was 'a high probability of systemic corruption' by elected members of the Turks and Caicos Islands.[13] The Cayman Islands are struggling to bridge a structural budget deficit, and the British Crown Dependencies face EU pressure to replace their 'harmful' corporate tax regimes and also join the automatic information exchange system of the EU's STD. Unlike in 2001, when a friendly US administration rode to their rescue, the SIE tax havens lack powerful political allies who will intervene on their behalf.

Jersey case study

In 2009, in the midst of global financial market crisis, the value of deposits held in Jersey fell by approximately 20 per cent, and the value of funds under administration fell by 30 per cent (McRandle, 2010a). The island's OFC had already been hit the previous year by falling demand for securitised debt: two Jersey law firms, Ogiers and Mourants, were leading specialists in these debt instruments. In May 2009, a panel of economic advisers to the island's Chief Minister warned that a £60m 'black hole' structural deficit is likely by 2012 (*Jersey Evening Post*, 2009), and in October 2009 the Chief Minister reported that after consultation with a UK government minister he had been advised that 'the UK felt that other Member States are increasingly unlikely to accept their stance that the fiscal regimes in the Crown Dependencies are fully compliant with the EU Code of Conduct on Business taxation' (Le Sueur, 2009). For the first time in decades, Jersey faces the possibility that its OFC industry might not be sustainable at its current scale: a plan B is required (Body, 2010).

Jersey, however, displays many of the problems of 'collective myopia' noted by MacKinnon et al. (2007). Echoing Hassink's (2005: 253) observations elsewhere, having previously been able to rely on large taxable profits of the multinational banks and law firms, the States of Jersey were under scant pressure to attract investment in other sectors or pay anything more than lip-service to economic restructuring. The island's tourism industry has been largely crowded out (Hampton and Christensen, 2007) and talk of attracting inward investment into new sectors, including information technology, a full-

---

13 The Commission of Enquiry report is available at www.fco.gov.uk/en/news/latest-news/?view¼PressS&id¼20517220.

service university, or 'creative industries' (McRandle, 2010b), appears wishful thinking.

At the level of functional lock-in, the OFC sector, which directly accounts for around one-quarter of the economically active population and over 50 per cent of gross value added in the local economy, dominates the labour and commercial property market, and crowds out prospects for diversification: 'financial capital appears to be able to out-compete other industries, particularly tourism, to gain dominance within the local political economy' (Hampton and Christensen, 2007: 1,014).

Considering the issue of political lock-in, Christensen and Hampton (1999: 186) described the sector's capture of the island's polity: 'Having established predominance, the financial services sector used its political power to secure additional fiscal and regulatory advantages'. Political power is exerted through a number of players, including Jersey Finance (the OFC's marketing arm), plus a large number of industry associations representing banks, law firms, trust and company administrators, hedge funds, the local branch of the Institute of Directors, the Jersey Chamber of Commerce and Industry, and powerful labour unions representing staff employed in the sector. These actors have been highly successful in securing favourable regulatory and tax treatment, even to the extent that they have been able to draft and dictate financial laws (Mitchell et al., 2002). Palan et al. (2010: 187) argue that the political independence of Jersey and similar islands 'is more apparent than real, for their developmental and social goals are subject to the whim of foreign capital'. Senator Stuart Syvret, a senior politician in the States of Jersey, described its government as a 'legislature for hire' (BBC, 1996).

Concerning cognitive lock-in by decision-makers in Jersey, Hampton and Christensen (2007: 1,011) described how 'key players (in Jersey) failed to comprehend the long-term implications of the crowding-out issue and lacked the political power to represent their interests'. For many decades Jersey's key politicians have assumed that the EU could not extend its powers to include Crown Dependencies and that the UK government would intervene to protect their autonomy on tax matters. This is clearly no longer the case: the powers of the EU Code of Conduct Group on Business Taxation extend to the Crown Dependencies and the Group has required their respective governments to remove 'harmful tax practices' such as the 'ring-fencing' of tax-exempt status to non-resident companies.

Despite clear evidence that their existing tax regimes constituted harmful tax practices as defined by the EU, Jersey officials are largely dismissive of efforts to strengthen international cooperation. For example, the Chief Executive Office of Jersey Finance, Geoffrey Cook (2009), commented that:

> An unlikely alliance of tax hobbyists, left wing newspapers, trades
> unions, and development agencies has catalysed around calls for

greater concentration of the means of wealth creation in the hands
of governments, and implicitly greater taxation of business and
wealthy individuals through the outlawing of wealth structuring and
planning, together with restrictions on cross border capital flows.
They hope that their own constituencies will be beneficiaries of this
new 'contract', with the authors; the tax hobbyists, gaining fame
and funding, and their supporters feeling validated in their enduring
distrust of the wealthy and their advisers.

Despite having been warned in 2006 by a number of experts, including one
of the authors of this paper,[14] that proposed amendments to their corporate
tax regime (the so-called Zero-Ten tax policy) would be rejected by the Code
of Conduct Group, in 2007 the States of Jersey adopted measures that were
indeed deemed unacceptable in 2009.

Similarly, the Jersey authorities continue to refuse to adopt automatic
information exchange within the framework of the EU's Savings Tax Directive.
This decision, confirmed in November 2009, runs counter to their claims to be
a transparent and well-regulated jurisdiction that cooperates with combating
cross-border crime. In practice, Jersey's lack of financial market transparency,
its weak international treaty arrangements for information exchange and its
unwillingness to cooperate with the EU led to its being ranked 11th out of
60 in Tax Justice Network's 2009 Financial Secrecy Index (Financial Secrecy
Index, 2009). Although the tide appears to have shifted significantly against
tax avoidance (Blackhurst, 2010), the Jersey authorities remain committed
to business as usual, indeed during discussions in March 2010 between one
author and Members of the States of Jersey, he was told that the expectation
is that a change of UK government in mid 2010 will reverse the tide of EU
measures against tax havens;[15] but even so, Jersey has been badly affected by
the severe tax competition between the Crown Dependencies, and now faces
having to implement considerable tax hikes in the short- to medium-term to
cover the missing revenue.

Conclusions

Tax havens have, in the recent past, shown an ability to resist successfully
external attempts to close down their activities (Palan et al., 2010). However,
the powerful coalitions of interests involved in initiatives launched since the mid
2000s are strongly motivated to take action, not least because of the budgetary
crises facing so many developed and less-developed countries. For this reason
it would be unwise for small islands hosting significant OFCs to ignore the
stronger international cooperation measures being promoted by the EU and

14 John Christensen was Economic Advisor to the States of Jersey from 1987 to 1998.
15 Personal communication with John Christensen, March 2010.

the OECD, and the potential changes to international financial reporting standards for multinational companies. Cumulatively these measures could radically strengthen the international financial architecture and significantly increase transparency, which will inevitably diminish opportunities for corporations and individuals to use tax havens for tax avoidance. It would equally be unwise for small islands to count on being able to muster the political support they were able to draw upon when resisting the 2000 OECD anti-tax haven initiative (Palan et al., 2010), as the focus for political change no longer lies on blacklisting specific jurisdictions, but on targeted measures designed to increase financial market transparency and strengthen international cooperation on tax matters. Examples of such measures include the tax information exchange treaties being promoted by the G20 and the OECD, and the international financial reporting standard for country-by-country reporting by multinational companies that the OECD has committed to adopt as a guideline before the end of 2010 (Houlder, 2010b).

Some tax haven islands, including Jersey, are already facing unprecedented budgetary pressures; but they have limited scope for reducing their dependence on offshore financial services. With approximately one-quarter of its economically active population directly employed in the OFC, and the majority of the remaining workforce employed in secondary sectors such as construction, distributive trades and catering, there is virtually no alternative skills base on which new industries can draw. This path dependence has been reinforced by the extraordinarily high costs of land and labour, which have crowded out pre-existing industries. Taking measures to diversify the local economy will therefore require politically unpalatable steps to reduce the domestic cost base significantly.

Unlike Vlcek (2008) – who appears broadly optimistic, arguing that the 'pessimism' of Hampton and Christensen (2002) concerning the OFCs' future did not happen and that they are in fact thriving – we have argued here that the present context is radically altered. Specifically, this paper has argued that tax havens hosted in small islands cannot ignore the exogenous shock to global financial capitalism caused by banking crises in 2007 and 2008, or the subsequent economic crises that have engulfed many countries in what is likely to be the most protracted recession since the 1930s. Recognition of this new world, and the implicit exogenous shock, is even seen in the (otherwise arguably timid) Foot Review (Foot, 2009a, 2009b) of the UK's offshore centres.[16]

Small island hosts of offshore finance cannot just hope that the status quo might somehow be maintained, or that the new international coalitions will somehow dissipate, leaving them free to remain as hosts of lucrative tax haven

---

16 Interestingly, the Foot Review remit did not include London, arguably the largest and most significant offshore finance centre (and tax haven) in the global financial system.

activity. Path dependency theory would suggest that the past actions and policy choices of the small island hosts themselves have contributed significantly to the serious predicament that they now find themselves in, and consequently the extremely limited economic development possibilities that remain open to them.

We would suggest that the future may be austere for many small island hosts of offshore finance. In the worst case scenario, islands could face a crash of real estate and land prices, significant emigration off-island where the most mobile leave (as in the recent cases of Iceland and Ireland) and a deep financial crisis of the local state. For non-independent island economies such as the UK Overseas Territories – or conceivably Crown Dependencies such as Jersey – this could result in increased direct control from the UK. For independent small island jurisdictions, the economic crisis could require IMF emergency loans to keep the economy afloat. In many cases, we would suggest that the outlook for small island hosts of offshore finance is bleak as there is scant evidence of the existence of a practical or realistic alternative 'plan B'.

References

ABC Radio Australia (2009) 'Tax haven clean-up hurts the Pacific', 27 Aug., www.radioaustralia.net.au/pacbeat/stories/200908/s2668920.htm (accessed 23 March 2011).

D. Acemoglu, S, Johnson and J. Robinson (2002) 'Reversal of fortune: geography and institutions in the making of the modern world income distribution', *The Quarterly Journal of Economics* 117 (4), pp. 1,231–94.

H. Armstrong and R. Read (2006) 'Geographical "handicaps" and small states: some implications for the Pacific from a global perspective', *Asia Pacific Viewpoint* 47 (1), pp. 79–92.

G. Austin (2008) 'The "reversal of fortune" thesis and the compression of history: perspectives from African and comparative economic history', *Journal of International Development* 20, pp. 996–1,027.

G. Baldacchino (2006) 'Managing the hinterland beyond: two ideal-type strategies of economic development for small island territories, *Asia Pacific Viewpoint* 47 (1), pp. 45–60.

BBC (1996) 'Close up: a storm in a haven', broadcast on BBC2, 13 Nov.

— (2010) 'Topshop's flagship London store hit by tax protest', BBC News, 4 Dec., www.bbc.co.uk/news/uk-11918873.

G. Bertram (2007) 'Reappraising the legacy of colonialism: a response to Feyrer and Sacerdote', *Island Studies Journal* 2 (2), pp. 239–54.

C. Blackhurst (2010) 'How the tide turned against the tax avoiders', *London Evening Standard*, 11 March, www.thisislondon.co.uk/standard/article-23814309-how-the-tide-turned-against-the-tax-avoiders.do.

P. Body (2010) 'What's in store now that the UK sees any kind of blatant tax planning as unacceptable?' *Jersey Evening Post*, 18 Feb., www.thisisjersey. com/2010/02/18/whats-in-store-now-that-the-uk-sees-any-kind-of-blatant-tax-planning-as-unacceptable/.

L. Briguglio (1995) 'Small island states and their economic vulnerabilities', *World Development* 23 (9), pp. 1,615–32.

J. Christensen and M.P. Hampton (1999) 'A legislature for hire: the capture of the state by Jersey's offshore financial centre', in Mark Hampton and Jason Abbott (eds.), *Offshore Finance Centres and Tax Havens: The Rise of Global Capital* (Basingstoke: Macmillan), pp. 166–91.

G. Cook (2009) 'A taxing fundamentalism'. Comment by Geoff Cook, Jersey Finance website, www.jerseyfinance.je/Media/Comments-from-Geoff-Cook/A-Taxing-Fundamentalism/.

D. Evans (2009) 'Coca-Cola, Oracle, Intel use Cayman Islands to avoid US taxes', Bloomberg, 5 May, www.bloomberg.com/apps/news?pid¼206011 03&sid¼aWoQkk2WY1oc.

J. Feyrer and B. Sacerdote (2009) 'Colonialism and modern income: islands as natural experiments', *The Review of Economics and Statistics* 91 (2), pp. 245–62.

Financial Secrecy Index (2009), www.financial.secrecyindex.com.

Financial Times (2009) 'Closing the havens'. Editorial, 16 Aug., www. financialtaskforce.org/2009/08/17/closing-the-havens/.

M. Foot (2009a) *Progress Report of the Independent Review of British Offshore Financial Centres*, April (London: HM Treasury).

— (2009b) *Final Report of the Independent Review of British Offshore Financial Centres*, Oct. (London: HM Treasury).

Global Financial Integrity, Christian Aid, Global Witness, Tax Justice Network (2009) 'The links between tax evasion and corruption: how the G20 should tackle illicit financial flows, Civil Society proposals to the G-20 in advance of the Pittsburgh Summit', www.financialtaskforce.org/wp-content/uploads/2009/09/illicit_financial_flows_asks_for_g20-2.pdf.

G. Grabher (1993) 'The weakness of strong ties: the lock-in of regional development in the Ruhr area', in G. Grabher (ed.), *The Embedded Firm: On the Socio-economics of Industrial Networks* (London: Routledge).

A. Gurria (2009) 'The end of the tax haven era', *The Guardian*, 31 Aug., www.guardian.co.uk/commentisfree/2009/aug/31/economic-crisis-tax-evasion.

M.P. Hampton (1996a) *The Offshore Interface. Tax Havens in the Global Economy* (Basingstoke: Macmillan).

— (1996b) 'Creating spaces. The political economy of island offshore finance centres: the case of Jersey', *Geographische Zeitschrift* 84 (2), pp. 103–13.

M.P. Hampton and J. Christensen (2002) 'Offshore pariahs? Small island economies, tax havens and the re-configuration of global finance', *World Development* 30 (9), pp. 1,657–73.

— (2007) 'Competing industries in islands: a new tourism approach', *Annals of Tourism Research* 34 (4), pp. 998–1,020.

R. Hassink (2005) 'How to unlock regional economies from path dependency? From learning region to learning cluster', *European Planning Studies* 13 (4), pp. 521–35.

R.J Hay (2005) 'Beyond a level playing field: free(r) trade in financial services'. Paper presented at the STEP Symposium, London, 19–20 Sept., p. 6.

V. Houlder (2009) 'Ports in a storm', *Financial Times*, 18 Nov.

— (2010a) 'OECD hails tax haven crackdown', *Financial Times*, 19 Jan., www.ft.com/cms/s/0/c9c2af7e-050a-11df-aa2c-00144feabdc0. html#axzz1jpjy1KVr.

— (2010b) 'Treasury aims to end tax outflows', *Financial Times*, 11 Feb., www.ft.com/cms/s/0/e070175a-163c-11df-8d0f-00144feab49a.html.

L. Hutchinson-Jafar, (2009) 'Caribbean fears witch-hunt in tax haven crackdown', *Jamaica Observer*, 8 May, www.jamaicaobserver.com/ magazines/Business/html/20090507T220000-0500_151005_OBS_ CARIBBEAN_FEARS_WITCH_HUNT_IN_TAX_HAVEN_ CRACKDOWN.asp.

International Herald Tribune (2009) Editorial: 'If Switzerland can ...', 21 Aug., p. A16.

Jersey Evening Post (2009) 'Another black hole', 6 May, www.thisisjersey. com/2009/05/06/another-black-hole/.

La Tribune (2009) 'Ils veulent en finir avec les paradis fiscaux', 4 March, p. 1, www.latribune.fr/journal/archives/edition-du-0403/155766/ils-veulent-en-finir-avec-les-paradis-fiscaux.html.

Le Monde (2009) 'Londres ou New York sont aussi des paradis fiscaux', interview with John Christensen, 24 March, www.lemonde.fr/la-crise-financiere/article/2009/03/24/john-christensen-londres-ou-new-york-sont-aussi-des-paradis-fiscaux_1171954_1101386.html.

T. Le Sueur (2009) 'Letter to members of the States of Jersey relating to discussions with UK government about the position of the EU Code of Conduct Group on Business Taxation', www.taxresearch.org.uk/ Blog/2009/10/14/the-crown-dependencies-do-not-comply-with-the-eu-code-of-conduct/.

D. MacKinnon, A. Cumbers, A. Pike and K. Birch (2007) *Evolution in Economic Geography: Institutions, Regional Adaptation and Political Economy*, Working Paper 12, Nov., Centre for Public Policy for Regions, University of Glasgow.

H. McRandle (2010a) 'Fall in deposits and funds last year', *Jersey Evening Post*, 26 Feb., www.thisisjersey.com/2010/02/26/sharp-fall-in-deposits-and-funds-last-year/.

— (2010b) 'Creative industries to replace finance?', *Jersey Evening Post*, 11 March, www.thisisjersey.com/latest/2010/03/11/creative-industries-to-replace-finance/ (accessed 14 March 2010)

A. Markoff (2009) 'Part 1: the early years—1960's: the Cayman Islands: from obscurity to offshore giant', *Cayman Financial Review*, 14 (first quarter), www.compasscayman.com/cfr/cfr.aspx?id¼108.

R. Martin and P. Sunley (2006) 'Path dependence and the evolution of the economic landscape', *Journal of Economic Geography* 6 (4), pp. 395–438.

N. Mathiason (2009) 'Financial hurricane shakes the tax havens', *The Observer*, Business Section, 6 Sept., p. 7.

A. Mitchell, P. Sikka, J. Christensen, P. Morris and S. Filling (2002) *No Accounting for Tax Havens* (Basildon, Essex: Association for Accountancy and Business Affairs).

D. Mitchell (2001) 'CFP strategic memo on OECD strategy', Centre for Freedom and Prosperity, Washington, 15 May, www.freedomandprosperity.org/Papers/m05-15-01/m05-15-01.shtml (accessed 14 March 2010).

R. O'Brien (1992) *Global Financial Integration. The End of Geography* (London: Pinter).

OECD (1998) *Harmful Tax Competition: An Emerging Global Issue* (Paris: OECD).

R. Palan (2003) *The Offshore World. Sovereign Markets, Virtual Places and Nomad Millionaires* (Ithaca: Cornell University Press).

R. Palan, R. Murphy and C. Chavagneux (2010) *Tax Havens: How Globalization Really Works* (Ithaca: Cornell University Press).

Y. Park (1982) 'The economics of offshore finance centres', *Columbia Journal of World Business* 17 (4), pp. 31–35.

B. Quérée (2009) 'Tax crisis as EU attacks', *Jersey Evening Post*, 14 Oct., p. 1.

R. Sanders (2002) 'The fight against fiscal colonialism. The OECD and small jurisdictions', *The Round Table* 91 (365), pp. 325–48.

P. Scott (2001) 'Path dependence and Britain's "coal wagon problem"', *Explorations in Economic History* 38 (3), pp. 366–85.

J. Sharman (2006) *Havens in a Storm. The Struggle for Global Tax Regulation* (Ithaca, NY: Cornell University Press).

Tax Justice Network (2005) *The Price of Offshore* (London: TJN).

W. Vlcek (2007) 'Why worry? The impact of the OECD harmful tax competition initiative on Caribbean offshore financial centres', *The Round Table* 96 (390), pp. 331–46.

— (2008) 'Competitive or coercive? The experience of Caribbean offshore financial centres with global governance', *The Round Table* 97 (396), pp. 439–52.

World Bank (2005) *A Time to Choose. Caribbean Development in the 21st Century*, Report No. 31725-LAC (Washington, DC: World Bank).

M. Zaki (2010) *Le Secret Bancaire est Mort, Vive l'évasion Fiscale?* (Lausanne: Éditions Favre).

Chapter 9

Contingent liability or moral hazard after the global financial crisis: Cayman, Westminster and global finance

William Vlcek

Introduction

This chapter considers two aspects of United Kingdom (UK)-Overseas Territory (OT) relations that achieved some prominence in recent years and are potentially interconnected. The first concerns the matter of government finances and the degree to which an OT government can pursue its own revenue-generating activities and accrue a quantity of sovereign debt, before it encounters the second aspect. The second issue discussed here concerns the position of the UK for what it argues is its 'contingent liability' arising from the actions and activities of an OT. In other words, how far can an OT go – financially, legally, politically – along a path before the UK would be 'obligated' to bail it out, an action that in the aftermath of bank bailouts during the global financial crisis is politically fraught in Westminster. The specific OT discussed in this chapter is the Cayman Islands, with the analysis drawing on a set of confidential interviews held in November 2010 in George Town, Grand Cayman, as well as reports and public documents produced by the governments in Westminster and George Town over the past decade.[1]

The next section provides a brief history/background to Cayman as an OT and as an offshore financial centre (OFC), including a few observations on the impact of the global financial crisis and the nature of an OFC as understood in the Foot Review, which was produced to assess the impact of the global financial crisis on a selection of UKOTs and Crown dependencies. The third section considers the issue of government finance, presenting first the case made in the Foot Review and the subsequent report commissioned by the government of the Cayman Islands at the direction of the Foreign and Commonwealth Office

1   Fieldwork for this chapter was generously supported by a research grant from the Carnegie Trust for the Universities of Scotland.

(FCO) to assess the specific case of Cayman. While specifically about Cayman, and therefore not directly transferable to the situation in any other OT, this case offers some points of reference for consideration by the governments of other UKOTs. The fourth section moves into the specific topic of 'contingent liability'; I will henceforth refrain from the use of 'scare quotes' anticipating readers' understanding that I find the concept problematic in the context of the political relationship between Britain and an OT. In part, the term represents the fear that should an OT default on its governmental (sovereign) debt the UK risks being obligated to reimburse the bondholders. This concern is fundamental to UK perceptions of Cayman government debt, as examined in the third section – though arguably, as discussed below, the Foot Review represented a specific political economic viewpoint about offshore finance as a service industry in Cayman as much as it reflected a concern that Westminster could find itself subject to claims from bailiffs seeking payment for delinquent OT debts. The chapter closes with a few concluding observations.

Setting the scene

The Cayman Islands has been a unique territory since Europeans first arrived in the 16th century. These three small islands (Grand Cayman, Little Cayman, and Cayman Brac) are located 240 kilometres south of Cuba and 268 kilometres northwest of Jamaica with a population estimated by the CIA's *World Factbook* at 51,384.[2] Acknowledged as a British colony in the 17th century, the Cayman Islands territory was not suitable for the plantation economy prevalent on the other Caribbean islands and consequently developed into a home for escaped slaves and those Europeans (some with slaves) that found the ungoverned nature of the Cayman Islands preferable to other Caribbean colonies. Cayman also served as a source of supplies for the privateers and pirates operating in the Caribbean during the 18th century, a historical label occasionally applied today to the financial services sector).[3] Because of its small size, limited economic power and small population, the Cayman Islands was structured as a 'colony of a colony' under the Governor of Jamaica until 1962 when Jamaica headed down the path to sovereign independence and the Cayman Islands resolved to retain its relationship with the UK as an OT (Bodden, 2007).

The pivotal feature behind the acquiescence on the part of the UK towards restructuring and reforming the political relationship with the Cayman Islands, at that particular time and continuing today, is the fact that Cayman is not, and never has been, 'aid dependent'. On the contrary, this small territory's

---

2   See www.cia.gov/library/publications/the-world-factbook/ (accessed 12 May 2011).
3   For example, C. Mortished (2004) 'Pirates of the Caribbean refuse to play ball on tax havens'. Times Online, http://business.timesonline.co.uk/article/0,,8210-996741,00.html (accessed 26 March 2004).

viability as an independent sovereign state is not of concern (see McIntyre, 1996: 253), because in the late 1950s the Cayman economy benefited from inflows of US dollar remittances sent home by the men serving in the US merchant fleet. In turn the development of the offshore financial centre has continued to negate any need for direct financial support from the UK. 'One thing seems crystal clear and that is the UK's willingness to entertain the Cayman Islands' request was primarily based on the fact of the islands financial independence' (Bodden, 2010: 85). In sum, the government of the UK had no problem with Cayman continuing as a dependent territory because there would be little direct financial cost from the relationship. It is only in recent years that the concept of contingent liability has emerged to motivate direct action by the UK with regard to negative events in its OTs, for example, the Turks and Caicos Islands in 2009 (Clegg, 2010).[4]

In terms of the historical development of Cayman as an OFC it has never collected income tax, relying instead on import tariffs and duties in addition to the remittances of the Caymanians serving with US merchant ships under a special visa regime between the Cayman Islands and the US following World War II. Economic independence and development as a territory of the UK would be achieved via the emulation of the financial services industry then emerging in the Bahamas and Bermuda; the first step was the enactment of legislation on companies to attract foreign capital (Cayman Islands National Archive, 1960–1). And it should be acknowledged that this strategy for an offshore financial services industry was initiated at a time when jurisdiction was held over a population of approximately 8,000, a rather small foundation on which to build what was to become a world-leading financial centre.

The later history of the Cayman Islands offshore financial centre has been related in a number of works (Roberts, 1995; Hudson, 1998; Montgomery, 2001; Vlcek, 2008b: 126–30) and general publications (Doggart, 1982; Doggart, 1997; Doggart, 2002; Williams et al., 2005; General Accounting Office, 2008). And the popular media frequently adopted Cayman as a trope representing a foreign haven for illicit and illegal money. But one perspective – of offshore finance before the economic crisis took hold (and global finance unravelled, unwound and precipitously declined) – was fairly benign. In 2007

---

4   As discussed further in the fourth section of this chapter, the concept of contingent liability in the OTs was raised publicly by the National Audit Office (1997). This concept has a longer history, however, within the UK government. In a lecture, presented at the Institute of Commonwealth Studies in 2006, Mike Summers, member of the Falkland Islands Legislative Council, described some of the difficulties encountered when crafting UK legislation to license fishing activity in the Falklands Interim Conservation Zone. Significantly, in 1987 he found 'politicians and civil servants more worried about contingent liabilities and multi-lateral agreements than real development' (Summers, 1996).

a special report on offshore finance in *The Economist*, entitled 'Places in the sun',[5] related the travails of regulators in controlling 'hot money' and pursuing financial criminality in the case of OFCs serving as intermediate waypoints. The report also highlighted the extent to which multinational corporations successfully arbitraged between national tax regimes in order to minimise their total tax bill. This frequently involved an OFC part of the network in which the multinational corporate structure has evolved (see Desai, 2009). Tax arbitrage is not the sole rationale for establishing a subsidiary firm (international business company) in the Cayman Islands or the British Virgin Islands (BVI). The high incidence of Chinese International Business Companies (IBCs) in the Caribbean has been attributed as representing 'round tripping' or capital augmentation (Vlcek, 2008a; Sutherland et al., 2009). Beneath the surface detail of tax arbitrage that was highlighted at the 2009 G20 meeting in London (Guthrie, 2009; Morais, 2009) rests a far more complex structure developed over decades as multinational corporations have sought to operate profitably across the legal and financial systems of multiple jurisdictions.

Consequently, some global initiatives for international standards and best practices have been created over the past two decades to resolve some of the inconsistencies and variance between national regulatory regimes. The initiatives promulgating financial regulation and enforcement were one area identified in the Scope statement for the 'Independent Review of British Offshore Financial Centres' whose final report was released in October 2009.[6] The report set the scene by specifying the size of international financial flows through the nine jurisdictions reviewed – 'those Crown Dependencies and Overseas Territories with significant financial centres', specifically Guernsey, Jersey, Isle of Man, Anguilla, Bermuda, BVI, Cayman Islands, Gibraltar and Turks and Caicos Islands (Foot, 2009: 61–2). The inclusion of Anguilla and the Turks and Caicos Islands suggests to this author that there was a *political* justification for their inclusion, rather than the use of any quantitative economic evaluation to determine a 'significant financial centre' (Foot, 2009: 61). While the Turks and Caicos Islands territory has a separate line in the Bank for International Settlements (BIS) dataset for International Banking Statistics, the foreign assets on deposit were minute compared to the other centres. Between 1984 and 2010, foreign assets on deposit exceeded US$500 million in 14 quarters (2006;

5   'Places in the sun' special report, The Economist, 22 Feb. 2007, www.economist.com/node/8695139?story_id=8695139.
6   In the 'Terms of Reference' for the Foot Review the scope of the review was 'to identify opportunities and current and future risks (and mitigation strategies) to their long-term financial services sector, including: financial supervision and transparency; taxation, in relation to financial stability, sustainability and future competitiveness; financial crisis management and resolution arrangement; and international co-operation' (Foot, 2009: 61).

2007; fourth quarter of 2008; and fourth quarter of 2009 to the end of 2010). In the case of Anguilla, any data on foreign assets is subsumed by the synthetic jurisdiction 'West Indies UK'; which includes Anguilla, Antigua and Barbuda, BVI, Montserrat and St Kitts and Nevis.[7] Consequently, we should expect that the majority of assets reported on deposit for West Indies UK in the data reported to the BIS are in fact on deposit in the BVI financial centre, as the remaining jurisdictions possess small to non-existent offshore financial centres.

The Foot Review offered a comparison of the assets and liabilities of a set of financial centres, juxtaposing the UK OTs with Ireland, Luxembourg and Switzerland as representative 'competitor' jurisdictions (which may or may not be viewed as a competitor by any individual OT financial centre). A similar comparison is offered here in Table 1, using data from the *BIS Quarterly Review*, Table 6A, 'External positions of reporting banks vis-à-vis all sectors' (Bank for International Settlements, 2011).

The data column in Table 1, showing foreign assets on deposit for 2007, roughly represents the high-water mark prior to the financial crisis taking hold of the global economy. The data from 2005 provides an indication for the trend line in that jurisdiction prior to the global financial crisis, while the figures for the recorded holdings at the end of 2010 indicate the extent of post-global financial crisis recovery for the financial sector in these jurisdictions. The scope of this chapter prevents detailed analysis of any of the jurisdictions listed here as more detailed data on the specific circumstances for each case would be necessary before reaching any conclusions about the extent of recovery (as measured by foreign assets on deposit) in Cayman as compared to Gibraltar, Ireland or Jersey. Briefly, however, one factor involves the type of depositor – the figure for Cayman reflects the large presence of institutional accounts – while the BVI (West Indies UK) represents the assets for the IBCs registered in that jurisdiction. It is a similar situation for Hong Kong SAR and Mauritius, with a significant portion of the foreign assets on deposit in fact reflecting the assets for IBCs registered in those jurisdictions and operating in China and India respectively.

This comparative exercise, however, does not give much of a sense of the importance of these OFCs, and in particular Cayman, within the global financial system (Foot, 2009: 15–22). A network analysis graphic, produced in a study by economists at the BIS, situated the OFC as a significant intermediary node in the network for global flows of capital (McGuire and Tarashev, 2006: 35). Similarly, in October 2010 the International Monetary Fund (IMF) released a report, *Understanding Financial Interconnectedness*, which also made an effort to understand the network structures forming the global financial system and the potential for this situation of 'interconnectedness' to produce

7   The definition has been published in Dixon, 2001 and verified with BIS staff members in 2007, personal communication, 23 July 2007.

Table 1. Foreign assets on deposit (millions USD)

Jurisdiction	2005	2007	2010
European exemplars			
Ireland	612,557	1,188,240	832,657
Luxembourg	555,819	949,534	922,786
Switzerland	593,516	1,051,299	606,183
UK Overseas & Crown Territories			
Bermuda	77,632	102,669	87,467
Cayman Islands	1,242,949	1,905,316	1,726,006
Gibraltar	8,508	21,465	11,632
Guernsey	98,855	171,932	115,197
Isle of Man	19,582	37,527	32,805
Jersey	285,656	504,120	224,811
Turks and Caicos	484	536	584
West Indies UK (Anguilla, BVI)	64,666	112,789	119,546
Other leading OFCs			
Bahamas	195,324	248,323	367,611
Barbados	9,280	20,185	18,189
Hong Kong SAR	192,444	286,002	424,825
Mauritius	5,589	14,011	19,943
Singapore	277,617	421,738	469,500

Source: Bank for International Settlements, BIS Quarterly Review (June 2011), Table 6A

'systemic risk concentrations' as a result. The latter report provides a brief case example positioning a number of OFCs as nodes in the network for the Greek tragedy that was central to the EU sovereign debt crisis in the first half of 2010 (Moghadam and Viñals, 2010: 19).

Undoubtedly there is an indeterminate amount of illegal and illicit funds, embedded within these global capital flows, that represents a source for contingent liability in the OFCs, UK and elsewhere. The Foot Review's observation that 'Legislation is, however, only as good as its enforcement' (Foot, 2009: 52) is, in and of itself, a valid point, though it is a statement equally applicable to all legislation and not just those laws concerned with financial criminality. The externally-driven assessments for compliance, conducted either by the IMF or the Caribbean Financial Action Task Force (CFATF), were utilised to provide a point of comparison among the jurisdictions evaluated by the Review. For this analysis, however, the Foot Review report did not make a comparison to other jurisdictions with a financial centre or a significant financial services sector.[8] For example, one measure used for evaluating the success of detection activities in a jurisdiction is the number of Suspicious Transaction Reports (STRs) submitted by the financial services and non-financial services businesses required to do so, and the subsequent conversion of a suspicion into a court case leading to a criminal conviction. The size of these simple arithmetical measurements is variable, not simply in the case of UKOTs as the Foot Review found, but also among larger jurisdictions. The report notes that among the OTs

> ... the numbers of STRs in 2008 were lower than might be expected
> in Anguilla (30) and the British Virgin Islands (153), both of which
> have international business companies as their international niche.
> On the face of it, the number of STRs in the Turks and Caicos Islands
> also appears low (50) (Foot, 2009: 53).

For a wider perspective on this issue, consider that for calendar year 2009 the United States Financial Crimes Enforcement Network (FINCEN) reported that it had received 1,281,305 STRs, while in the UK the Serious Organised Crime Agency (SOCA) reported that for the period October 2008–September 2009 it received 228,834 STRs (Financial Crimes Enforcement Network, 2010; Serious Organised Crime Agency, 2009). The point here is that this simple method of counting STRs to evaluate a jurisdiction's accomplishments with respect to financial criminality, while measurable, is not indicative of the extent of criminal assets in the financial system or the actual effectiveness of the regime against financial crime. The large quantity of STRs in the US and

---

8 A more comprehensive analysis for the operation and impact of these regulatory measures in small jurisdictions with an OFC is provided by Sharman and Mistry, 2008.

UK does not result in a correspondingly larger quantity of court cases and convictions.[9]

A more direct evaluation of the implementation of financial service regulation at the front-end of the process – that is, the process of registering an international business company and opening a bank account – is far more instructive. In this 'audit study of compliance with the prohibition on anonymous shell companies', J.C. Sharman found that the 'usual suspects' (Bahamas, BVI, Cayman Islands, Dominica, Nauru, Panama, and Seychelles) would not establish a company for him without the proof-of-identity documentation required by customer due diligence regulations. On the other hand, corporate registration agents in the UK and the US readily agreed to establish a company without identity documents (Sharman, 2010: 133–4). Consequently, the fact that a jurisdiction reports a large quantity of STRs in no way reflects the everyday practice of its financial firms and the potential that they could be used for illicit purposes. Rather, in the case of the US, the excessive quantity of STRs represents the everyday practice of 'defensive filing' on the part of banks. This serves to protect their reputation while significantly increasing analysts' difficulties in identifying actual criminal suspicious conduct (Chaikin, 2009; National Audit Office, 2007: 23).

As listed at footnote 6, the Terms of Reference for the Foot Review contained four specific issue areas, where financial regulation and enforcement activities against financial crime were just one. The specific item of interest here, however, concerns government finance as approached under the heading of 'taxation, in relation to financial stability, sustainability and future competitiveness'. The OFCs were advised to achieve stability, sustainability and competitiveness by implementing 'a prudent approach to managing government finances by developing: a diversified tax base to maximise sources of revenue; mechanisms to measure and control public spending; and by building financial reserves during periods of economic growth' (Foot, 2009: 31). In other words, to implement or expand the tax regime in those jurisdictions which have little or no VAT or income (personal and corporate) tax. In the case of the Cayman Islands this recommendation generated a rebuttal study, as discussed in the next section.

Government revenue in the Cayman Islands

Government finances have been a recurrent point of contention between Westminster and the OTs and, in the midst of the regulatory fallout from the global financial crisis, the Foot Review recommended the introduction of direct

---

9   In fact, in the case of the US, it has been noted that a charge of money laundering is frequently included with any felony case involving financial or physical assets (Adams, 2000).

taxation in the Cayman Islands. The first paragraph of a *New York Times* article on the subject offers one perspective, 'What happens to a tax haven when it has to raise taxes? The Cayman Islands may soon find out' (Thomas, 2009). The suggestion that direct taxation is the solution to the post-global financial crisis budget difficulties in the Cayman Islands was strongly rejected in George Town. In fact, the Cayman Islands' government funded a study that arrived at the opposite conclusion to the Foot Review. It is, as it were, a situation of duelling economic experts: on behalf of the Chancellor of the Exchequer we have Michael Foot, previous Managing Director of the UK Financial Services Authority following a long career at the Bank of England, and in Cayman's corner is James C. Miller III, a former head of the US Office of Management and Budget who has also been Chair of the Federal Trade Commission (Foot, 2009; Rahn, 2010). Achieving contrary conclusions using similar data suggests that differing approaches were taken to conduct the analysis, starting with the initial assumptions and hypotheses guiding the analysis. In other words, the question over whether or not to introduce direct taxation in the Cayman Islands (or anywhere else for that matter) is not, in point of fact, an economic question. And, notwithstanding claims made for the political neutrality of rational economic analysis, tax policy is at its most fundamental a political question. In the classic liberal economics view, taxes are a 'deadweight loss' to the economy and may encourage individuals and firms to relocate in order to match their tax obligations with the public goods provided (Tiebout, 1956; Feldstein, 1999: 679; Edwards and Keen, 1996: 131). To underscore this point, note that the Foot Review was completed under the previous Labour government, which used it to support its case in promoting direct taxation and refusing to agree an additional Cayman government loan. In June 2010, under the Conservative-Liberal Democrat coalition government in Westminster, the FCO determined that the Cayman Islands' government had taken 'positive action' in its measures to 'restore public finances to a sustainable footing' and 'had agreed in principle' additional borrowing by Cayman (Foreign and Commonwealth Office, 2010).

The case the Foot Review made for the introduction of direct taxation was framed as one element in a process leading to 'a diversified tax base to maximise sources of revenue' (Foot, 2009: 13, 29). Based on the accompanying study, *Understanding Corporate Usage of British Crown Dependencies and Overseas Territories*, completed in September 2009 by Deloitte on behalf of the Foot Review, the OTs should restructure their domestic tax regimes closer to 'international tax norms' (p. 34) to include VAT and income taxes. Deloitte's analysis was qualified with the recognition 'that given the diverse tax regimes and industry bases ... a single template for all the jurisdictions might not be appropriate' (p. 35). A detailed study for each jurisdiction was therefore recommended. The Cayman Islands did so, and the alternative case made by the Miller Commission Report pointed out that, while the various forms of income tax could raise revenue, 'they would impose high risks for the Cayman economy' (Miller et al., 2009: 74). The Commission's recommendation is that Cayman should not introduce direct taxation, notwithstanding the interest of the FCO (and in turn the UK government) in it doing so. In the short term, an income tax would generate additional revenue, but the Commission's analysis found that such an increased tax burden would hinder the Cayman economy and direct taxation could serve to encourage the 'very mobile financial services industry' to relocate. Given the significant contribution of the financial sector to government revenue and national GDP in Cayman, as it presently stands, any increased revenue is likely to shrink rapidly as financial service firms relocate business and staff (Miller et al., 2009: 91–7).

Nonetheless, the objective here is not to argue the relative merits of these two sets of recommendations with regard to reforming, improving, or otherwise changing the fiscal governance and government revenue policy in the Cayman Islands. Rather, it is to underscore the political basis for these economic decisions, returning attention to the critical challenge identified by Susan Strange many years ago (Strange, 1994: 121) – that is, the pointed question that should be at the centre of our inquiry – *cui bono*, who benefits? This issue of financial sovereignty was an important feature during the negotiations between Westminster and George Town on constitutional reform.

> In my presentation to the Foreign and Commonwealth Office I made
> it quite clear that any debate regarding constitutional modernisation
> for the Cayman Islands must take into account the financial
> sovereignty of the Cayman Islands and recognise the fact that these
> Islands have never been grant-aided by the United Kingdom (Cayman
> Islands Legislative Assembly, 2003: 796; statement of the Leader of
> Government Business, W. McKeeva Bush).

The negotiating position was 'that the United Kingdom Government should not have control of our financial affairs through Orders in Council, that is, the Privy Council, or by legislation in the Commons'. Further, the Cayman Islands sought to have the OFC in Cayman kept in mind when the UK negotiated future international agreements that might impact its operation, expecting in fact that Cayman should be consulted in advance of any agreement by the UK government (Cayman Islands Legislative Assembly, 2003: 796). In the 2009 Constitution this was reflected in part at §32, 'Exercise of the Governor's functions', in which the Governor is directed to keep the Cabinet informed of any matter that 'may involve the economic or financial interests of the Cayman Islands' (Privy Council, 2009: 24). How this function is exercised in practice remains to be seen, particularly in the context of the continued operation of the Cayman financial centre and the existing tax regime. In turn, the situation depends in part on perceptions of the Cayman OFC, and OFCs more generally, in the UK (and globally), which leads to the concern that there may be a contingent liability.

A contingent liability or the 'unknown unknown' risk?

The concept of contingent liability has been one motivation for the action of the UK government towards the OTs for over a decade. Yet the question emerged during interviews in George Town, Grand Cayman – what exactly is meant by the concept, as used by the UK government? This question is understandable in the context of a community that revolves around matters of tourism, finance and investment.[10] In its more common usage in business and finance, contingent liability means 'The possibility of an obligation to pay certain sums dependent on future events'.[11] But this definition was not the precise meaning of the term when it was applied to the roles and responsibilities of the UK towards its OTs. As discussed in George Town that day, the UK understood that, in the case of a contingent liability located in an OT, it possessed a moral obligation, rather than a clear legal obligation, to step in and cover an OT debt.[12] And from one perspective this sense of moral obligation may easily be transformed into a moral hazard; certainly, one argument frequently made in offshore finance literature is that the success of the Crown Colonies and the OTs rests on their continuing relationship with the UK and the perception among depositors and investors that the reputation (and government) of the UK supports the financial institutions located in these jurisdictions as 'lender of last resort'. Nonetheless, the understanding of the concept expressed in that conversation identified the essence of the explanation for a contingent liability offered in the 1997 National Audit Office (NAO) report on *Contingent Liabilities in the Dependent Territories*. The legal advice provided to the FCO at the time stated that under 'English and Dependent Territory law, the governments of the Territories are answerable for their own actions'. In other words, there is no legal obligation embedded in the relationship between the OTs and the UK. Yet the NAO went on to assert that, in the event an OT found itself in a situation where it was unable to meet its debt obligations, 'the UK government may come under international, political or moral pressure to assist the Territories, *despite the lack of a legal basis for such a claim*' (National Audit Office, 1997: 13; emphasis added). In other words, a moral hazard exists such that other parties would expect, and perhaps demand, that the UK government came to the aid of an OT in dire straits.

At the same time, observations over any potential liability in the case of the Cayman Islands should be balanced by the fact that Cayman has never

---

10 I bring tourism up here because 'human rights' has been identified as a contingent liability in terms of OT compliance with human rights conventions ratified by the UK and, in the case of the Cayman Islands, with the contentious issue of homosexual conduct, the decriminalisation of homosexuality and the potential for litigation when discrimination is practised against homosexuals in Cayman society (see Vlcek, 2011).

11 See www.investopedia.com (accessed 12 May 2011).

12 Confidential interview, George Town, Grand Cayman, 10 Nov. 2010.

placed an obligation on HM Treasury. 'The colony has never throughout its history been grant-aided, nor, for that matter, has it been a regular recipient of development aid or European funds' (Bodden, 2007: xix). This observation was reflected in official UK government documents concerning the Cayman Islands, for example, this statement from a draft 'Brief to the Secretary of State' dated February 1962:

> The Cayman Islands are self-supporting financially and so far as we can judge will continue to be so. They are thus unlikely to become a financial burden on the British Government, apart perhaps from ad hoc assistance in the event of a natural disaster, such as a hurricane (CO 1031/3244, Folio 54, page 2, paragraph 4).

Which raises a rather simple question in the context of a UK-based discourse over contingent liability and, given the absence of any previous aid to Cayman from Westminster, what might actually happen following a natural disaster?

The recent past offers a test case: Hurricane Ivan devastated Grand Cayman in 2004 to the point that one report had the entire island submerged under water (Tonner, 2005: 30). In an oral history interview with the Governor of the Cayman Islands in 2005, reflecting over his time as Governor, Bruce Dinwiddy was asked:

> And there was the feeling afterwards [after Hurricane Ivan] that Britain didn't help us, and that it was because of what was perceived as Cayman's recalcitrance over the EU Savings and the Gibbs business and everything. Is there any connection at all with those things?[13]

To which Dinwiddy responded that he felt perceptions existed of less support having been received from the UK than was actually the case, but he was confident that any reluctance on the part of the UK government to provide aid to Cayman had 'absolutely no connection' to these other events dominating the news and public discourse in Cayman in 2003 and 2004 prior to the hurricane (Dinwiddy, 2005: Part 3, page 20). Additional comments on the question of UK support to Cayman following Hurricane Ivan are available from an oral history interview conducted with the Cayman Islands Representative in the UK at the time it struck. Jennifer Dilbert stated that she found staff at the UK Department for International Development were dealing with issues of greater magnitude than Hurricane Ivan's impact on Cayman.

> And, you know, putting it into perspective, we just didn't ... didn't come up on their radar. And they *did* say to me, at one point, that if

13 Brian Gibbs had been the head of the Cayman Islands Financial Reporting Unit and it was alleged an 'agent of the British Government' in Cayman directed him to destroy documents. The UK government-appointed Attorney General was also accused of reporting to MI6 (Doran, 2003).

they thought Cayman wasn't going to make it, they would have found
real help, but they knew that we'd do it, that we'd pull ourselves back
up, which, of course, we did, because we're fantastic people (Dilbert,
2006: 8).

In Dominic Tonner's narrative of how events unfolded in Cayman after
the hurricane, he noted 'the value of UK aid and assistance to Cayman was in
the hundreds of thousands, rather than the millions of dollars' (Tonner, 2005:
128). He then compared this approximate figure (because 'no firm numbers are
available') with the aid provided by the UK to Grenada after Hurricane Ivan,
which was US$7 million. Additional aid was provided to the Cayman Islands
by several other countries, however, the general feeling in Cayman was that
the UK could have done more, because it is after all the administering state
(Tonner, 2005: 132–4). In line with the viewpoint from the early 1960s detailed
above, some Westminster Members of Parliament took the view that aid to
the Cayman Islands was inappropriate, since 'substantially wealthy countries'
such as the Cayman Islands and Bermuda 'should be planning contingency
reserves to meet such disasters themselves'. In the House of Commons, the
Conservative MP for Banbury, Tony Baldry (then in opposition), made this
overall assessment, 'The idea that one should take money away from very poor
people in other parts of the world to give to the Cayman Islands is wrong'
(House of Commons, 2004: 11WH).

In other words, rather than speak of a contingent liability, it may be
more useful to frame the question in terms of risk, which in turn opens the
discussion to matters of risk assessment and risk mitigation.[14] And that was
the approach followed by the NAO in its follow-up report of 2007, *Managing
Risk in the Overseas Territories*. Nonetheless, while the terminology for the most
part shifted to risk and risk mitigation, the concern for 'a commitment to the
Overseas Territories which exposed [the UK] to potential liability' remained
prominent (National Audit Office, 2007: 9). Thus, a risk assessment for
the Cayman Islands would include hurricanes, and some amount of capital
reserves and insurance policies appropriate to the normally expected hurricane
season should be established (National Audit Office, 2007: 14–18). Additional
coverage in the extreme case of a once-in-a-century hurricane such as Ivan
might also be considered. At the same time, reasonable measures to reduce the
damage likely to be caused by a hurricane should be undertaken, for example,
rewriting building codes to improve the resilience of new construction to high

14 My textbook for Public Finance and Public Choice approaches this topic differently:
the authors differentiate between risk and uncertainty, where risk is predictable
using quantitative methods to determine a probability distribution curve, while
uncertainty is the case where 'knowledge of the relevant probabilities is lacking'
(Cullis and Jones, 1998: 150). In other words, uncertainty is the unknown
unknown.

winds and flooding (Tonner, 2005: 191–6). Similar action could be taken with regard to the other risks that might affect a Caribbean island OT, that is, quarantine against infectious diseases for animals and livestock brought to the island. Nonetheless, a contingent liability is not likely to emerge from a risk that can be assessed and mitigated; rather it is the improbable event, like Nassim Nicholas Taleb's black swan, that will produce it (Taleb, 2010). Such events have the potential to exceed the capacity of risk mitigation activities rapidly as experienced, for example, by many national economies in their efforts to react to the global financial crisis. Consequently, the challenge is not a contingent liability, as understood in the technical sense, but rather a moral hazard. Risk prevention and risk mitigation measures may be instituted and followed; nonetheless, unknown unknowns remain beyond the event horizon for which general preparations alone represent the extent of possible preventive measures. In other words, the solution is simply to follow the Scout Movement's motto, 'Be Prepared'.

Conclusion

This chapter offered an analysis of two inter-related components of the Cayman Islands' continuing relationship with the UK. The nature of government finance in Cayman, as presented by the Foot Review and the Miller Commission Report, was outlined and situated in the historical circumstances of the Cayman financial centre (a significant source of government revenue and national GDP). The historical perspective highlighted the independent, self-financing nature of OT government in Cayman, most specifically in the context of the response to and recovery following Hurricane Ivan in 2004. This highly specific example of a contingent liability laid bare the thin substance behind the claim for a requirement to respond to international or moral pressure in the event of a political, economic, or natural catastrophe in an OT. The UK government's concerns over contingent liabilities or local government financial practice in an OT are very much a reflection of domestic politics in the UK. Government policy in Westminster shifts in order to follow the interests of the political party/parties in power – in this case the debt ratio, approved for the government of Cayman, changed. This action has consequently raised doubts about the stability of any proposed future policy since the next election may lead to yet another shift in operational strategy towards the OTs (a risk to be mitigated by the OT?).

It is a similar situation with regard to the level of political will among the wider community of state financial regulation as, for example, with the variable results from previous OECD efforts against 'harmful' tax competition. Shifting international dynamics combined with changing national agendas (such as the role of US domestic political change in 2001 in the case of the OECD initiative) meant that the initial impetus to promote international financial regulatory reform and strict enforcement of the same was diluted (Vlcek,

2009; Vlcek, 2008c). Similarly, there appears to have been declining interest in aggressively regulating 'tax havens', which had been prominently predicted after the April 2009 G20 meeting, for the topic subsequently evaporated off the agendas and communiqués of later G20 meetings. Consequently, in the long run, the environment in which the UKOT with an offshore financial centre operates possesses the recurring aspect of a death foretold. In 1979 the supply of offshore financial centres was deemed to exceed demand – 'it seems possible, indeed probable, that there is little unsatisfied demand for new offshore centers' (McCarthy, 1979: 48). Similarly, while a wave of liberalisation was sweeping across global financial markets in the 1980s, another author declared that 'recent international developments ... appear to threaten the future survival of offshore banking centres' (Francis, 1985: 91). The OECD initiative against tax competition in 1998 prompted yet another declaration for the pending demise of offshore finance, 'With the passage of time, the death of tax havens seems to be inevitable' (Hishikawa, 2002: 417). More recently, the OECD acted on behalf of the G20 to produce a list categorising jurisdictions based on their implementation of the OECD's 'internationally agreed tax standard' (Organisation for Economic Co-operation and Development, 2009). This response to the global financial crisis, along with other measures seeking to establish global standards intended to rein in global finance and capital flows, portends an 'austere future' for the OTs and Crown Territories hosting an OFC and could even 'result in increased direct control from the UK' (Hampton and Christensen, 2011: 178; see also chapter 7). It is noteworthy that the latter two authors, individually and jointly, have reached essentially the same conclusion in every analysis published for over a decade (Hampton, 1994; Hampton and Christensen, 1999; Christensen and Hampton, 1999; Hampton and Christensen, 2002; Hampton and Christensen, 2003).

For some observers of the offshore world, therefore, hope springs eternal (Palan et al., 2010: 234–5), yet the dynamics of the global financial system in which OFCs occupy a pivotal niche, as demonstrated by the network analysis of the BIS and IMF, must itself be restructured to a greater extent than currently proposed before the decline and disappearance of the OFC can be anticipated. As long as there is a demand for the services they provide, there will continue to exist a firm, and location, with the supply of skills, resources and connections necessary to satisfy that demand. And if it is not one of the UK's Crown Territories or OTs that provides these financial services than it will most likely be a former British colony, such as the Bahamas, Hong Kong SAR, Mauritius or Singapore, because the common law heritage left by British colonial rule is conducive to the innovative and flexible needs of an OFC. The concern that a contingent liability may exist in the financial centres of UKOTs is in fact a global problem, in turn requiring a global solution. However, experience of international efforts over the past two decades suggests that a solution is not yet at hand.

References

T.E. Adams (2000) 'Tacking on money laundering charges to white collar crimes: what did Congress intend, and what are the courts doing?', *Georgia State University Law Review* 17 (2), pp. 531–73.

Bank for International Settlements (2011) *BIS Quarterly Review: Statistical Annex*. Basel: Bank for International Settlements. Available at www.bis.org (accessed 21 June 2011).

J.A.R. Bodden (2007) *The Cayman Islands in Transition: The Politics, History, and Sociology of a Changing Society* (Kingston, Ian Randle Publishers).

— (2010) *Patronage, Personalities and Parties: Caymanian Politics from 1950–2000* (Kingston, Ian Randle Publishers).

Cayman Islands Legislative Assembly (2003) *Official Hansard Report*, 2002 Session. Available at www.legislativeassembly.ky (accessed 1 Feb. 2012).

Cayman Islands National Archive (1960–1) *Attitude of the Smaller Dependencies of the West Indies Towards the Federation* (London: UK PRO reference CO 1031/4271).

D. Chaikin (2009) 'How effective are suspicious transaction reporting systems?', *Journal of Money Laundering Control* 12 (3), pp. 238–53.

J. Christensen and M. Hampton (1999) 'All good things come to an end', *The World Today* 55 (8/9), pp. 14–17.

P. Clegg (2010) 'Governance in the UK Overseas Territories: the case of the Turks and Caicos Islands', paper presented at the conference 'Turmoil and Turbulence in Small Developing States: Going beyond Survival', held at The University of the West Indies, St Augustine, Trinidad, 24–6 March.

J. Cullis and P. Jones (1998) *Public Finance and Public Choice* (Oxford: Oxford University Press).

Deloitte LLP, *Understanding Corporate Usage of British Crown Dependencies and Overseas Territories* (a report to the Independent Review of British Offshore Financial Centres, 23 Sept. 2009).

M.A. Desai. (2009) 'The decentering of the global firm', *The World Economy* 32 (9), pp. 127–1290.

J. Dilbert (2006) *Cayman Islands National Archive Oral History Programme*, George Town, Grand Cayman, Cayman Islands National Archive, last revised 12 July.

B. Dinwiddy (2005) *Cayman Islands Memory Bank*, George Town, Grand Cayman, Cayman Islands National Archive, last revised 21 Oct.

L. Dixon (2001) 'Financial flows via offshore financial centres as part of the international financial system', *Financial Stability Review* 10, pp. 105–16.

C. Doggart (1982) *Tax havens and their uses* (London; Economist Intelligence Unit).

— (1997) *Tax havens and their uses* (London: Economist Intelligence Unit).

— (2002) *Tax havens and their uses* (London: Economist Intelligence Unit).

J. Doran (2003) 'Briton quits top legal post over Cayman spy case', *The Times* (London), 11 March. Available at www.timesonline.co.uk/tol/news/world/article1118374.ece (accessed 24 June 2011).

J. Edwards and M. Keen (1996) 'Tax competition and Leviathan', *European Economic Review* 40, pp. 113–34.

M. Feldstein (1999) 'Tax avoidance and the deadweight loss of the income tax, *Review of Economics and Statistics* 81 (4), pp. 674–80.

Financial Crimes Enforcement Network (2010) *The SAR Activity Review: By the Numbers*. Issue 14 (Washington, DC: US Department of the Treasury). Available at www.fincen.gov (accessed 1 Feb. 2012).

M. Foot (2009) *Final report of the independent Review of British offshore financial centres* (London: HM Treasury). Available at www.hm-treasury. gov.uk/indreview_brit_offshore_fin_centres.htm (accessed 1 Feb. 2012)

Foreign and Commonwealth Office (2010) *Cayman Islands: restoring public finances* 2010, last revised 8 June. Available at www.fco.gov.uk/resources/en/news/21480373/22300409/bellingham-cayman-islands-080610 (accessed 1 Feb. 2012).

C.Y. Francis (1985) 'The offshore banking sector in the Bahamas', *Social and Economic Studies* 34 (4), pp. 91–110.

General Accounting Office (2008) *Cayman Islands: Business and Tax Advantages Attract U.S. Persons and Enforcement Challenges Exist* (Washington, DC: General Accounting Office). Available at www.gao.gov (accessed 1 Feb. 2012).

J. Guthrie (2009) 'Why tax havens make such great scapegoats?', *Financial Times* (London), 2 April, sec. UK. Available at www.ft.com/cms/s/0/074e5e3e-1f1e-11de-a748-00144feabdc0.html (accessed 1 Feb. 2012).

M.P. Hampton (1994) 'Treasure islands or fool's gold: can and should small island economies copy Jersey?', *World Development* 22 (2), pp. 237–50.

M.P. Hampton and J. Christensen (1999) '*Treasure Island* revisited. Jersey's offshore finance centre crisis: implications for other small island economies', *Environment and Planning A* 31, pp. 1,619–37.

— (2002) 'Offshore pariahs? Small island economies, tax havens, and the re-configuration of global finance, *World Development* 30 (9), pp. 1,657–73.

— (2003) 'A provocative dependence? The global financial system and small island tax havens', in: F. Cochrane, R. Duffy and J. Selby (eds.), *Global Governance, Conflict and Resistance*, pp. 194–215 (Basingstoke: Palgrave Macmillan).

— (2011) 'Looking for plan B: what next for island hosts of offshore finance?', *The Round Table: The Commonwealth Journal of International Affairs* 100 (413), pp. 169–81.

A. Hishikawa (2002) 'The death of tax havens?', *Boston College International & Comparative Law Review* 25 (2), pp. 389–418.

House of Commons (2004) *The Caribbean*, Westminster Hall, 2004–2005 ed., London, *Hansard*, last revised 2 December. Available at www. publications.parliament.uk/pa/cm200405/cmhansrd/vo041202/ halltext/41202h01.htm (accessed 1 Feb. 2012).

A.C. Hudson (1998) 'Reshaping the regulatory landscape: border skirmishes around the Bahamas and Cayman offshore financial centres', *Review of International Political Economy* 5 (3), pp. 534–64.

I. McCarthy (1979) 'Offshore banking centers: benefits and costs', *Finance and Development* 16 (4), pp. 45–8.

P. McGuire and N. Tarashev (2006) 'Tracking international bank flows', *BIS Quarterly Review: International banking and financial market developments* 4, pp. 27–40.

W.D. McIntyre (1996) 'The admission of small states to the Commonwealth', *The Journal of Imperial and Commonwealth History* 24 (2), pp. 244–77.

J.C.I. Miller, D. Shaw and K. Jefferson (2009) *Addressing the Challenge of Fiscal Sustainability of the Cayman Islands: Final Report of the Independent Commission*, George Town, Grand Cayman. Available at www.gov.ky/ portal/page?_pageid=1142,4836309&_dad=portal&_schema=portal (accessed 1 Feb. 2012).

R. Moghadam and J. Viñals (2010) *Understanding Financial Interconnectedness*, 100410 (Washington, DC: International Monetary Fund). Available at www.imf.org/external/np/pp/eng/2010/100410.pdf (accessed 1 Feb. 2012).

M. Montgomery (2001) 'A portrait of success: the rise of the Cayman Island as an offshore financial center', *Revista Mexicana del Caribe* 6 (12), pp. 33–83.

R.C. Morais (2009) 'Critics say tax haven crackdown falls short', *Forbes*, 23 June. Available at www.forbes.com/2009/06/23/offshore-tax-evasion-switzerland-personal-finance-taxes-havens.html (accessed 1 Feb. 2012).

National Audit Office (1997) *Foreign and Commonwealth Office: Contingent Liabilities in the Dependent Territories*, HC 13 Session 1997–8 (London: The Stationery Office).

— (2007) *Foreign and Commonwealth Office: Managing Risk in the Overseas Territories* (London: The Stationery Office). Available at www.official-documents.gov.uk/document/hc0708/hc00/0004/0004.asp (accessed 1 Feb. 2012).

Organisation for Economic Co-Operation and Development (2009) *A Progress Report on the Jurisdictions Surveyed by the OECD Global Forum in Implementing the Internationally Agreed Tax Standard*, Paris, OECD Publications, last revised 2 April. Available at www.oecd.org (accessed 1 Feb. 2012).

R. Palan, R. Murphy and C. Chavagneux (2010) *Tax Havens: How Globalization Really Works* (Ithaca and London: Cornell University Press).

Privy Council (2009) *The Cayman Islands Constitution Order 2009*. Statutory Instruments, 2009 No. 1379, At the Court at Buckingham Palace, last revised 10 June. Available at www.legislation.gov.uk/uksi/2009/1379/contents/made (accessed 1 Feb. 2012).

R.W. Rahn (2010) 'Saving Cayman: the Miller Commission', *Cayman Financial Review*, 14 April. Available at www.compasscayman.com/cfr/2010/04/14/Saving-Cayman--The-Miller-Commission/ (accessed 1 Feb. 2012).

S.M. Roberts (1995) 'Small place, big money: the Cayman Islands and the international financial system', *Economic Geography* 71 (3), pp. 237–56.

Serious Organised Crime Agency (2009) *The Suspicious Activity Reports Regime Annual Report 2009* (London: Serious Organised Crime Agency). Available at www.soca.gov.uk/about-soca/library (accessed 1 Feb. 2012).

J.C. Sharman (2010) 'Shopping for anonymous Shell companies: an audit study of anonymity and crime in the international financial system', *Journal of Economic Perspectives* 24 (4), pp. 127–40.

J.C. Sharman and P. Mistry (2008) *Considering the Consequences: The Development Implications of Initiatives on Taxation, Anti-money Laundering and Combating the Financing of Terrorism* (London: Commonwealth Secretariat).

S. Strange (1994) *States and Markets* (London and New York: Pinter Publishers).

M. Summers (2006) *Good Government and Development in the Falkland Islands*, address to the Institute of Commonwealth Studies, London, 16 June 2006 (copy on file with the author).

D. Sutherland, A. El-Gohari and B. Mathews (2009) 'Round Tripping' or 'Capital Augmenting' OFDI: Chinese Outward Foreign Direct Investment and the Caribbean Tax Havens, paper presented at the *3rd China Goes Global Conference*, Harvard University, Cambridge, USA, 30 Sept.–2 Oct.

N.N. Taleb (2010) *The Black Swan: The Impact of the Highly Improbable* (London: Penguin Books).

L. J. Thomas (2009) 'Offshore haven considers a heresy: taxation', *New York Times* (New York) 4 Oct. Available at www.nytimes.com/2009/10/04/business/global/04cayman.html (accessed 1 Feb. 2012).

C.M. Tiebout (1956) 'A pure theory of local expenditures', *The Journal of Political Economy* 64 (5), pp. 416–24.

D. Tonner (2005) *Ivan: The Full Story - The storm that changed a nation forever*, George Town, Grand Cayman, Focus Communications.

W. Vlcek (2008a) 'From road town (BVI) to Shanghai: FDI, IBCs and global capital flows'. Paper presented at the Third Biennial Oceanic Conference on International Studies (OCIS), School of Political Science and International Studies, held at University of Queensland, Brisbane Australia, 2–4 July.

— (2008b) *Offshore Finance and Small States: Sovereignty, Size and Money* (Basingstoke: Palgrave Macmillan).

— (2008c) 'Competitive or coercive? The experience of Caribbean offshore financial centres with global governance', *The Round Table* 97 (396), pp. 439–52.

— (2009) 'The Caribbean confronts the OECD: tax competition and diplomacy', in A.F. Cooper and T.M. Shaw (eds.), *The Diplomacies of Small States* (Basingstoke: Palgrave Macmillan).

— (2011) 'Sovereignty games in the British Caribbean: the experience of the Cayman Islands', paper presented at the conference, Micropolities in the Margins of Europe – Postcolonial Sovereignty Games, held at University of Greenland, Nuuk, 18–19 April.

O.H. Williams, E.C. Suss and C. Mendis (2005) 'Offshore financial centres in the Caribbean: prospects in a new environment', *The World Economy* 28 (8), pp. 1173–88.

Chapter 10

Self-governance deficits in Caribbean non-independent countries

Carlyle Corbin

Introduction

Although much of the Caribbean has achieved political independence, the region remains one of the most constitutionally diverse in the world, with three distinct sets of non-independent Caribbean countries (NICCs). These comprise: 1) non-self-governing territories (NSGTs); 2) self-governing autonomous countries (SGCs); and 3) integrated jurisdictions (IJs). The nature of these increasingly complex political arrangements presents significant challenges to the sustainability of democratic governance in the wider Caribbean region, and to the Caribbean integration process. This analysis provides an updated composition of the Non-Independent Caribbean reflecting recent political and constitutional changes including the dismantling of the Netherlands Antilles; constitutional modifications in the British-administered territories in the Caribbean; and political status and internal constitutional deliberations in United States-administered Puerto Rico and the US Virgin Islands. The contemporary composition of the Non-Independent Caribbean is now markedly different from that which prevailed before 2010 (Corbin, 2001: 139). In this connection, the present examination provides illustration of the self-governance deficit in NICCs, and devises a political formula based on the existent power relationship between the individual non-independent country and the respective metropole. It is precisely the nature of this relationship which must be assessed in order to determine the level of preparedness of an NSGT for a full measure of self-governance, or whether a NICC which is said to have already achieved a full measure of self-governance through autonomy or integration has in fact met the criteria for either option as defined by internationally recognised standards.

Changing composition of the non-independent Caribbean

The composition and categorisation of the non-independent Caribbean reflects periodic political and constitutional changes. As such, these overseas countries and territories continue to evolve, often under increasingly complex dependency, autonomous or integrated arrangements ranging from some internal colonial reform to political fragmentation. Internationally recognised classifications used to define those which are non self-governing, self-governing or integrated remain the most accurate benchmark in assessing self-governance for the Caribbean. The categorisation did not change significantly during the 1990s and through most of the first decade of the new century – a reflection of only internal constitutional developments having taken place in some of the NICCs (Corbin, 2009b: 254).

It was only in the last quarter of 2010 that the categorisation of the non-independent world altered to reflect noteworthy political changes in a number of the countries. This has resulted in corresponding modifications in nomenclature for the benefit of further clarity. Thus, the 'self-governing territories' are better described as 'self-governing autonomous countries' (SGCs) in recognition of their non-'territorial' status consistent with a certain level of autonomy. Similarly, the term 'Integrated Territories' (ITs) formerly used has been modified to 'Integrated Jurisdictions' (IJs) to reflect the fact that the French departments were no longer 'territories' in the classic sense following the attainment of full political integration into the French Republic; while the new Dutch 'public entities' are only partially integrated.

Non Self-Governing Territories (NSGTs)

Seven of the 16 territories formally listed by the United Nations (UN) as non self-governing are located in the Caribbean/Atlantic (Anguilla, Bermuda, British Virgin Islands, Cayman Islands, Montserrat, Turks and Caicos Islands, and the US Virgin Islands). Although some internal constitutional adjustments have been made or are ongoing in a number of NSGTs, the powers delegated to the NSGTs – as opposed to devolved to them – have proven to be clearly reversible (as in the case of the Turks and Caicos Islands), with the imbalance of power remaining intact, reinforced and strengthened.

Despite their democratic deficiencies, many of these territories are part of various regional cooperation mechanisms through membership in regional organisations such as the Caribbean Community (CARICOM), the Organisation of Eastern Caribbean States (OECS), and the UN Economic Commission for Latin America and the Caribbean and its regional subsidiary, the Caribbean Development and Cooperation Committee (CDCC). Two (Anguilla and Montserrat) share the Eastern Caribbean currency with independent states of their sub-region, whilst others maintain separate currencies (Bermuda and Cayman Islands). The British Virgin Islands and

Turks and Caicos Islands – dependencies of the United Kingdom – use the US dollar.

No legitimate acts of self-determination have been undertaken in the Caribbean NSGTs in several decades. A political status referendum in 1993 in the US Virgin Islands conducted under administering power law on an excessive number of seven options yielded inconclusive results, whilst four attempts to draft a constitution based on the present dependency status proved unsuccessful with a draft constitution based on the current dependency status resulting from a fifth constitutional convention awaiting revision by the middle of 2011. Regarding Puerto Rico, a number of referenda have been held on political status options during the 1980s and 1990s serving to reinforce the political stalemate which has delayed the self-determination process. The latest referendum process being pushed by the pro-integrationist government in the Commonwealth in 2011 would give the voters a choice between retaining a territorial status and one which is non-territorial, with a second phase between integration and independence if the non-territorial option is originally selected.

For the British-administered territories, referenda have rarely been used to help shape their status with the 1995 Bermuda vote on 'independence – yes or no' as the only modern illustration – and even then only one option was on the ballot. As a result of strong civil society pressure, a referendum was held in the Cayman Islands in 2009 on the 'modernised' constitutional order. Referenda were not utilised in the case of the earlier 2006 Turks and Caicos Islands Constitutional Order (before its suspension by the UK), in the British Virgin Islands Constitutional Order of 2007, or the Montserrat Constitutional Order which came into force in the autumn of 2011. Instead, these were endorsed by the respective legislative bodies of the three dependencies. Meanwhile, subsequent calls by the leader of the Turks and Caicos Islands Progressive National Party (PNP) for a referendum on a new, lesser autonomous, constitutional order completed for the territory by the British halfway through 2011, in the wake of the suspension of elected government in 2006, were readily dismissed by the British Government. In any event, none of the internal constitutional reforms were meant to alter the underlying power dynamic and political status of the territories in question, and the Turks and Caicos Islands Constitutional Order of 2011 significantly reverses much of the delegated autonomy contained in the previous 2006 version. In the final analysis, none of these internal constitutional procedures could be considered as legitimate acts of self-determination.

Notwithstanding, it is often projected that these territories are content with their respective political dependency arrangements, and that they exercise a full measure of self-governance. However, this is not consistent with the objective reality in the territories where varying degrees of dissatisfaction with the democratic deficiencies of the prevailing political arrangements have been expressed by elected leaders with varying degrees of support from civil society.

The fact remains that the existing constitutional arrangements emerging from the colonial reform process fall well short of international standards for full self-governance with absolute political equality.

Self-Governing Autonomous Countries (SGCs)

It is in the category of self-governing autonomous countries (SGCs) that noteworthy changes have occurred. Emerging from the dismantlement of the erstwhile autonomous country of the Netherlands Antilles occurring on 10 October 2010 was the addition of the two new self-governing autonomous countries (SGCs) of Curaçao and Sint Maarten, and the creation of three partially integrated jurisdictions (IJs) – termed 'public entities' – of the Netherlands (Bonaire, Sint Eustatius and Saba). This has resulted in three new European Union (EU) borders in the Caribbean with resulting implications for Caribbean integration, security and sovereignty. Unlike the UK reticence toward referenda, the changes in the former Dutch autonomous country of the Netherlands Antilles were initiated by respective referenda in each of the five islands comprising the erstwhile autonomous country between 2000 and 2005, and after subsequent extensive deliberations with the Dutch Government on the terms and conditionalities of the changes. The referendum process was not flawless, however, as the results – particularly in the smaller islands of Bonaire and St Eustatius – were subject to differences in interpretation between the Dutch and island officials with Bonaire attempting a second referendum with a fuller range of political options (OTR, 2010a: 1).

Accordingly, the number of SGCs in the region increased from three to four, with the new autonomous models in Curaçao and Sint Maarten joining Aruba which had initiated the fragmentation process in 1986, but which was not affected by added controls by the Kingdom government applied to Curaçao and Sint Maarten. The legitimacy of the fourth Caribbean self-governing model in Puerto Rico has been increasingly questioned in the international discourse (Corbin, 2001: 239), whilst the integrationist and independence parties, and the free association wing of the Commonwealth party, dismiss the autonomist nature of the model as insufficient to meet contemporary international standards of autonomous governance.

The political fragmentation of the former autonomous Netherlands Antilles described above, and the addition of the three Dutch 'public entities' to the existent three French integrated departments of Guadeloupe, Martinique and French Guiana, doubled to six the number of integrated jurisdictions (IJs) in the Caribbean, fully or partially integrated with member states of the EU (France and the Netherlands).

Integrated Jurisdictions (IJs)

Additional changes in the governance structure of the French overseas (integrated) department of Guadeloupe and its erstwhile dependencies constituted a separate political fragmentation process with respect to the islands of (French) St Martin and St Bartholomey (St Barts), both of which heretofore had been under the administrative jurisdiction of Guadeloupe. Recent arrangements now provide for separate collectivity status for St Martin providing direct ties with France rather than via Guadeloupe, with the evolution of a similar status for St Barts in progress in mid 2011.

The possibility of a fundamental shift from political integration to a more autonomous arrangement for Martinique and French Guiana (similar to the model of French Polynesia) was considered by the voters of the two overseas departments in referenda in 2010. This was a year after labour unrest due to low wages and high prices arose in the French Antilles as a whole, and in La Réunion (Indian Ocean). The vote was overwhelmingly against more autonomy with 79 per cent saying 'no' in Martinique, 55 per cent of the electorate having participated, while 70 per cent of the voters were against more autonomy in French Guiana, with 48 per cent of eligible voters casting ballots. No referendum was held in Guadeloupe. Media reports reflect that the reluctance of the people to pursue more autonomy was fuelled by fears that a change of status would lead to a reduction in financial support from Paris – a position which French President Nicolas Sarkozy made quite clear in public statements in the run-up to the referendum (France 24, 2010: 1). Some regarded the timing and nature of the presidential statement as unwarranted interference. It was further argued that the negative vote was influenced by a lack of information and clarity about the type of autonomous model on offer.

As a consequence of the referenda, the respective political statuses of Martinique and French Guiana will remain unchanged, albeit with internal adjustments promised by the French Government being undertaken aimed at providing more flexibility within the integrated framework. On the other hand, the emerging new collectivities of St Martin and St Barts, the new partially integrated jurisdictions of the Netherlands (BES), as well as the new self-governing autonomous countries of Curaçao and Sint Maarten, are all still evolving in the early stages of their new status arrangements, with a number of issues to be sorted out, including:

- The relationship with the EU of the new, partially integrated Dutch 'entities' and the emerging French collectivities in relation to whether the L'Outre-Mer with the EU (formerly Ultra-Peripheral Territory status) should be sought. This would allow for the full extension of EU law in contrast with the Overseas Countries and Territories (OCT) status which is designed for the autonomous countries.

- The disposition of a new Caribbean Guilder that would be pegged to the US dollar to replace the Netherlands Antilles Guilder, and that would be shared by the new SGCs of Curaçao and Sint Maarten respectively, through a joint central bank (*Daily Herald*, 2010: 1). Alternatively, the outright adoption of the US dollar (not the Euro) remains under active discussion in the three SGCs, with Aruba seriously considering a possible switch to the US dollar from its dollar-pegged 'Florin' currency which had been the national currency for 25 years.

- The implications of the adoption of the US dollar as the official currency of Bonaire, St Eustatius, and Saba – rather than the Euro – even as the three jurisdictions have become partially integrated with a Eurozone state, along with limitations on their voting rights, political representation and social benefits within the Kingdom. Further, the applicability of Dutch and EU laws were having predictable inflationary and other impacts (Amigoe, 2010: 1).

These recent changes and implications in dependency and autonomous governance are reflected in Tables 1 and 2 denoting the present composition of the non-independent Caribbean, Atlantic, Pacific and other regions.

Applicable international standards of political equality

International instruments

The international norms establishing minimum standards for a full measure of self-governance are derived primarily from international law and principles beginning with the UN Charter, coupled with subsequent international conventions and UN resolutions providing greater specificity. The Covenant of the League of Nations pursuant to Article 23 was the first international instrument to deal with the evolution of peoples under non self-governing arrangements, with its reference to securing 'just treatment of the native inhabitants' of such territories (Igarashi, 2002, 7). Thus, the UN at its adoption in 1945 provided international legitimacy to the companion processes of self-determination and decolonisation through concrete references in its Charter. Accordingly, both chapter I of the UN Charter on Purposes and Principles, and chapter IX on International Economic and Social Co-operation, highlight the critical importance of 'equal rights and self-determination of peoples'.

The Declaration on Non Self-Governing Territories contained in Chapter XI of the UN Charter gives definition to the principle of self-determination. Accordingly, the Charter affirms that those UN member states which administer territories which have not yet attained a full measure of self-government recognise, *inter alia*, the obligation to ensure the cultural integrity of the people

Table 1. Non-Independent Island Countries

Caribbean/Atlantic/Other (2011)		
Non-Self Governing Territories (as listed by the UN)	**Self-Governing Countries (recognised by the UN)**	**Integrated Juristictions (partially or fully)**
Anguilla (UK) (b, d, f)	Aruba (Neth.) (f)	Guadeloupe (Fr.)
Bermuda (Atlantic, UK) (b)	Sint Maarten (Neth.) (g)	Martinique (Fr.)
Virgin Islands (UK) (b, d, f)	Curaçao (Neth.) (g)	French Guiana (Fr.)
Cayman Islands (UK) (b, f)	Puerto Rico (US) (e, f)	Saint Barthélemy (Fr.)
Montserrat (UK) (c, d, f)	St Eustatius (Neth.)	Saint Martin (Fr.)
Turks & Caicos Islands (UK) (b, f)	Greenland (Denmark) (a)	Bonaire (Neth.)
US Virgin Islands (US) (f)	Faroe Islands (Denmark) (a)	Saba (Neth.)
St Helena (South Atlantic, UK)		

a) Model contains attributes of substantial autonomy with shared citizenship of the metropole including political rights and representation
b) Associate membership of The Caribbean Community (CARICOM)
c) Full member of CARICOM
d) Associate member of the Organisation of Eastern Caribbean States (OECS)
e) The metropole has determined that Puerto Rico is an un-incorporated territory. As such, Puerto Rico would be placed in the category of non self-governing territories if the UN makes the adjustment
f) Associate member of the UN Economic Commission for Latin America and the Caribbean; and the Caribbean Development & Cooperation Committee
g) International Organisation participation, previously held by the former Netherlands Antilles, to be determined for the two autonomous countries of Curaçao and Sint Maarten

Table 2. Non-Independent Island Countries

Asia/Pacific (2011)		
Non-Self Governing Territories (as listed by the UN)	**Self-Governing Countries (recognised by the UN)**	**Integrated Jurisdictions (voluntarily or annexed)**
American Samoa (US) (c)	Northern Mariana Islands (US) (c)	Hawaii (US)
Guam (US) (c)	Cook Islands (NZ) (c, e)	Alaska (US)
Kanaky/New Caledonia (Fr.) (a, c)	Micronesia Fed. States (US) (b, d)	Rapa Nui (Chile)
Tokelau (NZ) (f)	Niue (NZ) (c, e)	
Pitcairn (UK)	Belau/Palau (US) (b, d)	
	Te Ao Maohi/Fr. Polynesia (Fr.) (a, c)	
	Wallis and Futuna (Fr.) (a, c)	
	Marshall Islands (US) (b, d)	

a) Model contains aspects of autonomy with shared citizenship of the metropole
b) Free associated state with separate citizenship, full membership in the UN and limitations on defence and foreign affairs
c) Associate member of the UN Economic and Social Commission for Asia and the Pacific (ESCAP)
d) Full member of ESCAP
e) Substantial autonomy with shared citizenship of the metropole
f) Associate member of the UN Educational, Scientific and Cultural Organisation (UNESCO)

concerned, and to foster their political, economic, social and educational advancement. The obligation includes the development of self-government through free political institutions (UN Charter, 1945: 46–7). Similar provisions are contained in Chapter XII of the Charter governing the territories which were formerly under the trusteeship system, although this category is presently vacant. Chapters I, IX and XI of the UN Charter have been repeatedly cited as the basis for prescriptive remedy to address the persistent democratic deficits inherent in the remaining dependency governance arrangements. The Chairman of the UN Decolonisation Committee in 2005 elevated the global discussion on the issue in characterising decolonisation as the unfinished agenda of the UN, and emphasised the criticalness of bringing the remaining dependent territories in line with a full measure of self-governance consistent with international principles (Hunte, 2005: 1).

In addition to the UN Charter, other international instruments apply great weight to the international legal mandate of the promotion and subsequent realisation of full political equality as a fundamental human right. The most relevant of these instruments are the International Covenant on Civil and Political Rights (ICCPR) and the International Covenant on Economic and Social Rights (ICESR), both of which affirm the right of peoples to self-determination. Of particular note is Article 1 of both conventions, recognising the responsibility of administering states to promote the realisation of the right to self-determination. Both conventions are generally accepted as pre-emptory norms of *jus congens* (Aguon, 2008: 140–1). The Convention on the Elimination of Racial Discrimination (CERD) has similar provisions giving further weight to the international legal basis for the realisation of self-determination which is intended to culminate in a full measure of self-governance. Orellana argues that 'the self-determination of peoples was among the purposes and principles on which the Charter of the United Nations (1945) was based … (and) while not every statement of political principle in the (UN) Charter creates legal obligations, the inclusion of self-determination – especially in the context of purposes – placed it in a privileged position for subsequent interpretations regarding its legal meaning and consequences' (Orellana, 1998: 6).

Implementation of UN Resolutions

Resolutions adopted by the UN General Assembly since its first session in 1946 provide a lengthy and comprehensive legislative authority to carry out the mandate through prescriptive remedies in addressing the democratic deficits which characterise the dependency arrangements classified as non self-governing under the United Nations Charter (Hunte, 2005: 2). Whilst many of the territories achieved full self-government pursuant to these UN resolutions – and were removed from non self-governing designation – others remain formally listed as such, while some have been relegated to the dependency periphery (Corbin, 2009a: 84) where adjustments to their arrangements may have rendered them below the threshold of full self-governance but outside international scrutiny as there is no standard UN process of re-evaluation save a resolution to this effect proposed by a UN member state before the world body.

The implementation of these prescriptions contained in long-standing UN resolutions slowed significantly in the early 1990s following the independence of Namibia and the end of the Cold War, with a new perception increasingly propagated by the states which administered territories that the self-determination process culminating in decolonisation was an issue whose time had passed. In this vein, the UK withdrew its cooperation from the UN Decolonisation Committee in 1986 (Thomson, 1986: 1), with the US following suit in 1991 (Bolton, 1991: 1).

The persistence of self-governance deficiencies in the dependency arrangements therefore should not come as a surprise given the ineffective implementation of the UN's decolonisation agenda which had still not been completed in 2011 – more than 50 years after the UN adopted the Decolonisation Declaration in 1960. In the 2010 independent expert assessment of how far the Second International Decade for the Eradication of Colonialism's plan of action had been carried out, the implementation deficit was systematically examined (OTR, 2010: 7–12).

Despite the dearth of implementing action and repetition of bureaucratic process, the resolutions remain an integral component of the ever-growing legislative authority. This constitutes the applicable standards of political equality, and complements the relevant international instruments, to form a set of clearly defined minimum standards key to the identification of self-governance deficits in non-independent countries. These applicable resolutions have been continuously reaffirmed and refined by the UN General Assembly from its first session in 1946 to its most recent 65th session in 2010. The resolutions included a number of landmark instruments, such as the 1960 Decolonisation Declaration which was the main legislative instrument underpinning the independence movements in Africa and much of the Caribbean and Asia/Pacific. When Namibia gained independence at the beginning of the 1990s, the process of decolonisation slowed, with only one territory, Timor Leste, achieving a full measure of self-government since then, even as two international decades were adopted by the UN General Assembly to bring about full self-governance consistent with the ever-expanding legislative authority. The Assembly adopted a third International Decade for the Eradication of Colonialism (IDEC) at the end of 2010 with consultations on a new plan of action ongoing into 2011 (UN General Assembly Resolution, 2010c: 1–2).

As the UN commemorated the 50th anniversary of the Decolonisation Declaration in December 2010, the prevailing understanding that full self-governance was to be achieved through independence, free association or integration continued to be endorsed by UN General Assembly resolutions. These affirmed, *inter alia*, the right of the peoples of the dependent territories to self-determination in conformity with 'the legitimate political status options', based on the principles clearly defined in (UN) General Assembly 1541 (XV) and other relevant resolutions and decisions (UN General Assembly Resolution, 2010b: 1–2). On behalf of Cayman Islands civil society, Pineau affirmed prior to the 2011 UN Caribbean Regional Seminar on Decolonisation in St Vincent and the Grenadines that 'UN guidelines for self-determination are as applicable today as they were when they were first drafted' and expressed the view that civil society did 'not regard the introduction of a new administrative arrangement between the administering power and her territory as a sincere attempt to advance the progress towards self-determination' (Pineau, 2011: 5–8).

Notwithstanding these recognised criteria, significant democratic deficits remain in place in the NSGTs' and autonomous countries' governance arrangements, despite the international standards long affirmed by the world community. Although these standards of political equality remain in force, there is little indication that self-governance indicators have been utilised in the 'case-by-case' approach of international examination of each territory – at least, in the few cases where case-by-case examination has been applied. Yet, an objective determination of self-governance sufficiency can only be made if specific indicators of minimum standard are utilised.

Assessment of the self-governance mandate

A 2006 assessment of the prevailing legislative authority, completed at midterm of the Second International Decade for the Eradication of Colonialism, provided a critical analysis of the implementation of the relevant UN resolutions to that point (OTR, 2006: 1–5). This offered new insights on emerging thought regarding the parameters for full self-governance, and reflected an increasing measure of flexibility in the 21st century for the remaining island territories. Within the realm of a more flexible approach to assessing the prevailing governance arrangements, proper care was taken in the assessment to maintain adherence to minimum standards of self-governance so as to avoid the temptation of lending legitimacy to the deficient dependency arrangements, for the sake of political and bureaucratic expediency.

However, the lack of implementation of the prescribed measures contained in UN resolutions created an unfortunate political vacuum. It therefore became somewhat expedient, as early as the 1980s, to re-define existent dependency arrangements as acceptable forms of self-governance without regard for the applicability of self-governance standards. This began with the UK's 1986 formal withdrawal from co-operation with the UN Decolonisation

Committee (Thomson, 1986: 1), with the US following suit in the early 1990s (Bolton, 1991: 1). Since that time this colonial accommodation strategy has accelerated through challenges to the continued applicability of international law and principles to contemporary self-governance (Corbin, 2009b: 260–6). Thus, a number of dependency models reflecting self-governance deficiencies were devised, put into effect and subsequently projected as self-governing alternatives for the dependent territories (Corbin, 2009a: 89–92). No model, however, was considered to be fully self-governing. Simultaneously, the British declared the autonomist option of free association, as a recognised legitimate political status option defined in Resolution 1541 (XV), to be no longer 'on offer' to the dependencies under its administration (Rammell, 2003: 1–2) – a decision the distinguished Caribbeanist, Sir Howard A. Fergus, referred to as 'uncompromising'. (Fergus, 2011: 6)

The choices, then, were narrowed down to either continued dependency or independence with a short transitional period. This position was at odds with long-standing international principles and consensus resolutions of the General Assembly which recognised the legitimacy of the three options of independence, free association and integration. However, the earlier referenced strategic withdrawal of cooperation from the UN decolonisation review process by the UK removed the opportunity for member states to gain clarification on the inconsistency of supporting resolutions affirming the legitimacy of free association for the territories under UK administration at the same time as informing them that it was not 'on offer.'

In the case of the current autonomous countries in the region, the existence of residual powers of unilateral action on the part of the dominant partner in the autonomous arrangements were projected as either consistent with a more flexible governance model (in the case of the erstwhile Netherlands Antilles) or outside of international oversight (in the case of Puerto Rico, French Polynesia, et al.). These conditions have relegated the 'autonomous' country model in the Caribbean to the 'dependency periphery' (Corbin, 2009a: 84–5), without sufficient self-governance to meet the established criteria, but yet beyond the jurisdiction of the UN decolonisation review process.

On the whole, international human rights mechanisms in Geneva could prove an effective alternative approach to thoroughly examining and subsequently addressing the decolonisation dilemma given the implementation deficit concerning UN General Assembly resolutions and in view of the limited resources made available to service the UN decolonisation agenda. In this connection, the proposed programme budget for the Decolonisation Unit of the UN Department of Political Affairs for the biennium 2012–13 recommends the abolition of two posts, from five to three persons, even as the UN General Assembly has called for increased emphasis in the decolonisation area by adopting the Third International Decade for the Eradication of Colonialism (UN Budget, 2011: 28; UN General Assembly Resolution, 2010c: 1–2), and reporting requirements on the implementation of the decolonisation mandate have been eliminated.

The 2006 assessment earlier cited examined resolutions as far back as 1952–3 which had initiated the process of identifying a full measure of self-governance through the political options of independence, internal self-government and integration. It was recognised, even at this early stage, that for the standard for internal self-government to be met, 'freedom from control or interference by the government of another State in respect of the internal government' of the territory was required along with the need for 'complete autonomy in respect of economic and social affairs' (UN General Assembly Resolution, 1952: 1). In 1953, the UN emphasised in its resolution that 'self-government can be achieved by association with another State or group of States if this is done freely and on the basis of absolute equality' (UN General Assembly Resolution, 1953: 1).

These important baseline principles, adopted and applicable during the period, were used as the foundation for assessing the acquisition of a full measure of self-governance in Puerto Rico, Greenland, Netherlands Antilles and Suriname during the 1950s. Based on the prevailing doctrine of the time, these erstwhile dependencies had become sufficiently autonomous to have them de-listed from non self-governing status (OTR, 2006, 2). The modality of their deletion from UN oversight, however, did not provide for an administrative mechanism to facilitate a later reassessment of the new 'autonomous' political arrangements in the light of changing political circumstances warranting such re-consideration. Thus, the re-listing of a former non self-governing territory has only occurred in the case of New Caledonia in 1986 (UN General Assembly Resolution, 1986: 1).

Prevailing standards of self-governance

The adoption of the landmark Decolonisation Declaration of 1960 (Resolution 1514 XV), and its companion resolution of the same year on a full range of equality options (Resolution 1541 XV), gave further clarity to emerging prerequisites for the attainment of a full measure of self-government sufficient to remove a territory from the UN list of non self-governing territories. The Declaration re-emphasised the right to self-determination whilst requiring the transfer of all powers, without any conditions or reservations, to the people of the territories in advance of an act of self-determination. This obviated the prevailing unilateral applicability of administering power laws and regulations, including those governing voter eligibility, which influence the electoral process and lead to results not necessarily reflective of the people's wishes in that territory.

Resolution 1541 (XV) further refined the principle of 'absolute political equality', earlier identified in 1953, with the identification and elaboration of the three options of independence, free association and integration. This established a standard for full self-governance, which remains applicable on its merits, and is the norm against which present non self-governing arrangements are judged. Although a subsequent resolution in 1970 (Resolution 2625 XXV) made reference to other political status options freely determined by the people as a method leading towards the fulfilment of self-determination, it in no way implied that the minimum level of political equality, as identified in the three recognised options, would be set aside. Thus, it was never the intention of the General Assembly to legitimise political dependency models which did not provide for a full measure of self-government (OTR, 2006: 3). Resolution 2625 (XXV) has often been misrepresented as a sort of legislative authority for colonial accommodation and legitimisation, but this interpretation has been readily dismissed as inconsistent with the attainment of real self-governance for the remaining island dependencies.

Measures for the achievement of self-governance

Although UN resolutions in the 1970s and 1980s intensified the re-affirmation of principles earlier adopted, resolutions subsequently adopted further defined the actions necessary in implementing the mandate. They can be grouped in a number of substantive areas:

•   *Self-determination and democratic governance*
The resolutions continually call for a specific timetable that people of the territories can follow to exercise their right to self-determination, and for the administering powers to expedite a process which will prepare the people to exercise freely and without interference their right to self-determination, consistent with internationally recognised principles. To this end, consistent references focus on fostering awareness among the people regarding the political status alternatives available to them through political education programmes, with the role of the UN, the administering power and the elected territorial government clearly defined and the necessary financial support as appropriate. Given the lack of implementation, the UN in its resolutions increasingly began to affirm its statutory role in the self-determination process, initially mandating its Decolonisation Committee, and more recently its 'appropriate UN bodies', to embark on a public awareness campaign aimed at assisting the peoples of the territories in gaining an understanding of their legitimate political options (UN General Assembly Resolution, 2010b: 4).

Beginning in the 1990s, continued reference was made to the three legitimate political status options clearly defined in General Assembly Resolution 1541. Not surprisingly, by 1997, the reference was modified, in the interest of colonial accommodation, to 'legitimate status options *including* those defined in Resolution 1541 (XV) (emphasis added). This was corrected in 1999 by returning to the original text, to be modified a few years later, in service of the same interests. In any case, the UN consistently calls for the 'faithful observance' of the relevant international instruments as related to the self-determination process.

In the first few years of the 21st century UN resolutions were being passed which made a strong link between self-determination, decolonisation and human rights, that is, it was felt that human rights were not being fully defended and safeguarded unless a proper process of self-determination and decolonisation was taking place. Accordingly, the resolutions during the period stressed that 'in the process of decolonisation, there is no alternative to the principle of self-determination which is a fundamental human right as recognized under the relevant human rights conventions' (UN General Assembly Resolution, 2010b: 4–5). Later in the decade, reference was added to the applicable human rights conventions, and calls for collaboration by the UN decolonisation mechanism with the Human Rights Committee (under the ICCPR) as well as with the Permanent Forum on Indigenous Issues (PFII). Collaboration of the UN Decolonisation Committee with the UN Economic and Social Council and its relevant subsidiary bodies was also called for consistently, even as actual collaboration was limited to a report compiling responses to requests for information on assistance to the NSGTs from the wider UN system (UN General Assembly Resolution, 2010b: 4–5).

International acknowledgement of the necessity for people of the territory to participate in the process also strengthened during this period, as well as the role of the UN in the promotion of full self-governance. In this regard, the resolutions recognised that 'negotiations to determine the status of a territory must take place with the active involvement and participation of the people of the territories, and that the views of the people of the territories in respect to their right to self-determination should be ascertained under the supervision [later changed to "under the aegis"] of the United Nations' (UN General Assembly Resolution, 2010b: 2).

This assertion that the UN had a direct role to play in the conduct of a self-determination process further strengthened the mandate by reaffirming the international legal primacy of that procedure, serving to make the important differentiation between a true process of self-determination and an internal consultation leading to some constitutional reforms. Accordingly, for example, New Caledonia's credible, if imperfect, self-determination process leading to a political status referendum can be contrasted with the internal constitutional review process in the UK-administered territories pursuant to the UK's 1999 overseas territories policy (FCO, 1999: 1–72). The French territorial process recognises the relevancy of international law and principles, whilst the UK and US processes are effectively silent on these tenets given that they were not designed to change the political status of the dependencies in the true sense. The US Virgin Islands constitutional convention process – dormant since 2010 – is also illustrative of a process of internal colonial reform even as the parameters of the prevailing dependency status were challenged by a number of provisions of the draft constitution (James, 2009: 1–4).

• *Ownership of natural resources and preservation of cultural heritage*
UN resolutions have identified as a critical element the right of the people to the ownership of their natural resources, including their marine resources. In this connection, the UN has made specific reference to the natural resources as the heritage of the people of the territories, and has expressed concern for any activities aimed at exploiting the natural and human resources of the territories to the detriment of the people's interests. There have also been calls for the states which administer territories to protect and conserve their environments. In this vein, the need for the preservation of the people's identity and cultural heritage has also been identified.

• *Financial support*
The UN has also identified expanded budgetary aid to the territories as critical to their development and, to this end, has called for concrete programmes of assistance and human resource development to be developed in order to advance the territories' economic progress, as well as programmes aimed at addressing social development concerns.

• *Presence of military bases*
The presence of military bases in non self-governing territories has been recognised historically by the UN as an impediment to the right to self-determination. To this end, the importance of the return of land from military or other external appropriation was a consistent theme in respect of a number of Caribbean and Pacific territories (UN Decision, 2002: 1–2). Alarmingly, this focus has been dormant for the last decade amidst impending militarisation build-ups, particularly in the Pacific NSGT of Guam.

• *Participation in the international process*
The participation of the territories in programmes and activities of the UN system of organisations, as well as regional institutions such as development banks, has been consistently recommended. The UN resolutions also endorsed the territories' participation in programmes and activities of the UN system, and their participation as observers in UN world conferences in the economic and social sphere. Accordingly, the UN further confirmed the applicability to these territories of the UN world conferences' plans of action (POA) and their eligibility for participation in UN programmes emanating from these POAs (UN General Assembly Resolution, 2010a: 2–5). Further, the UN resolutions recognised the role of the states which administer territories to promote their self-governance, and to this end, expressed concern for the unilateral authority exercised by the administering powers to legislate for the territories and to apply treaties to them, without their consent and often against their will. The

UN also acknowledged the importance of internal constitutional evolution as part of the preparatory process towards the attainment of full self-governance.

Identification of self-governance deficits in Caribbean non-independent countries

International principles recognise the existence of geographical and ethnic or cultural distinctness as factors in determining whether or not there is a mandate for international review of the level of self-governance in a dependency arrangement. The consequence of such a determination is the further examination of other elements of 'an administrative, political, juridical, economic or historical' basis with respect to whether the dependency is arbitrarily placed ... in a position or status of subordination' (UN General Assembly Resolution, 1960: 1). In this connection, the most appropriate measure of determining the present degree of self governance, and of identifying any existent self-governance deficit, can be made in examining the specific elements of the power relationship between the metropole, on the one hand, and the non-independent jurisdiction on the other. In such an assessment, the political relationship between the two entities would be judged against the international standard of full and absolute political equality as set forth in the principles contained in Resolution 1541 (XV), providing realistic conditions which must be established before full self-governance can be confirmed.

UK-administered territories

An initial look at the six Caribbean/Atlantic dependencies under UK administration is instructive – this dependency model focuses on the metropole's direct role in the daily governing process via the reserved and other constitutional powers set aside for a governor, periodically dispatched from the metropole but not elected by the people. The appointment of a native governor from the territory concerned is not afforded within this model, presumably reserved for a governor-general under associated statehood (no longer on offer). Consultation with the people of the dependency on the appointee of the British governor, as has been suggested repeatedly by dependency heads of government, remains out of the question.

Under the prevailing model, the unelected governor maintains a veto power over the elected legislative council, headed by an elected Chief Minister or Premier, who has the ability to annul, and/or decline to assent to legislation adopted by the elected legislative body of the territory. This occurred in Anguilla in 2011 where the governor refused to assent to the budget adopted by the elected legislative body (Proclamation, 2011: 1), noting that he 'had been instructed to reserve the 2011 Appropriation Bill for the signification of Her Majesty's pleasure in December 2010'. This resulted in an inordinate delay in the required fiscal measures being passed by the House of Assembly. The Cayman Islands experienced a similar delay (Caycompass, 2011: 1). The model also provides for the governor's total control over external affairs, internal security and the civil service, even as some degree of reversible delegation of power (particularly in regional affairs) has been made in the 'modernised' constitutions of the Turks and Caicos Islands (now suspended); the British Virgin Islands; and the Cayman Islands. These came into force in the latter part of the last decade. Similar delegation is also reflected in the new Montserrat constitutional order that were enforced in 2011.

The additional authority of the governor to impose legislation unilaterally on the territory without the consent and often against the will of the elected government (UN General Assembly Resolution, 2010b: 2) has been termed the 'nuclear option' in the UK House of Commons (Corbin, 2009c: 7–9). Quite apart from the self-governance deficit that this scenario suggests, such powers granted to an unelected official from the metropole are illustrative of a clear imbalance of power and democratic deficiency. Fergus, in his presentation to the 2011 Caribbean Regional Seminar on Decolonisation, pointed out that 'colonialism with its idea of client state and subordinate people is inherently undemocratic', arguing that 'there is no reason why … glaring elements of authoritarianism should not be removed' from the political relationship, and that 'no country is too poor to afford democracy' (Fergus, 2011: 2–7).

Mitchell has made the related point that 'when an Order-in-Council is made affecting our basic right to self-government, without public information, consultation and consent, a wrong is done … to the people of the British overseas territories' (Mitchell, 2011: 2). On the power of the unelected governor to refuse to assent to legislation adopted by the elected government of an overseas territory, Mitchell observed that the procedure was 'unacceptable because it is undemocratic, redundant and anachronistic' (Mitchell, 2011: 3). He similarly concluded that the UK power to legislate for the overseas territories 'in relation to its domestic issues is a process generally to be condemned when it occurs (and) any recommendation to this effect is retrograde, colonialist and undemocratic' (Mitchell, 2011: 16).

US-administered territories

Appointed government from the metropole was replaced by elected administrative executive authority in Puerto Rico in 1953 and in the US Virgin Islands in 1970. Direct authority from Washington was retained, however, via the unilateral application of US laws and regulations in such areas as: affirming the metropole's jurisdiction over marine resources; immigration and customs controls at the borders of the respective territories; and the primacy of selected US Constitution provisions, with curbs on the territories' political power and the level of political representation vis-à-vis the US political system amongst other limitations. This power imbalance in the US dependency model, through the US Congressional plenary authority, to unilaterally apply US laws to both territories (as well as to the three Pacific non-independent countries of American Samoa, Guam and the erstwhile autonomous Northern Mariana Islands) is a function of the US Constitution's territorial clause [(USC, Article IV, Section 3(2)] which governs territories which are appurtenant to, but not part of the US. In this regard, the five territories have active non-voting delegates in the US House of Representatives and no representation of any kind in the US Senate. This compares with the absence of representation in the UK House of Commons for the UK-administered territories in the Caribbean. In both the US and UK dependencies, there is no vote for the people of the respective dependencies in the metropole's elections.

Dutch autonomous countries

The self-governing countries of Aruba and the five-island grouping of the erstwhile Netherlands Antilles as autonomous countries in the Kingdom of the Netherlands, combined relative autonomous powers with aspects of political integration, for example, shared citizenship (Igarashi, 2002: 62–5) This was similar to the constitutional arrangement between Greenland and the Faroe Islands vis-à-vis the Kingdom of Denmark. Both Dutch and Danish autonomous models were characterised by voting representation in the parliaments of the Netherlands and Denmark, respectively, coupled with the exercise of effective autonomy. The relevant provisions of the Dutch Kingdom Charter which provide for unilateral intervention in the autonomous countries in the Caribbean, including higher supervision in financial matters, have historically been highlighted as aspects of the autonomous relationship which required re-assessment in relation to consistency with the principle of full political equality and self-governance. With the dismantling of the model in 2010, a number of laws have been enacted for newly autonomous Curaçao and Sint Maarten consistent with the relevant articles of the Kingdom Charter. This has resulted in a lesser autonomous model than that which had been the basis for UN recognition of the Antilles as self-governing in 1955, raising the question of whether the new model is sufficiently autonomous.

The remaining three jurisdictions of Bonaire, Saba and St Eustatius, which have been partially integrated by the Netherlands as 'public entities', are now being governed pursuant to Article 134 of the Dutch Constitution relating to the supervision of 'public bodies' which 'may be established and dissolved by or pursuant to an Act of (the Dutch) Parliament. The Dutch Constitution provides that '[t]he duties and organisation of such bodies, the composition and powers of their administrative organs and public access to their meetings shall be regulated by Act of Parliament, [that] [l]egislative powers may be granted to their administrative organs, by or pursuant to Act of Parliament, [and that the] supervision of the administrative organ shall be regulated by

Act of Parliament'.[1] Such are the mechanisms of partial political integration which limit internal decision-making but do not provide full rights in the political system of the metropole in which the jurisdictions are projected to be politically integrated. Given the requirement of full political rights as a necessary prerequisite of legitimacy for full self-governance through political integration, present limitations to political power in the metropole suggest that the Dutch 'public entity' model at this stage of its development is not yet in compliance with international norms.

In this context, it should be noted that a proposal to extend such voting rights to the three 'entities' in the Dutch Senate (First Chamber) elections was approved by the Dutch Council of Ministers in March 2011. If ultimately adopted, this would complement voting rights extended to the 'public entities' in the Dutch Lower House of Parliament (Second Chamber) upon the change of political status in October 2010. However, the extension of these rights can only come about through a change in the Dutch Constitution, requiring a majority vote by both Houses of the Dutch Parliament, and a second two-thirds vote in the Second Chamber. A timetable for this process had not been determined by mid 2011, and full political equality remains very much unfinished business. Meanwhile, inequalities for the people of the three island jurisdictions are also apparent in the social services sector which is not on par with the metropole. Further, increased economic inflation has been apparent as a result of the swift applicability of Dutch laws to the BES islands, higher in the second quarter of 2011 than in the first, with the rate highest on St Eustatius, at 10.5 per cent, up from 7.0 per cent in the first quarter. The rate on Saba and Bonaire also rose in the second quarter (*Caribseek*, 2011: 1).

Whether examining the acknowledged and recognised democratic deficits in the non self-governing territories, the self-governance deficiencies in the autonomous models, or the political and social inequalities in the integrated/ partially integrated political status arrangements, it is clear that a systematic examination of the specific elements of the power relationships with the metropole is a most effective measure in determining the extent to which these models conform to international principles of full self-governance. Accordingly, the adherence to the principles of political integration of the French overseas departments and the 'public entities' of the Netherlands, for example, would be assessed according to standard interpretations of '... complete equality between the peoples ... with equal status and rights of citizenship, and equal guarantees of fundamental rights and freedoms without any distinction or discrimination; both should have equal rights and opportunities for representation and effective participation at all levels in the executive, legislative and judicial organs of government' (UN General Assembly Resolution, 1960: Annex).

1   See www.servat.unibe.ch/icl/nl00000_.html.

Development of self-governance indicators

Derived from this examination of the applicability of international standards are areas of assessment which have been identified in the development of self-governance indicators for non self-governing territories, self-governing autonomous countries and integrated jurisdictions. For the classic dependencies classified as non self-governing, where the self-governance deficit is generally recognised, the areas of assessment are focused on the level of preparation for the process of achieving a full measure of self-governance. Ratuva (University of the South Pacific) emphasised the qualitative nature of 'Readiness for Decolonisation' indicators incorporating a number of factors including degree of progress towards political evolution and self-determination, interest and commitment of the metropole, political will of the people concerned in their own political evolution, internal governance capacity (including level of economic resources), and the extent of UN support among other factors (Ratuva, 2000: 3–4). In applying the self-governance indicators to the three subsets of non-independent jurisdictions, specific levels of attainment can be assessed for each indicator.

In effect, self-governance indicators for the non self-governing territories (NSGTs) reflect the nature of the power relationship between the metropole and the territory concerned. Accordingly, the indicators of Preparedness for Self-Governance (PSG) are informed by Ratuva, and broadened to incorporate a number of additional areas reflective of increasingly intricate dependency arrangements made more complex by internal reform processes. Accordingly, the measurements for specific indicators for NSGTs are contained in Table 3. The indicators of assessment for the self-governing autonomous countries (SGCs) and for the integrated jurisdictions (IJs) – as well as for the dependencies in the periphery – are informed by different factors, since self-governance in these cases is perceived to have been achieved already to varying degrees through sufficient autonomy or political integration, respectively. The focus of concentration is, therefore, on the intricacies of the existing political and constitutional arrangement with the metropole, and whether the respective arrangements adhere to the international standards of self-governance defined by international principles. Accordingly, measurements for specific indicators of self-governance for the autonomous countries are set forth in Table 4, whilst measurements for the integrated jurisdictions are in Table 5.

Table 3. Self-governance indicators for non Self-Governing Territories

Indicator	Measurement
a) Degree of awareness of the legitimate political status options and self-determination process	1) Little or no awareness 2) Some degree of awareness 3) Significant degree of awareness 4) High level of awareness and preparedness for self-determination
b) Nature and degree of unilateral authority of the metropole to legislate for the territory, including the applicability of treaties	1) Absolute authority by metropole to legislate 2) Consultation with metropole in advance of legislating 3) Existence of process to assess impact of laws/treaties to territory 4) Mutual consent required before applying laws/treaties
c) Extent and evolution of governance capacity	1) Direct rule by metropole 2) Some degree of elected representation 3) Significant degree of representation 4) High degree of decision-making by elected government
d) Extent of ownership and control of natural resources by the territory	1) Metropole exercises absolute control over natural resources 2) Some degree of shared ownership/control of natural resources between territory and metropole 3) High degree of shared ownership 4) Natural resources owned/controlled by territory
e) Degree of economic dependence of the territory on the metropole	1) Territorial economy dependent on direct aid from metropole 2) Territory receives some aid from metropole but generates significant revenue from its economy 3) Territory generates most revenue from its economy but receives project assistance from metropole 4) Territory has self-sufficient economy but may receive technical assistance from metropole

f)	Extent and nature of military presence in the territory	1)	Metropole can establishment and expand military presence including expropriation of land for military purposes without consulting territory
		2)	Metropole consults with territory before establishment/expansion of military activities
		3)	Metropole abides by territorial environmental and other laws in establishment/expansion of military presence
		4)	Territory has authority to determine the extent and nature of military presence and to receive compensation
g)	Extent of commitment of metropole to genuine process of self-determination	1)	Metropole dismisses relevance of self-determination and regards political development of territory as a purely domestic process, governed only by the laws of the metropole
		2)	Metropole acknowledges existence of the self-determination process but regards it as subordinate to domestic process of metropole
		3)	Metropole recognises relevance of international law and uses it as a guideline for self-determination process
		4)	Metropole co-operates with UN in developing genuine process of self-determination for territory with UN participation
h)	Level of UN engagement in self-determination process	1)	UN adoption of resolutions on UN role in the self-determination process with publication of information on self-determination process
		2)	UN outreach to UN Information Centres, tertiary institutions and civil society for dissemination of information on self-determination
		3)	UN observation of public education programme on self-determination process in the territory
		4)	Direct UN involvement in the education programme on self-determination and the conduct of the act of self-determination

i) Level of participation of territory in international and regional organisations	1) Limited awareness of eligibility of the territory for participation in international and regional organisations 2) Substantial awareness of international and regional organisation eligibility but limited participation 3) Significant participation in international and regional organisations 4) Full participation in programmes of international and regional organisations

A framework for the political formula for Non Self-Governing Territories (NSGTs) would reflect: a+b+c+d+e+f+g+h+i = PSG (Preparation for Self-Governance).

Table 4. Self-governance indicators for Self-Governing Autonomous Countries

Indicator	Measurement
a) Extent of mutual consent between the metropole and the self-governing country (SGC)	1) High degree of unilateral authority of the metropole to intervene in a range of areas 2) Limited degree of unilateral authority of the metropole to intervene in a range of areas 3) Limited degree of unilateral authority of the metropole to intervene in a few defined areas 4) Intervention permitted only on the basis of mutual agreement
b) Application of laws, international agreements and regulations from the metropole to the SGC	1) Metropole's absolute authority to legislate 2) Consultation with metropole in advance of applying laws and regulations 3) Existence of process to assess impact of laws/treaties to territory 4) Mutual consent required before applying laws/treaties
c) Extent of ownership and control of natural resources, including marine resources of the SGC	1) Metropole exercises absolute control over natural resources 2) Some degree of shared ownership/control of natural resources between territory and metropole 3) High degree of shared ownership 4) Natural resources owned/controlled by territory

d)	Freedom of the SGC to modify the prevailing political status and to determine its internal constitution without external interference	1) Metropole can veto recommended changes 2) SGC can change political status and internal constitution only with agreement of metropole 3) SGC must consult with metropole on changes to political status and internal constitution 4) Full authority of SGC to change political status and adopt internal constitution
e)	Degree of economic dependence of the SGC on the metropole	1) SGC dependent on direct aid from metropole 2) SGC receives some aid from metropole 3) SGC has high degree of economic self-sufficiency 4) SGC enjoys full economic self-sufficiency
f)	Nature of military activities in the SGC	1) Metropole has unilateral authority over its military activities 2) Metropole must consult with SGC regarding military activities 3) Extent and nature of military activities only by mutual consent 4) SGC concurrence on military activities with full disclosure from metropole

The framework for the political formula for Self-Governing Countries (SGCs) would reflect a+b+c+d+e+f = FMSG (Full Measure of Self-Governance).

Table 5. Self-governance indicators for Integrated Jurisdictions

Indicator	**Measurement**
a) Degree of political equality including equal status and rights of citizenship, and equal guarantees of fundamental rights and freedoms without any distinction or discrimination	1) Direct governance by metropole with symbolic representation 2) Limited political power 3) Substantial political power with some exceptions 4) Full political equality

b)	Extent of equal political participation and representation in the metropole	1) No political participation and representation of IJ in metropole 2) Limited degree of political participation and representation 3) Large degree of political participation and representation 4) Full political participation and participation
c)	Degree of economic and monetary integration with the metropole	1) Extent of economic integration determined by metropole 2) Limited economic integration with metropole 3) Substantial economic integration with metropole 4) Full economic integration with metropole
d)	Degree and nature of autonomy for regional economic and technical co-operation	1) Economic engagement and technical co-operation controlled by metropole 2) Limited power of IJ for economic engagement 3) IJ can enter into economic and technical agreements with metropole 4) IJ can enter into economic and technical agreements in their own right
e)	Right to self-determination	1) No right to self-determination and to change political status 2) Right to self-determination understood but not explicit 3) Right to self-determination understood but subject to consultation 4) Right to self-determination clearly recognised and defined

A framework for the political formula for Integrated Jurisdictions would reflect: $a+b+c+d+e$ = FMSG (Full Measure of Self-Governance).

Conclusion

The exercise in the development of self-governance indicators for non-independent, small island countries in the Caribbean (and Pacific) examines the basic elements of the power relationship between the metropole and the respective island jurisdictions. In this regard, the use of 'Small Island Developing States – Specific Governance Assessments' of the UN Development Programme (UNDP) is cited as an important initiative, with its focus on five primary areas of Caribbean democratic governance for independent countries of the region. The development of self-governance indicators for non-independent countries complements the UNDP work, and would provide a specific measurement to determine the level of self-governance not covered within the framework of the SIDS-specific governance assessments which are focused on independent Caribbean states' internal governance.

The present initiative is a country-specific measurement designed to monitor progress in the implementation of the international mandate of self-determination and the resultant achievement of full and complete decolonisation. The endeavour is informed by the earlier work done by the former UN Commission on Human Rights on the development of a Racial Equality Index (REI) which recognised, *inter alia*, the importance of the 'operationalisation of the rights into a set of indicators, small enough to be feasible and allow good handling, but detailed enough to capture the essential rights' (UNHCHR, 2006: 9). Consistent with the REI, the self-governance indicators refer to the 'essential dimensions' of decolonisation incorporated in the self-determination and decolonisation instruments discussed previously, with the relevant categories translated into quantitative measures creating a multidimensional index covering the areas identified in Tables 3–5 above.

Accordingly, the establishment of objective indicators for non-independent countries, reflecting the specific elements of the individual political arrangement concerned, sets the stage for an assessment of each non self-governing territory, self-governing country or integrated jurisdiction. The assessments would determine sufficiency of self-governance; identify any democratic deficits which may exist; and create modalities for bringing these arrangements into international compliance with recognised standards of political equality. Such a process of assessment is critical for avoiding legitimisation of the command and absolute power of the 'constitution of imperium' (Lipschutz, 2009: 1–8) that is inconsistent with democratic principles. The intention of the initiative is to provide a set of flexible indicators policymakers can use to enable them to assess the intricacies of the prevailing governance arrangements against a set of parameters identified by the international in order to advance democratic governance.

References

J. Aguon (2008) 'Other arms: the power of a dual rights legal strategy for the Chamoru people of Guam using the Declaration on the Rights of Indigenous Peoples in US Courts', *University of Hawaii Law Review* 31 (1), pp. 113–54.

Amigoe Newspaper (Curacao) (2010) 'Protest BES against tax changes', 8 Sept. Available at http://amigoe.com (accessed 1 Feb. 2012).

J.R. Bolton (1991) Letter to Peter Coleman, Governor of American Samoa, 27 March, Archives of the Offshore Governors' Forum, Washington, DC.

Caribseek News (2011) 'Sharp rise in Dutch Caribbean inflation in second quarter', 5 Aug., Available at http://news.caribseek.com/Sint_Eustatius/article_96756.shtml (accessed 19 Sept. 2011).

N. Connolly (2011) 'UK refuses to sign off on budget', 23 May. Available at www.compasscayman.com/caycompass/2011/05/23/UK-refuses--to-sign-off-on-budget/ (accessed 19 Sept. 2011).

C. Corbin (2001) 'Direct participation of Non-Independent Caribbean Countries in the United Nations – a method for self-determination', in A.G. Ramos and A.I. Rivera (eds.), *Islands at the Crossroads: Politics in the Non-Independent Caribbean*, pp. 136–59 (Kingston-Miami: Ian Randle Publishers).

— (2009a) 'Dependency governance and future political development in the Non-Independent Caribbean', in A. Cooper and T. Shaw (eds.), *The Diplomacies of Small States: Between Vulnerability and Resilience*, pp. 81–95 (Basingstoke: Palgrave Macmillan).

— (2009b) 'A view of the metropole', in P. Clegg and E. Pantojas-Garcia (eds.), *Governance in the Non-Independent Caribbean – Challenges and Opportunities in the Twenty-First Century*, pp. 253–68 (Kingston-Miami: Ian Randle Publishers).

— (2009c) 'Constitutional reform and political identity in the Non-Independent Caribbean', *Caribbean Perspectives*, January 2009.

Daily Herald (Sint Maarten) (2010) 'Caribbean guilder will not be ready by 10-10-10', 26 July. Available at http://demo.thedailyherald.com/islands/1-news/6250-caribbean-guilder-will-not-be-ready-by-10-10-10.html (accessed 19 Sept. 2011).

H. Fergus (2011) 'Modernizing a British colonial constitution: limitations and possibilities', paper presented to the United Nations Caribbean Regional Seminar on the implementation of the Third International Decade for the Eradication of Colonialism: goals and expected accomplishments, St Vincent and the Grenadines, 31 May–2 June. Available at www.un.org/en/decolonization/pdf/dp_2011_howard.pdf (accessed 19 Sept. 2011).

Foreign and Commonwealth Office (1999) *Partnership for Progress and Prosperity: Britain and the Overseas Territories*, Cm 4264, March (London: The Stationery Office).

France 24 (2010) 'French Guiana, Martinique vote against more autonomy', 10 Jan. Available at www.france24.com/en/20100111-french-guiana-martinique-vote-against-more-autonomy (accessed 19 Sept. 2011).

J.R. Hunte (2005) Opening Statement of the Chairman to the Organisational Session of the United Nations Special Committee on

Decolonisation, Official Records of the United Nations Decolonisation Committee, New York, 17 February.

M. Igarashi (2002) *Associated Statehood in International Law* (New York: Kluwer Law International).

G. James (2009) Statement of the President of the Fifth Constitutional Convention of the US Virgin Islands to the United Nations Fourth Committee, 6 October, Official Records of the Fifth Constitutional Convention of the US Virgin Islands.

R.D. Lipschutz (2009) *The Constitution of Imperium* (Boulder: Paradigm Publishers).

D. Mitchell (2011) 'New perspectives in oppression: the British Foreign and Commonwealth Office and proposals for constitutional reform in the Overseas Territories of Anguilla, Montserrat and the Turks & Caicos Islands', 28 April. Available at http://donmitchellcbeqc.blogspot.com/ (accessed 19 Sept. 2011).

M.R. Orellana (1998) 'Human rights talk ... and self-determination too!', *Notre Dame Law Review* 73 (5), pp. 1391–412.

OTR (2006) 'Criteria for the cessation of transmission of information under Article 73(e)', *Overseas Territories Review* V (5), Aug.

— (2010a) 'Self-determination or annexation: the case of Bonaire, *Overseas Territories Review* IX (2), Feb.

— (2010b) 'An analysis of implementation of the United Nations Decolonisation Mandate during the Second International Decade for the Eradication of Colonialism (2001–2010) and strategies for completion of the Decolonisation Mandate', *Overseas Territories Review* IX (5), Sept.

W. Pineau (2011) 'A Cayman Islands civil society perspective', paper presented to the United Nations Caribbean Regional Seminar on the implementation of the Third International Decade for the Eradication of Colonialism: goals and expected accomplishments, St Vincent and the Grenadines, 31 May–2 June 2011. Available at www.un.org/en/ decolonization/pdf/dp_2011_wil.pdf (accessed 19 Sept. 2011).

Proclamation, Office of the Governor, Anguilla (2011) 'Proclamation of Her Majesty's Assent to the budget', Office of the Governor of Anguilla, 31 March.

B. Rammell (2003) Letter to Hon W McKeeva Bush, Leader of Government Business, Cayman Islands, 12 Nov., Office of the Constitutional Secretariat, Government of the Cayman Islands.

S. Ratuva (2000) 'Towards decolonisation in the Pacific in the New Millennium', paper presented to a Pacific Regional Seminar organised by the United Nations Special Committee on Decolonisation, Majuro, Marshall Islands, 16–18 May.

J.A. Thomson (1986) Letter to Ambassador Abdul Koroma, Chairman of the United Nations Special Committee on Decolonisation, 30 Jan., Archives of the United Nations Association of the Virgin Islands.

United Nations (1945) *Charter of the United Nations*. Available at www. un.org/en/documents/charter/index.shtml (accessed 19 Sept. 2011).

UN Budget (2011) *Proposed programme budget for the biennium 2012–2013 Part II*, Political Affairs, Section 3, United Nations Document A/66/6 Section 3, 31 May.

UN Decision (2002) United Nations Decision 57/525, 'Military activities and arrangements by colonial powers in Territories under their administration', United Nations General Assembly Official Records, Fifty-seventh Session, Supplement No. 49, A/57/49 Vol. II. 2003.

UNHCHR (2006) 'Report of the High Commissioner for Human Rights containing a draft basic document on the development of a racial index', United Nations Economic and Social Council, Commission on Human Rights, Sixty-second Session, E/CN.4/2006/14, 31 Jan.

United Nations General Assembly Resolution 567 (VI) (1952) 'Future procedure for the continuation of the study of factors which should be taken into account in deciding whether a territory is or is not a territory whose people have not attained a full measure of self-government', United Nations General Assembly Official Records, Sixth Session, 18 Jan.

— Resolution 742 (VIII) (1953) 'Factors that should be taken into account in deciding whether a Territory is or is not a Territory whose people have not yet attained a full measure of self-government', United Nations General Assembly Official Records, Resolutions adopted on Reports of the Fourth Committee, 27 Nov.

— Resolution 1541 (XV) (1960) 'Principles which should guide Members in determining whether or not an obligation exists to transmit the information called for under Article 73e of the Charter', United Nations General Assembly Official Records, Resolutions adopted on Reports of the Fourth Committee, 15 Dec.

— Resolution 41/41 (1986) 'Implementation of the Declaration on the Granting of Independence to Colonial Countries and Peoples', United Nations General Assembly Official Records, Resolutions adopted without reference to a Main Committee, 2 Dec.

— Resolution 62/118 (2007) 'Questions of American Samoa, Anguilla, Bermuda, the British Virgin Islands, the Cayman Islands, Guam, Montserrat, Pitcairn, Saint Helena, the Turks and Caicos Islands and the

United States Virgin Islands', United Nations General Assembly Official Records, Resolutions adopted by the General Assembly on the report of the Special Political and Decolonization Committee (Fourth Committee), 17 Dec.

— Resolution 64/104 (2009) 'Questions of American Samoa, Anguilla, Bermuda, the British Virgin Islands, the Cayman Islands, Guam, Montserrat, Pitcairn, Saint Helena, the Turks and Caicos Islands, the United States Virgin Islands', United Nations General Assembly Official Records, Resolutions adopted by the General Assembly on the report of the Special Political and Decolonization Committee (Fourth Committee), 10 Dec.

— Resolution 65/110 (2010) 'Implementation of the Declaration on the Granting of Independence to Colonial Countries and Peoples by the specialized agencies and the international institutions associated with the United Nations', United Nations General Assembly Official Records, Resolutions adopted by the General Assembly on the report of the Special Political and Decolonization Committee (Fourth Committee), 10 Dec.

— Resolution 65/115 (2010) 'Questions of American Samoa, Anguilla, Bermuda, the British Virgin Islands, the Cayman Islands, Guam, Montserrat, Pitcairn, Saint Helena, the Turks and Caicos Islands, the United States Virgin Islands', United Nations General Assembly Official Records, Resolutions adopted by the General Assembly on the report of the Special Political and Decolonization Committee (Fourth Committee), 10 Dec.

— Resolution 65/119 (2010) 'Third International Decade for the Eradication of Colonialism, Official Records', Resolutions adopted by the General Assembly on the report of the Special Political and Decolonization Committee (Fourth Committee), 10 Dec.

Afterword

This book has highlighted both the continuities and changes that have framed relations between the non-self governing territories of the Caribbean and Pacific with their respective metropolitan powers in recent years. On the one hand, there has been a general conservatism on both sides that has restricted the possibility of radical reform of the links that bind the islands to their sovereign centres, but on the other concerted attempts have been made to revise, re-energise and retune these links.

What is certainly clear is that among the island territories considered in this book, any impetus there has been in relation to gaining independence has been diminishing for some time. Despite the continued enthusiasm of some of their politicians and oft-repeated criticisms of the 'colonial' powers and their level of influence, the people have shown little appetite for re-visiting the issue. The key factor is that most citizens feel that the existing (albeit quite varied) systems of governance are still better than independence despite the tensions that come to the fore and the reductions in autonomy that sometimes result. In many respects, the territories, overseen from Europe and the US, have a privileged position in the international system. Their citizens have a final guarantee against autocracy and economic collapse; many territories receive sizeable monetary assistance that has helped them in creating relatively high levels of GDP per capita; and nationals possess the citizenship of their metropolitan powers. In the case of the British, Dutch and French territories, they also have the freedom of movement across the European Union. As a consequence, there has not been a radical restructuring or breaking of these long-standing ties.

Nevertheless, even though independence is not on the agenda, constitutional change (within certain parameters) certainly is. Indeed, the last several decades have seen a continual process of reform and revision. For example, most of the United Kingdom Overseas Territories have adopted new constitutions that have awarded greater local executive power over areas such as foreign affairs and law and order. While in the French territories – both in the Caribbean and Pacific – a series of reforms have been instituted pivoting around Articles 73 and 74 of the French Constitution. As a consequence, there is now a series of different statuses better tailored to the particular needs of each territory. However, perhaps the most notable development has been the attempt by some territories to form more direct relationships with their respective metropolitan powers. So those islands, formerly part of the Netherlands Antilles (Curaçao, Sint Maarten, Bonaire, Saba and St Eustatius) and Guadeloupe (St Martin and St Barthélemy), have broken away from their neighbours and established direct links with The Hague and Paris. However, even in these cases where there has been significant structural reform, the re-balancing of powers has been relatively moderate. In part, this is because the territories are cautious about starting a process of reform, which could then lead to independence or at least fewer protections and preferences from the metropole, and in part because the metropolitan powers wish to retain certain key powers to protect their own interests. Indeed, in the Turks and Caicos Islands (in response to serious allegations of corruption) and in Curaçao and Sint Maarten (in an attempt to improve financial and judicial standards), there has been some repatriation of powers back to the metropolitan governments. More generally, there is now a sense that, after a period of active reconsideration of territory-metropole relations, it is a case of this far and no further in regard to the question of additional autonomy, and this will almost certainly remain the case for some time to come.

Because it seems we are nearing a time when no further extension of autonomy may be possible, efforts are being made to renew and strengthen the day-to-day aspects of the territory-metropole relationship, as well as dealing with perceived weaknesses in the territories' systems of political and economic management. So, at present, both the British and Dutch governments are attempting to formalise a discourse that emphasises the positive aspects of the relationship. They are also trying to engage fully with the territories and make sure that government departments in London and The Hague are aware of, and respond to, the needs of the territories in a timely and effective way. By doing this, there is hope that standards of governance and the levels of political maturity can be improved and that economic vulnerabilities can be mitigated. On the latter issue all three European metropolitan governments have made and are making significant efforts to strengthen economic management and to encourage greater self-sufficiency. The United Kingdom's recent interventions in Anguilla and the Cayman Islands, to limit their budget deficits after suffering serious economic problems, are cases in point; so too, its continued support for the sometimes-controversial offshore financial sector. There is a clear recognition that territory-metropole relations which were once seen as temporary must now have a strong functional basis and clear rationale in order to survive. This is of course to be welcomed.

However, territory-metropole relations have always been difficult to maintain at optimum levels as we have seen from the essays in this book. Beyond the constitutional systems, which are imperfect compromises between countries and territories with different interests, these relations are hard work. There are stresses and strains on an institutional and personal level between the territories and their metropoles; between departments of the same government;

and even within departments. So it takes significant effort to make sure all aspects of the relationship are working in an effective way. Unfortunately, this has not always been the case. Perhaps the best examples of this have been when metropolitan governments have slowly lost interest in the territories (which are admittedly not high priorities), or have just become worn down by the day-to-day demands of the relationship. Also, metropolitan governments are conscious that some of their territories remain colonised in the view of the United Nations and are therefore cautious about imposing their will, even when serious problems develop in the territories. So, there is certainly a risk that the relatively effective (if not always popular) territory-metropole relations today will become less effective in the medium term and this would certainly be damaging for all involved. Thus the present efforts of the metropolitan powers to re-engage with their territories must be maintained, no matter what troubles and frustrations may lie ahead.

Index

Lightning Source UK Ltd.
Milton Keynes UK
UKOW05f1001200314

228497UK00001B/39/P

9 780956 954602